CW01375807

# TEACHING TODAY
# woodcraft

# TEACHING TODAY
# Woodcraft
## Gwyn Hughes

Batsford Academic and Educational Ltd   London

**Acknowledgment**
My thanks go to the following for their support and assistance: to my headmaster for his support and encouragement, to my design department staff, to Stan Tomlinson — invaluable department technician and photographer, to Betty Flavell for meeting all the typing requirements, to Doncaster Metropolitan Borough Council Advisory Staff, and finally to my wife Jan and our children for those long periods of absence during the past few months.

J G H  Doncaster 1981

© Gwyn Hughes 1981
First published 1981

All rights reserved. No part of this publication may be reproduced, in any form or by any means, without permission from the Publisher

Typeset by Tek-art Ltd, SE20
and printed in Great Britain by
R.J. Acford Ltd
Chichester, Sussex
for the publishers
Batsford Academic and Educational Ltd
an imprint of B.T.Batsford Ltd
4 Fitzhardinge Street
London W1H OAH

ISBN 0 7134 3960 2

# CONTENTS

*Introduction* 6

1 **Teaching principles — what basis for teaching** *9*
Seeking the relevant parts from traditional courses *10*
Designing new courses *11*
Trying to predict a child's future needs *12*

2 **An approach to material selection and presentation** *20*
Learning *20*
Ideas *24*
Safety *26*
Skills and techniques *28*
Tools *37*
Machines and portable powered tools *39*
Material *41*

3 **Organization and management in a workshop** *43*
Organization *43*
Management *47*

4 **The range of work — a chapter of ideas** *51*
Communication *54*
Resources *54*
Pupil ideas *55*
Applying the problem solving model *57*
Examination courses *59*
Project work *60*

*Conclusion* 69
*References* 70
*Bibliography* 70
*Index* 71

# INTRODUCTION

Wood continues to retain its popularity amongst the materials derived by man from the natural resources within his environment. For generations wood has been used alone and its visual and tactile qualities have enhanced the forms produced.

Traditionally, wood is associated with furniture but nineteenth-century crafts saw wooden utensils and implements as well as folk furniture. The farm wagon also represents a fine example of a complex arrangement of wooden parts by a craftsman of the same period. Here the form of the cart evolved through generations of craftsmen developing their understanding of the material and its working properties in relation to function.

For the cabinet maker, the long-established shapes of furniture remained, until late in the nineteenth century, influenced partially by the type of wood used. These shapes reflected the sturdy qualities of oak up to the eighteenth century, the elegance of walnut during the late seventeenth century and further lighter structures were achieved with mahogany from the mid-eighteenth century onwards.

Since then new ideas on the part of designers and the introduction of new materials have brought a significant change in the role of wood for furniture. Natural resources have diminished and new, sometimes more durable and more versatile, man-made boards have been developed using wood in thin sheets bonded together with synthetic resin adhesives.

The visual and tactile qualities have been retained as a surface veneer on man-made boards.

Such a change has demanded new constructional ideas and the introduction of metals and plastics as allied materials in order to resolve the problems arising. Today wooden forms are produced from solid timber, man-made boards and by lamination.

The significant factor is change, and the nature of society itself over the past two decades has shown rapid change alongside technological advance. Man's values and established systems have been questioned or found to be inadequate to cope with the increasing complexity of modern living.

Within our schools a similar pattern can be identified. The teacher of workshop subjects during the early part of the twentieth century, was associated with an industrial background or a specialist course of training set apart from the academic institutions of his colleagues in the staff room. His skill as a craftsman and his approach to pupils reflected the craftsman/apprentice relationship in the world of work. The emphasis on skills and techniques was high and within education generally, low intellectual content was ascribed to practical activity. The role of workshop activities was vocationally biased and considered as being more suitable for the less able child.

However, the needs of the twentieth century, the changing nature of knowledge, the advent of mass production and of a mass culture renders many of the traditional values of a craft workshop questionable. The hand skills and techniques, the craftsman/apprentice learning situation, are no longer as relevant to the needs of modern industry. The teaching of outmoded skills and techniques is hardly likely to encourage pupils to become aware of new skills and knowledge.

The craft teacher's approach to the curriculum, biased towards skills and techniques emphasized the value of workmanship. To ensure the highest possible standards in this respect, the projects undertaken were generally pre-determined by the teacher with each stage in the making process being carefully monitored.

Change in curriculum content and in the organization of secondary schools has encouraged a reassessment of the role of practical activities. The craft teacher's reliance on initial training is being tested fully within a design, or similar faculty structure, teaching boys and girls together in mixed ability groups as part of integrated courses. Here change is the significant factor once again and the craft teacher has the task of reassessing the role and content of the curriculum for workshop activities, within the broader concept of design education.

This book aims at outlining those areas which should concern the teacher in the workshop today. Although aimed primarily at the wood workshop the content can be viewed as equally relevant for craft teachers generally. It is likely that these teachers are part of a team within a faculty structure. Therefore the role of workshop activities needs to be examined in relation to some overall concept of education rather than to splendid isolation and traditional skills and techniques.

Education and learning should be seen as synonymous and therefore each educational experience should be soundly based and subjected to some form of evaluation.

The changing nature of knowledge makes the

teacher's task often more akin to that of a co-learner alongside pupils. The pre-determined project is less likely to be the means of providing for a child's needs since it denies that child any opportunity to be involved in decision making.

The question of relevance is raised. How can workshop activities be relevant to the lives of children in the context of the real world? There is also the question of relevance in preparing children for their adult role in society.

It is unlikely that craft teachers now or in the future can survive, working in isolation. The pressures for integration within courses and within faculty structures, well established today in secondary education, represent a real threat to identity when considered in traditional terms.

Organization and management have become increasingly important as courses become integrated, linked or structured in modular forms. In practice, the craft teacher must have some educationally valid basis for the selection of material taught, the management of learning situations and the teaching approach adopted.

Overall, the proposals discussed in this book centre on the concept of developing a child's ability to learn through encouraging the development of individual ideas. It is also maintained that such ideas should be allowed to evolve within a sound course structure rather than within an apparently aimless experience.

Problem-solving situations offer the opportunity for developing models of thought based on the design process and its application in designing and making activities.

Further intuitive, imaginative and work-through-observation can assist to ensure that a good balance is achieved within a course structure.

There cannot be a prescription for all craft teachers but there can be a determination to encourage each individual to develop a personal approach based on sound philosophy. This philosophy relates to the role of workshop activities, through designing and making, as part of a child's general education.

The discussion engendered by this book will, it is hoped, raise questions and encourage personal thought, criticism and evaluation. Whatever the reader's thoughts may be at this stage there can be little doubt about the need to consider workshop activities as part of a broader context. In this book that broader context is design education.

# 1 Teaching principles – what basis for teaching

The traditional concept of teaching within the wood workshops was based on developing skills and techniques. This was achieved quite successfully through the teacher's pre-determined project. The standard of workmanship achieved was effectively controlled by the teacher's demonstrations of techniques and the child following precise instructions in the manner of an apprentice.

It is not the intention here to dispute the need for skills and techniques but rather to identify other, equally important aspects of a child's educational needs that should be included as part of workshop activities.

The traditional approach places making as the primary activity. This also implies that the ability to make is the only requirement of adult life that workshop activities can provide. Assessed in these terms, craft subjects generally offer the low-ability child the opportunity to make, and the potential apprentice a good vocational grounding. However if workshop activities are made available to children of all abilities then the emphasis on making as the primary activity is questionable. It seems more relevant to suggest that the whole of life is not to do with making but more to do with acting upon decisions made.

The central role in life now and later for a child is that of decision making. Consequently, to have any real relevance, the form of workshop activities in secondary education must evolve from decision making as a central concept.

Within the traditional approach, the teacher plays the role of the designer and the master craftsman making decisions at appropriate stages in order to guide his charge along the pre-determined route.

Decision making in relation to a product offers a useful opportunity to consider the work of a designer more closely. The latter is generally concerned with three factors:

1 Taking what is relevant from the past.

2 Making maximum use of what is available in the present.

3 Trying to predict some future state.

This analysis can be considered relevant for the workshop teacher today. The task of selecting the content of a course and then producing a suitable structure can raise considerable difficulties. A suitable starting point could be based on the following:

1 Seeking the relevant parts from traditional courses and retaining them.

2 Designing new courses to include 1 above and to develop other aspects of work that are relevant and important in terms of a child's educational needs.

3 To try and predict needs beneficial to a child's future and to ensure that the course caters for those needs.

These three factors warrant closer attention when placed in the context of the workshop today.

*Figure 1* Giles Cartoon. Reproduced with the permission of London Express News and Feature Services

## 1 Seeking the relevant parts from traditional courses and retaining them

The cartoon, by Giles, in Figure 1 illustrates the scene in the wood workshop during the 1950s and 1960s. Whilst the leadership role of the teacher is overstated the pupil's work was largely related to skills, techniques and materials, all pre-determined by the teacher. Pupil progress was monitored according to how well skills and techniques were being developed and mastered, and according to the standard of workmanship evident in the end product.

If the product was constant for each child then the teacher's assessment was based on a comparison within the group, based on a criteria linked very closely to the final form of the product.

Questions can be raised as follows in relation to this concept of workshop activities:

1 How valuable to a child is the constant use of pre-conceived teacher ideas and teacher directed work?

2 How is a child's maturation affected by 1?

3 How is a child's potential ability utilized in 1 above?

4 How can the teacher be assured that all the skills and techniques included are relevant?

5 Does the teacher acknowledge the existence of other skills omitted or neglected?

6 How valuable is the assessment of the end product when assessing the potential and the attainment of a child?

Figure 2 shows a typical working drawing from the 1960s and the product — a tea tray made in wood.

Some of the skills required here are as follows:

1 Reading a working drawing.
2 Preparing material to size.
3 Marking out and cutting out joints.
4 Shaping wood.
5 Fitting joints.

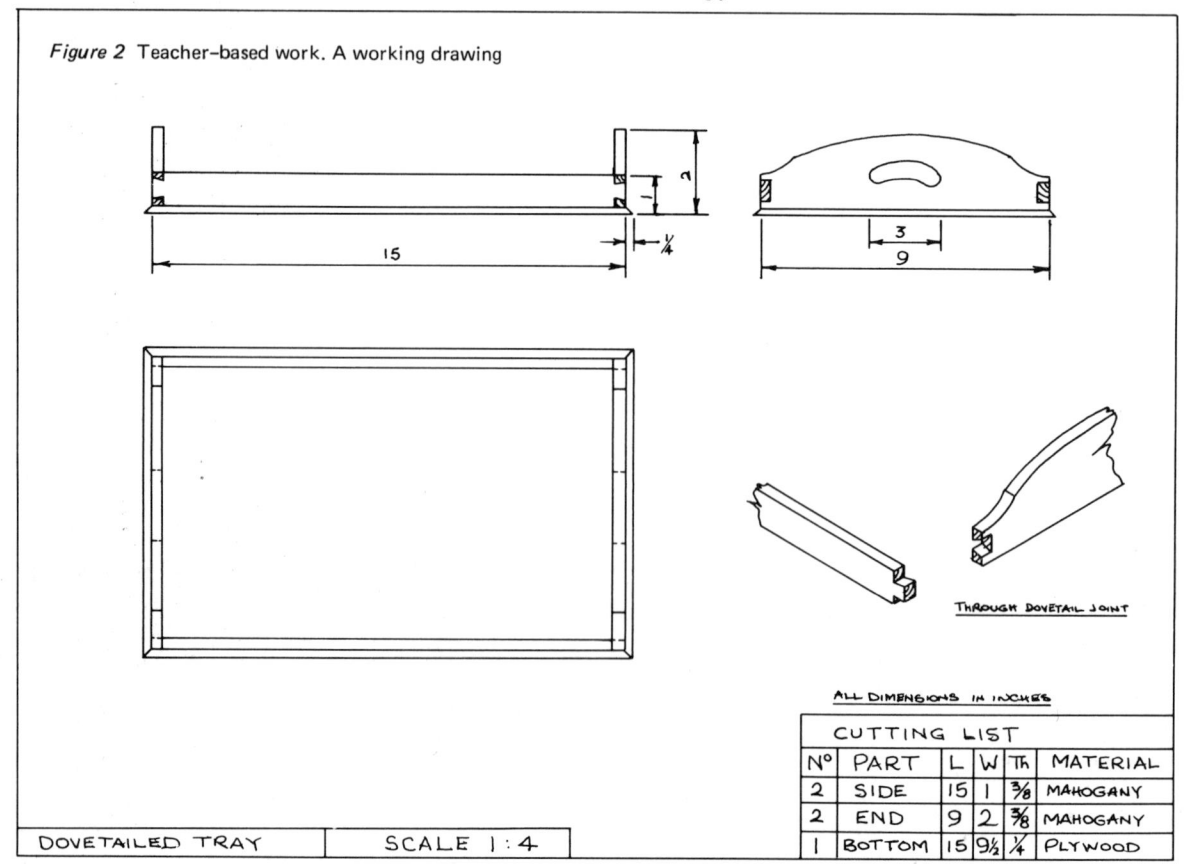

*Figure 2* Teacher-based work. A working drawing

DOVETAILED TRAY    SCALE 1:4

ALL DIMENSIONS IN INCHES

CUTTING LIST

| N° | PART | L | W | Th | MATERIAL |
|----|------|---|---|----|----------|
| 2 | SIDE | 15 | 1 | ⅜ | MAHOGANY |
| 2 | END | 9 | 2 | ⅜ | MAHOGANY |
| 1 | BOTTOM | 15 | 9½ | ¼ | PLYWOOD |

### Processes

1 Plane wood to size
2 Mark out lengths and shoot to line
3 Lay-out with face edge upwards and face side inwards. Letter corners for reference
4 Gauge side height on end pieces
5 Mark out tails
6 Cut out tails
7 Mark out pins from tails
8 Cut out pins
9 Mark out and cut handles. Shape ends
10 Clean and polish inside surfaces. Fit joints. Glue together
11 Shape bottom, fit, polish
12 Clean up and finish

6 Surface finishing.
7 Gluing and assembly.

Each skill and technique was demonstrated by the teacher (the craftsman) and then repeated by the pupil (the apprentice) until the product was completed.

Here again similar questions arise:

1 What does a working drawing represent to (a) the teacher, as part of a child's education? (b) the child, as part of workshop activities?

2 How does the teacher determine that the skills and techniques required here are relevant to the needs of all children?

3 Do these skills and techniques represent a stage within a pre-determined sequence? If so, on what basis was the sequence determined initially?

Figure 2 can also be considered as a structure for work, the list of processes representing the sequential nature of work in the workshops. The list also represents the teacher's approach to learning, although it was unlikely to be viewed in those terms at the time. Far more likely that the list should be considered as a sequence of operations compiled by the teacher in order to ensure the successful completion of a product.

The major hazard for the teacher was the pupil's individual work rate so that in practice the more able children completed the sequence in advance of the remainder of the group.

This approach to workshop activities must be considered as part of the past since many changes have occurred in the past two decades. Consider the following influences:

**1958** The Crowther Report emphasized the advantage of providing intellectual challenge through practical activities where academic courses failed to generate response.

**1967-72** Schools Council Curriculum Development Project Technology (11-18).

**1969** Schools Council Working Paper 26 — Education through the use of Materials.

**1969-72** Schools Council Research and Curriculum Development Project Art and Craft Education (8-13).

**1968-73** Schools Council Research and Curriculum Development Project Design and Craft Education (13-16+).

**1976-78** Schools Council Modular Courses in Technology.

**1979** Royal College of Art enquiry into Design in General Education.

The wealth of material available as the outcome of these projects has been channelled into an area of the school curriculum where change seems to have been heralded as the way ahead for the future.

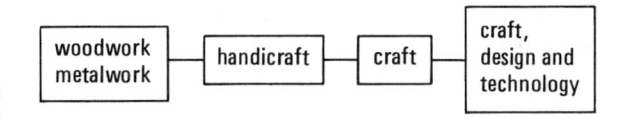

woodwork metalwork → handicraft → craft → craft, design and technology

The changes in name have also reflected a change in direction as a result of research and curriculum development projects.

The developing involvement of the Design Council in design education at secondary level, the importance of engineers to the national economy and the core curriculum philosophy, all exert their influences on the workshop teacher today. The outcome can be an inspired teacher or a confused individual striving to satisfy such a variety of needs.

For the teacher, progress can only be made in such circumstances, through a careful analysis of the established workshop skills, and the identification and inclusion of relevant new skills in a revised course structure.

**2 Designing new courses in order to develop aspects of work relevant to a child's educational needs**

The traditional approach mentioned in 1 identifies the needs of a child as being primarily the development of skills and techniques in relation to making, with the emphasis on the end product.

In practice the children who continued to work with craft materials beyond the age of 13 years were generally the less able since the value of the subject was not accepted in either intellectual or examination terms, as being of real value to the more able child.

Questions arise here immediately.

1 Why should the content of workshop activities be relevant only to the needs of less able pupils?

2 Cannot the range of skills and techniques be expanded to be relevant to all abilities up to the age of 16 years as part of a general education?

3 Cannot the activity of designing and making be considered a valuable part of a child's education?

New courses suggest change. Change in both the nature of knowledge and in the manner it becomes available.

Here the teacher needs to identify the needs of children both within the school curriculum and in terms of their future life generally as members of society.

Professor Eggleston suggests that

the capacity to adapt, to initiate, to modify, to solve problems and make decisions is likely to be the central human contribution to life in the coming decades. [1]

Where then does the teacher in the wood workshop begin?

A simple answer at this stage would be to think away from wood and materials generally.

## 3 Trying to predict a child's future needs

Making a start

For the established teacher and the newly trained probationary teacher there is a need for developing a professional approach to teaching. This entails extending the concept of teaching from the confines of the workshop into a much broader educational context. For the established teacher this suggestion may represent coping with change, whilst for the young teacher it means identifying the basis from which developing a philosophy for teaching may be possible.

It must be stressed that a prescription does not exist which is of equal value for each individual teacher. Emphasis must be placed on encouraging each teacher to analyse, synthesize and evaluate in determining the educational value and role of workshop activities. For that reason the skills required from each teacher at this stage relate to a thought process; a thought process which seeks out the relevant, essential issues.

This can be achieved by stating the broader context more specifically. This context is one of workshop activities within design education and pursued through a problem solving approach. As a basis for problem solving activity we have the design process.

As a starting point for the design process we find the task of compiling a design brief, a statement which is the outcome of having established that a need exists. The first task for the teacher is to work to a brief or a series of briefs in order to determine what the nature of the work itself should be. The implication is that each teacher can only establish clearly the basis for workshop activities by considering the parameters of such a problem quite extensively.

Design brief

What is the first problem? Is it to define the brief or to establish whether the brief is sufficiently explicit for analysis to commence?

Since most problems are generally ill-defined, it seems likely that the task of stating the brief precisely is the most urgent.

At this stage the teacher's brief must include the following:

1 The teacher's role in a broad educational context.
2 The child's educational needs.
3 The school's management and organization.
4 The department's management and organization.

Here the brief is to analyse rather than to resolve a problem. The identification of relevant components of a problem is an essential prerequisite to offering a means of resolving a problem.

**Model 1** indicates the general role of a teacher concerned with child growth and development. The context here is broad rather than specific. The immediate observation to be made is that although each component has been identified in isolation,

*Figure 3* Design department structure

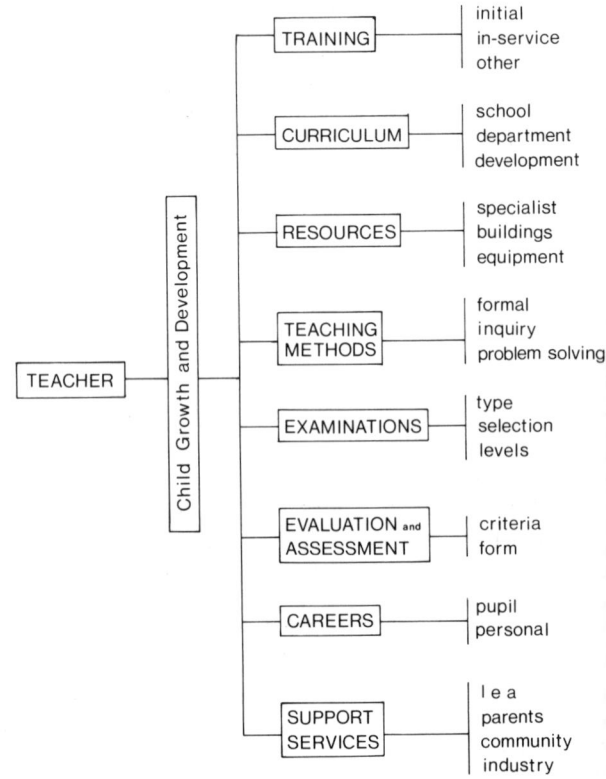

*Model 1* Role of the teacher

reality deems that each component is linked and interdependent. This suggests complexity for the teacher but also reinforces the need for analysis, identification and isolation in order to break a problem into simpler more manageable parts.

**Model 2** indicates possible major components within a child's needs during the course of secondary

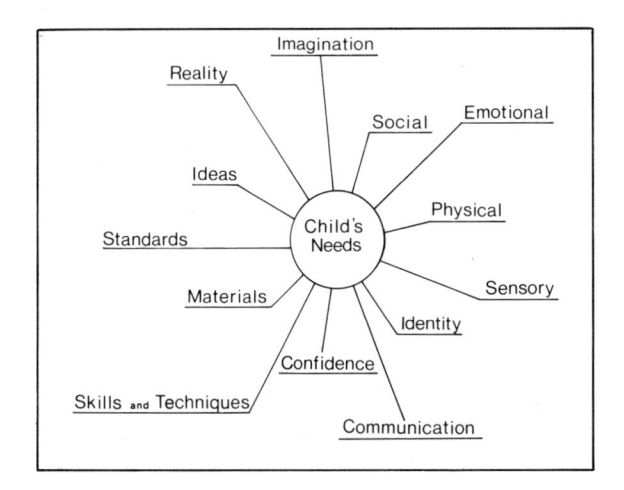

*Model 2* Child's needs during secondary education

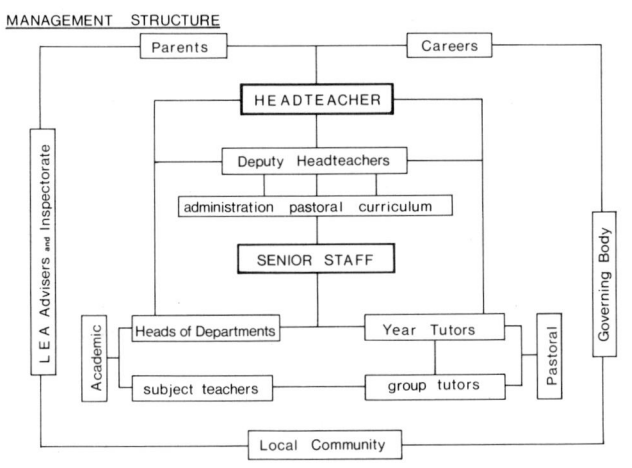

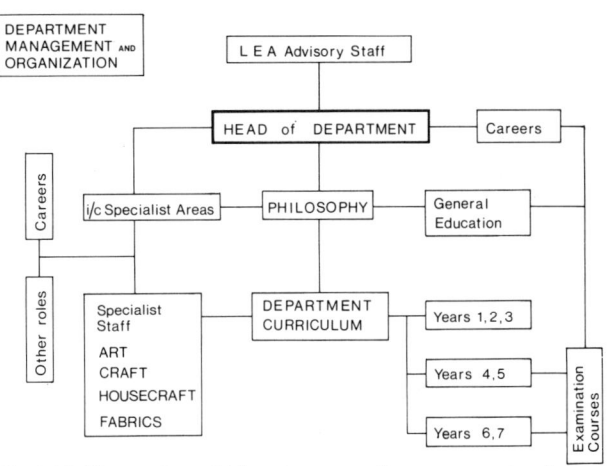

*Model 4* The teacher within a department's management and organization

*Model 3* The teacher within a school's management structure

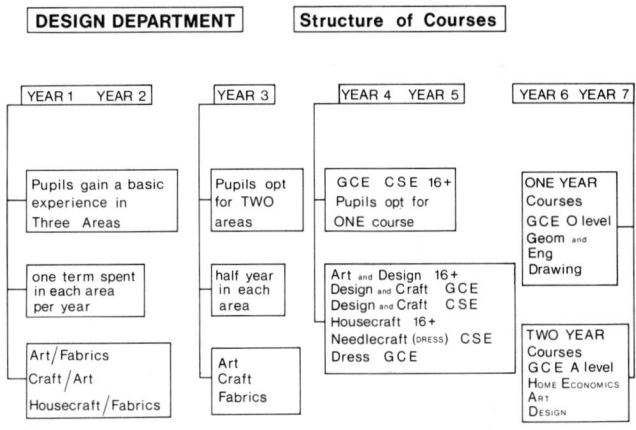

*Model 5* Craft within a design department's structure of courses

education. Here again complexity is evident and the interrelated nature of each component is unavoidable.

**Model 3** aims at identifying the position and role of the subject teacher within the management and organization of a comprehensive school. It is inevitable that the subject teacher is also involved in pastoral work (as a group tutor or form teacher) as part of a broader role as a teacher. Although the outcome of a broader role can perhaps only be explicitly defined as an increased work load, there are many tangible benefits to be gained in relation to the following:

1 Teacher/pupil relationship.
2 Development of a teacher's personal skills.
3 Career prospects.
4 Subject status in the school curriculum.
5 Awareness of a broader context.

**Model 4** offers an outline for a department or faculty structure. Here the subject teacher can see his/her place within a smaller, more immediate context. The head of a department holds or delegates responsibilty for the following areas:

1 Department philosophy.
2 Specialist subject areas.
3 Child's needs in terms of general education, examinations and careers.
4 Teacher needs in terms of careers, in-service training and other roles in the school.
5 Department curriculum.
6 External support services.

**Model 5** offers an example of a structure for courses within a design department comprising the specialist subject area indicated in Figure 3. Here the craft teacher could identify his/her role at both the basic course level in years one and two, and at the more specialized examination levels of years four, five and six. This model suggests a link between craft and art in the basic course. Such a link depends on the department staffing, the nature of the work areas and the attitude of mind amongst staff in relation to the department philosophy and the content of a basic course.

```
                          ┌─ ENVIRONMENT
                          │
                          ├─ AWARENESS
                          │
                          ├─ MATERIALS
                          │
                          ├─ SKILLS and TECHNIQUES
                          │
                          ├─ TOOLS and EQUIPMENT
DESIGN ── (CHILD GROWTH   │
EDUCATION   DEVELOPMENT   ├─ SAFETY
  │         and ASSESS-   │
MAJOR       MENT)         ├─ COMMUNICATION
COMPONENTS                │
                          ├─ PROBLEM SOLVING
                          │
                          ├─ TEACHING METHOD
                          │
                          ├─ PUPIL IDEAS
                          │
                          ├─ IMAGINATION
                          │
                          └─ METHODOLOGY
```

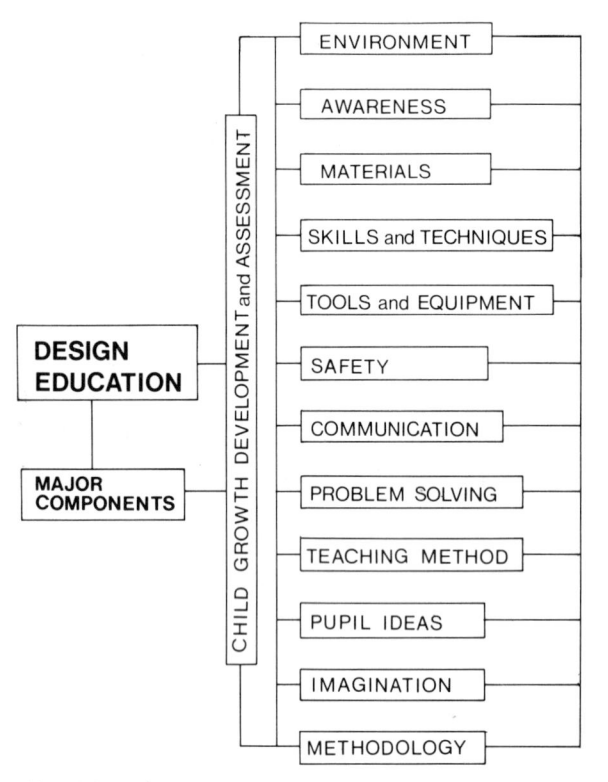

*Model 6* Design education – major components

Model 6 offers an analysis of design education for a typical Department comprising the specialist subject areas indicated in Figure 3. Here the craft teacher needs to find an appropriate role within the context of a department. However this analysis can be relevant within a single isolated workshop if the circumstances within a school promote isolation rather than integration.

Consider this analysis in more detail in order to develop a teacher's role within the broader context.

### Environment
Considered in the restricted sense, this refers to the specialist work area, in this case the wood workshop. The teacher's concern must be with the total working environment and its development as a stimulus for children in both their work and their organization of work.

In the broader sense of a total environment, here lies the source of inspiration, the source of reference and relevance for all aspects of workshop activities.

### Awareness
Both visual and social awareness are considered here. The former in relation to the development of a child's visual literacy and the latter to human behaviour.

In the workshop this means the organization and utilization of pupil and teacher awareness within the teacher/group situation.

Visual literacy must be seen as the development of a child's ability to look and see in depth rather than superficially. The value of paying attention to detail is relevant to all activities. The objective here should be to develop an attitude of mind which allows the child to be receptive to the need to pay attention to detail.

To achieve this behavioural pattern amongst children, teachers themselves should seek to develop their own level of awareness.

### Materials
The objective here is the development of an overall understanding of materials in terms of their source, manufacture, cost, economic use and working properties. This component is closely linked to skills and techniques since the development of an understanding of materials can stem from both a working knowledge and researched information.

### Skills and techniques
Skills and techniques need to be developed in relation to the pupil's age, experience, immediate and future needs within the total context of a child's journey from child to adult standards during secondary education.

The range of skills and techniques must include the development of sensory skills, communication skills, social skills, as well as specific performance in relation to tools and equipment.

### Tools and equipment
These are essential resources within the workshop. This component is closely linked to safety and awareness.

### Safety
This must be considered as a vital component for the workshop in terms of the personal well-being of both the pupil and the teacher. Whilst the development of a sensible approach to all aspects of safety within the workshop is the immediate behavioural objective for the teacher, the same attitude of mind should be projected beyond the workshop boundaries, to the total environment.

### Communication
Here is an essential component if ideas are to be discussed, concepts are to be developed and factual information given to children. The use of words and images is relevant here and children should be encouraged to communicate their ideas through the use of the most appropriate media.

The use of language across the school curriculum receives the workshop's major contribution here in the form of dialogue, group discussion, written notes and design folios. The use of sketches and standardized drawing techniques develop the ability to communicate ideas clearly and successfully both to oneself and to others.

### Problem solving
This component draws attention to the teaching approach adopted in the workshop.

Analysis, synthesis and evaluation are required within problem solving and decision making is an essential sub-component here.

The latter should be both child-centred and teacher-aided according to a child's needs.

Problem solving forms the basis for the application of the design (learning) process as a structure for learning within workshop activities.

Teaching method
This component is the responsibility of the teacher and should be determined by the needs of a particular learning situation.

It can be viewed as a vehicle for travelling into 'what is unknown for the child'. The teacher selects the most appropriate vehicle for the journey.

Pupil ideas
These are pupil responses in any situation whether related to a design brief or within a more formal demonstration by the teacher. The teacher's use of pupil ideas is central to the development of a particular piece of work and to the child's confidence generally.

A constant use of preconceived or teacher-directed work can stifle individual response and subsequently exclude a child from any worthwhile decision making.

Imagination
Here is a relevant component whenever no pre-conceived course of action exists.

The expression of imaginative ideas, whether completely successful or otherwise in adult terms, must be viewed as an essential emotional outlet for a child.

The fantasy world of a child needs to be acknowledged and can effectively offer a balance for work within a course which is heavily orientated towards function and product design.

Methodology
Closely linked to problem solving, this component can be viewed as essential for the organization of knowledge and its useful application within problem solving.

Furthermore the organization of the workshop environment, tools and equipment, safety requirements, communication and group management can benefit from a sound methodology.

In relation to a teacher's personal life, the ability to analyse, to organize and apply information usefully in decision making is essential for survival.

The penalties incurred as result of an ill-considered decision can be painful. The teacher's ability to make and implement decisions can only be developed through practice. The decision making skills of a child can only be developed through practice.

Whatever the extent of the decision it should be relevant to a child's needs at that moment in time and be supported by the broader aim to sow a seed that will mature and bear fruit in the later years of a child's life, both during and beyond school years.

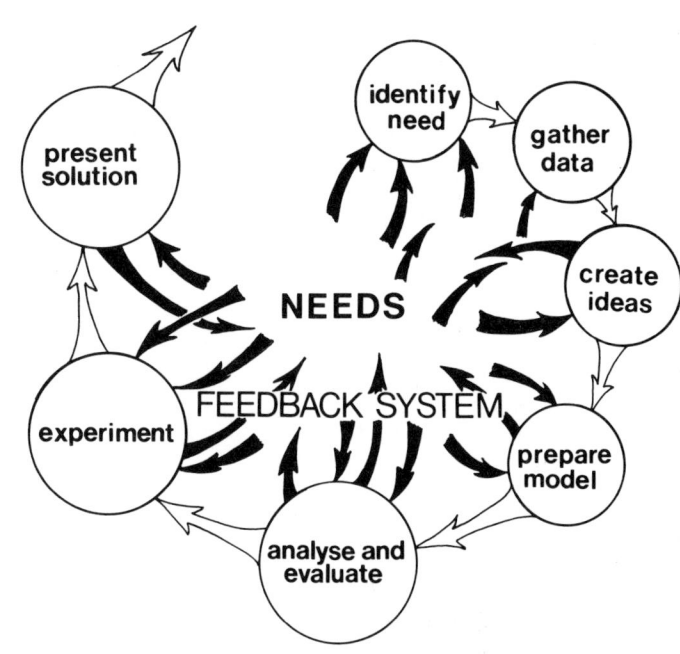

*Figure 4* The design process – engineering method. Taken from *Design Serving the Needs of Man* by George C Beakley. Reproduced with the permission of Macmillan Publishing Co. Inc.

Having considered the analysis offered by Model 6, two components – *Teaching method* and *problem solving* – are worthy of consideration in some depth in order to transfer the philosophy to the reality of a teaching situation.

Firstly, our total environment may be viewed as the outcome of man's conscious attempt to create a habitat for human beings. The environment can also be viewed as the outcome of man's attempts at resolving many problems. Environmental problems are generally considered to be the prerogative of architects, town-planners and civil engineers.

An example of the design process taken from the world of engineering (Figure 4) can serve as a useful illustration of the process within the real world.

Within education the following quotation from Bloom's 'Taxonomy of education objectives' offers food for thought.

..... we have the task of preparing individuals for problems that cannot be foreseen in advance, and about all that can be done under such conditions is to help the student acquire generalized intellectual abilities and skills which will serve him well in many new situations. [2]

There is a case therefore for placing emphasis on the process of learning as well as on the acquisition of skills, techniques and a body of knowledge.

Consider now the design process from the field of engineering as illustrated in Figure 4. The intention at this stage is not to suggest that such a model can be usefully transferred to a workshop situation, but to draw attention to components within the process.

Problems in real life are generally ill-defined so

that the designer has to decide what information is required in order to produce an edequate working brief. A similar experience awaits all of us within many problems in life generally and we are faced with the task of determining what the nature of the problem really is.

This seems to suggest that teaching methods in the workshop could usefully be directed towards a problem-solving approach which is relevant to the real world of both the professional engineer and the layperson. Each works at a level relevant to the problem in hand.

What is being suggested here is quite a contrast to the more traditional approach generally used in workshop activities. Here the process of designing is being introduced as a basis for activities where children are involved with the task of resolving a problem. They begin with a brief and conclude with a means of resolving the problem having taken part in decision making at each stage of the process.

One feature of the engineering process that needs emphasizing here is the feedback system. This reinforces the view that the problem solving process is dynamic and constantly being re-aligned in order to make allowances for individual needs and to admit any new, relevant information at any stage. This notion seems to be relevant to the needs of a teacher faced with a group of children.

The intention here is not to prescribe a process for use in the workshop but rather to encourage each individual teacher to evolve an approach which is based on a personal philosophy.

Developing a personal philosophy in relation to workshop activities seems to be a relevant objective for any craft teacher.

Consider now a model for thought applicable to workshop activities and then reference will be made later to its relevance to the real world and to the teacher's personal philosophy.

Figure 5 illustrates a basic model where the right hand side of the flow diagram relates quite readily to materials. The left hand side indicates the need to include additional skills into workshop activities. This side also implies that if any decisions are to be made in terms of materials, shape and size, construction and surface finishing then the teacher and the child should be involved in a dialogue. This dialogue can be informal and incidental to the process of making. However if the teacher wishes to emphasize the importance of this aspect of the work then a more structured approach is needed.

Figure 5 taken in conjunction with Figure 6 develops the approach further. Whilst Figure 5 isolates parts within problem solving. Figure 6 suggests most strongly that none of these parts can be treated in isolation. The interrelated nature of these parts must be understood and their isolation accepted only in order to make the problem more manageable. For the teacher these flow diagrams offer a structure for working. A structure which is based on a pattern of

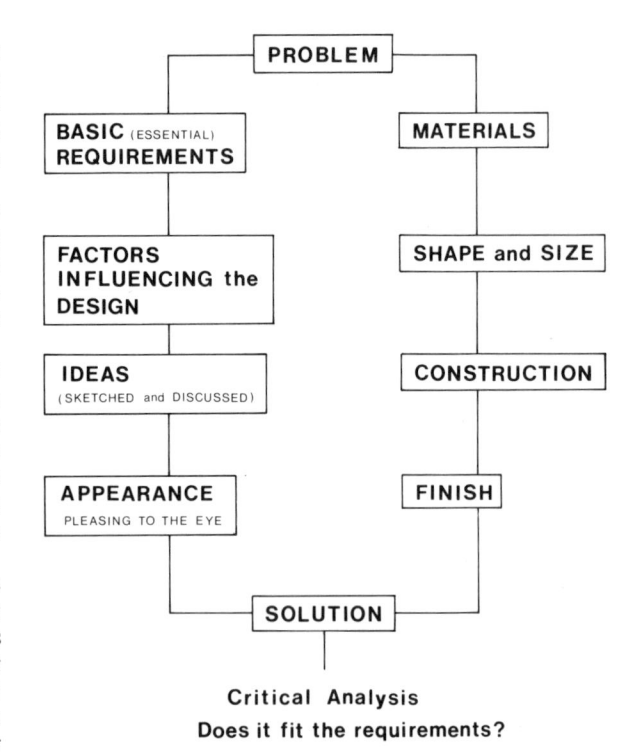

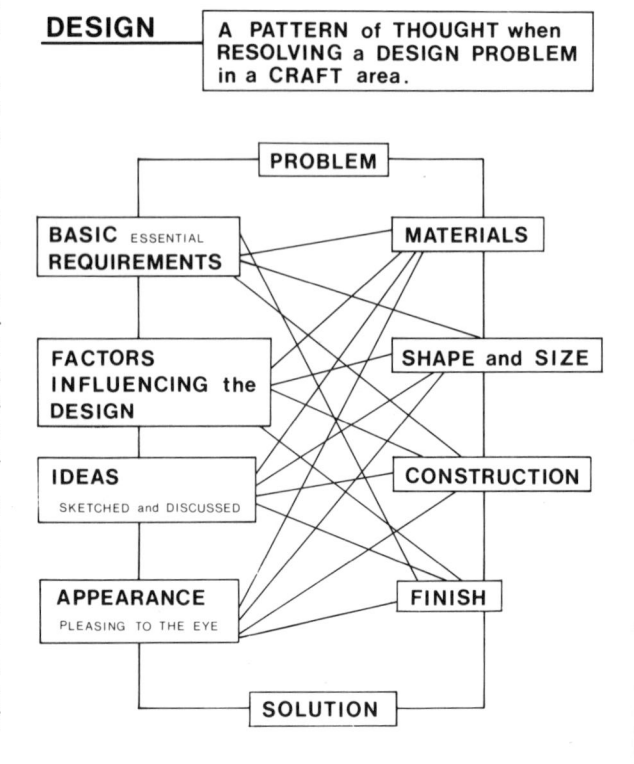

*Figure 5* Design - problem solving - a basic model

*Figure 6* A pattern of thought

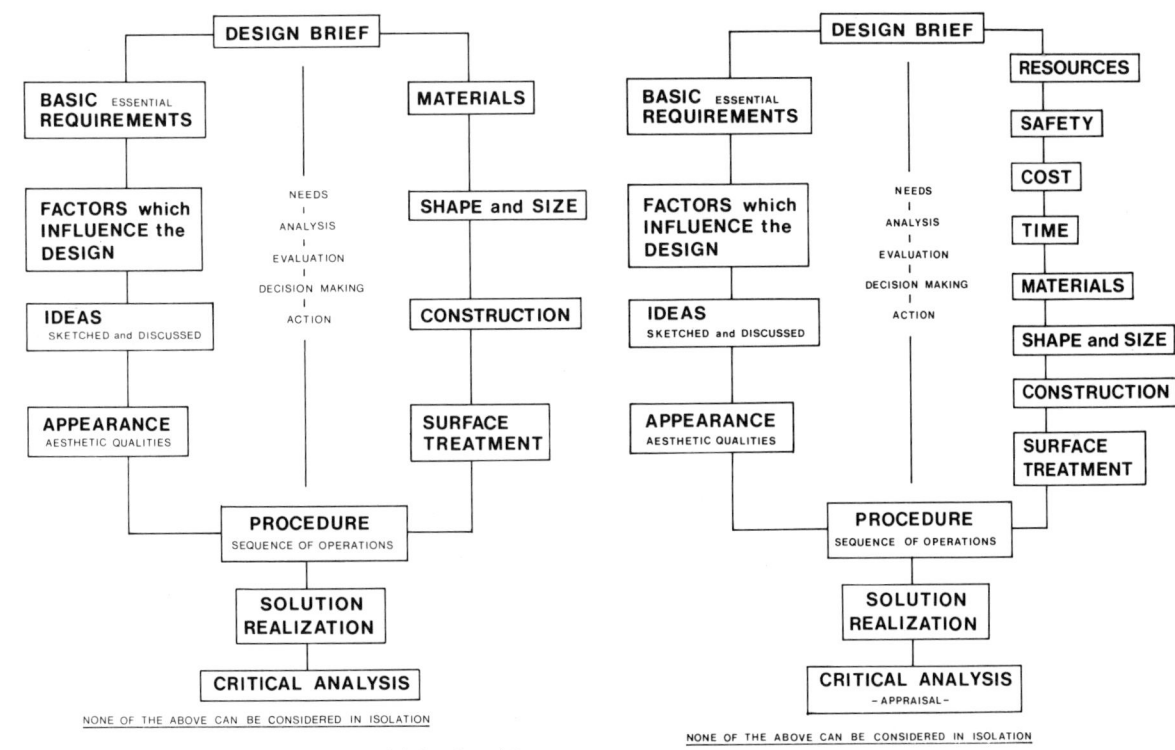

*Figure 7* Design – problem solving model developed from Figure 5

*Figure 8 Above right* Design – problem solving – a comprehensive model

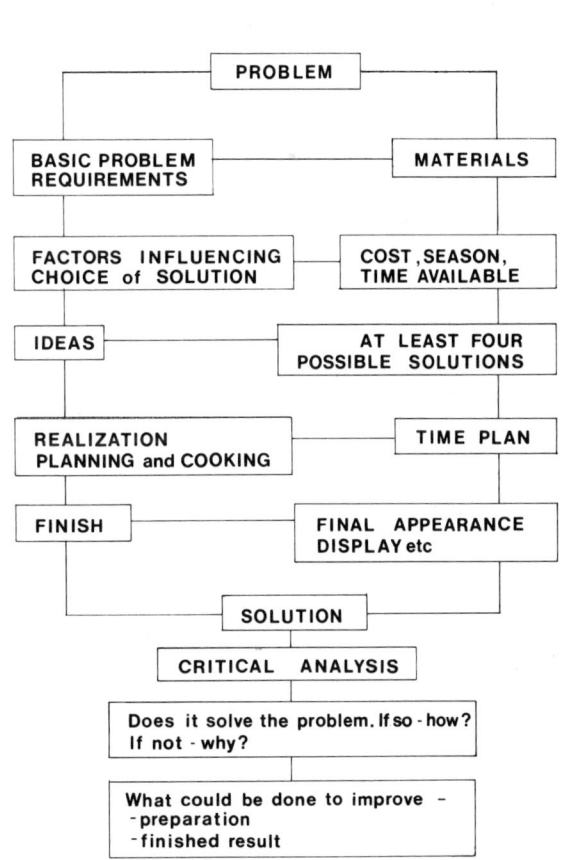

*Figura 9 Below right* Problem solving model produced by a home economics specialist to suit her own needs

thought when resolving a design problem in the workshop. This pattern relates quite favourably to the pattern shown in the engineering method in Figure 4.

The form of this model must be individual to the teacher and be modified to suit the needs of the child. Figure 7 offers a development from the initial model shown in Figure 5 and suggests a variation applicable perhaps to more able children.

Bearing in mind the interrelated nature of the thought process as indicated in Figure 6, a comprehensive model which a teacher can develop and use according to a child's ability is shown in Figure 8.

Within a department of faculty structure, where teachers are working together as part of a team, this modelling of a thought process can form the basis for like-mindedness amongst teachers. It can be argued that modelling relates to the process of learning and not to the end product, therefore it forms the only meaningful means of integration.

Consider the following two examples in Figure 9 and Figure 10 where specialist teachers have evolved a model to suit their own specialism and their own, developing personal philosophy.

It seems far more likely that a worthwhile dialogue can take place between specialist teachers if they can agree initially on the concept of modelling a thought process as part of problem solving.

In order to take this problem solving approach to a logical conclusion it is necessary to relate once again to the real world so that the child can begin to realize the value of such an approach.

It has already been suggested that the work of the engineer involves a thought process and that we as individuals employ a similar process in resolving our everyday problems. In order to clarify such a concept for children a clearer analysis is required which is quite readily associated with their everyday lives.

Figure 11 offers a simple analysis relating the thought process to decision making and identifying quite specifically broad areas of application in our everyday lives: *making, buying, organizing* and *forming an opinion.*

It seems that a child can quite readily identify his/her role within these activities.

However whilst Figure 11 extends the context quite naturally for the child, the teacher's needs require another dimension if a personal philosophy is to be developed.

Matchett's Fundamental Design Method may prove useful here. His aim is:

To enable a designer to perceive and to control the pattern of his thoughts and to relate this pattern more closely to all aspects of a design situation. [3]

In practice this means developing modes of thinking in order to cope with a variety of design problems. Matchett sets out

To enable designers to restructure their experience and thoughts to match both the essential and the variety of a design situation. [4]

He makes it quite clear that each person may select a different way of doing this. At the same time each

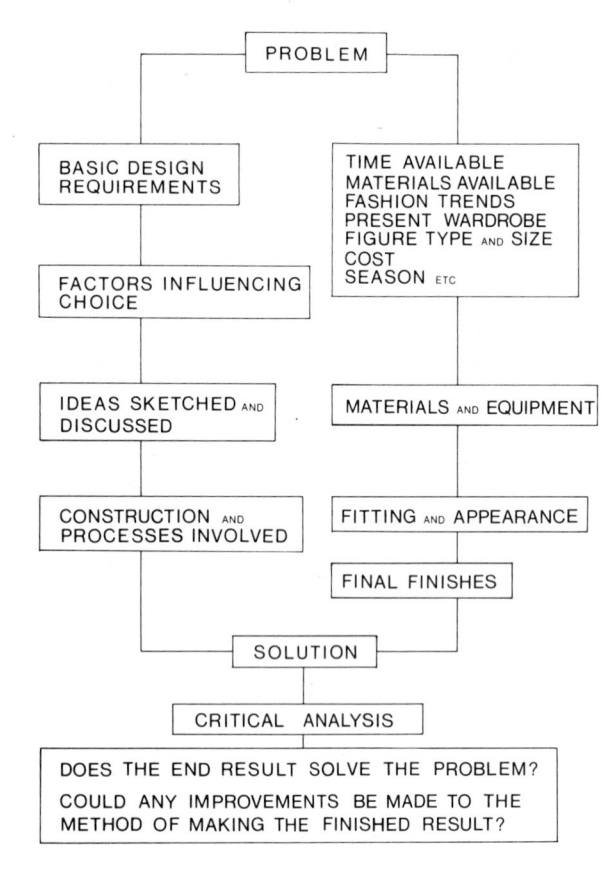

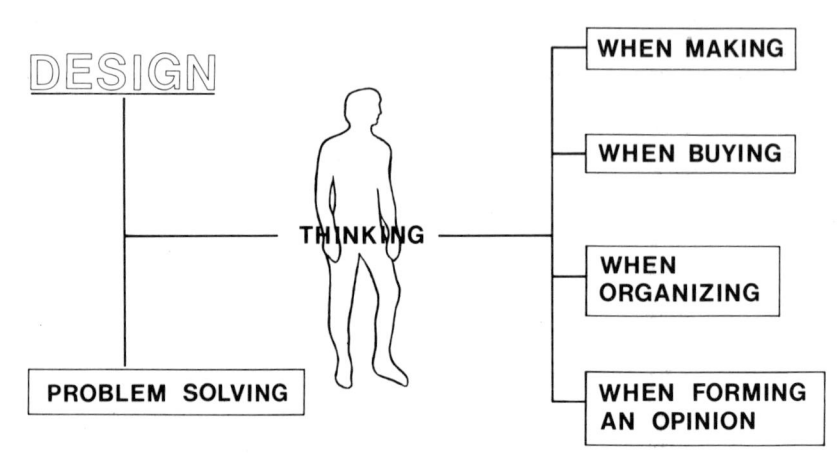

*Figure 10* Problem solving model produced by a fabrics specialist to suit her own needs

*Figure 11* Problem solving – the broader context. Adapted from Schools Council Design and Craft education project book *You are a Designer!*. Reproduced with the permission of the Schools Council and Edward Arnold (Publishers) Ltd

individual must develop their self-awareness and control of thought in order to be able to develop a personal strategy of thought for any situation.

The approach to workshop activities proposed in this chapter reflects this philosophy and encourages each teacher to develop control of thought and to encourage the same in a child.

Matchett's concept of the design process could serve a useful function for the teacher who is prepared to consider its implications in the context of workshop activities and to research further into Matchett's Design Method (see Bibliography reference).

Further food for thought can be found in the work of Karl Popper and his theory of knowledge.

He sees problem solving as the primary activity and survival as the primary problem to be resolved. He identifies the first task when dealing with a problem, as being to identify the reasons for its being a problem. He then suggests the notion of avoiding a common approach through a pre-determined format for all problems and stresses the need for constant feedback and successive adjustments during the problem solving process.

Popper refers to reality as the model where something is happening continuously and he sees the nature of our knowledge as being provisional, and permanently so. The truth cannot be proven at any stage since it is always possible that it will turn out to be false. Therefore in reality what is needed is the means of justifying a preferred choice.

He offers the problem solving process as a replacement for scientific method as illustrated in Figure 12 and supported further in the Bibliography.

A final word in this chapter extends the teacher's pattern of thought further to suggest the use of models in our everyday lives. A London Underground map, for example, is a model used to simplify a complex network of railway lines and stations in order to communicate essential information to the travelling public. This example is the outcome of a strategy of thought adopted by a designer in order to resolve a problem.

| SCIENTIFIC METHOD | PROBLEM SOLVING |
|---|---|
| 1 OBSERVATION and EXPERIMENT | 1 PROBLEM (usually rebuff to existing theory or expectation) |
| 2 INDUCTIVE GENERALIZATION | 2 PROPOSED SOLUTION (in other words a new theory) |
| 3 HYPOTHESIS | 3 DEDUCTION OF TESTABLE PROPOSITIONS FROM THE NEW THEORY |
| 4 ATTEMPTED VERIFICATION OF HYPOTHESIS | 4 TESTS attempted refutations by, among other things, observation and experiment |
| 5 PROOF or DISPROOF | 5 PREFERENCE ESTABLISHED BETWEEN COMPETING THEORIES |
| 6 KNOWLEDGE | |

*Figure 12* Popper's theory. Reproduced with permission from Popper by Bryan Magee, copyright Bryan Magee 1973, 1975, printed by Wm Collins and Sons Ltd (Fontana Books)

Similarly we are involved daily in determining strategies, modes of thought to resolve problems. We are all undeniably familiar with models of some kind whether they are maps, charts or catalogues used as models of what is for sale. We have a model in our mind of the clothes we wish to purchase, the food we consume and perhaps of the person we would like to marry.

If our lives depend upon relevant modes of thought being applied in particular circumstances then the role of the craft teacher should be to use that specialist subject area to encourage and develop modes of thinking as part of a child's education.

# 2 An approach to material selection and presentation

The function of this chapter is not to provide data of woodworking tools and techniques but rather to focus attention on how a child may be encouraged to learn through an approach to all aspects of workshop activities.

Emphasis is placed once again on analysis, synthesis and evaluation in relation to the process rather than to the end product itself. Here flow diagrams are used to identify key issues, in order to simplify and subsequently make the problem more manageable.

Courses' content will always remain the teacher's task and involvement in course planning ensures a high level of teacher commitment working from clearly identified objectives or criteria. In practice there is a need to monitor the constant feedback available and to modify the approach to content and structure accordingly, even when working within the constraints of an examination course.

For the teacher this amounts to a problem-solving situation where decisions have to be made and an appropriate course of action determined. The more difficult task is to develop this approach within the learning experiences available in the workshop.

Figure 13 identifies the major components within the problem facing the teacher.

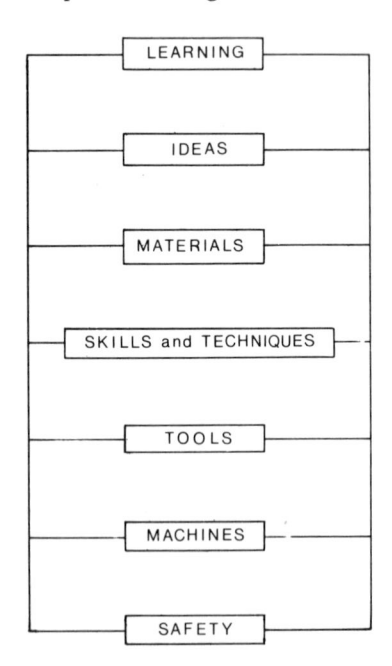

```
LEARNING
   |
IDEAS
   |
MATERIALS
   |
SKILLS and TECHNIQUES
   |
TOOLS
   |
MACHINES
   |
SAFETY
```

*Figure 13* Learning – major components

**Learning (see Figure 14)**
The teacher's role here is an important one. An appropriate starting point can be to consider the dialogue that occurs between the teacher and the child in a workshop.

If we extend this concept we are concerned with *discussion* which has an essential role to play in communication between the teacher and the child. Discussion is always valuable in a problem solving situation and is relevant to academic work as well as to practical activities. Here we are concerned with the practical, and discussion requires a child to think. Whatever the subject may be, thinking is an essential part of the learning process. Discussion may be two-way or general. The former can effectively take place between the teacher and a child whilst the latter can take several forms. General discussion is more complex and needs careful management by the teacher. It can involve a whole group of children in the workshop and each child is stimulated to translate ideas into words and to hear how other children and the teacher respond to these ideas. Here each child can be encouraged to express their own views and to listen to others. Group discussion is only one form of discussion that can take place in the workshop.

Informal discussion can occur spontaneously among a group of children where nobody is regarded as an authority on the problem involved. Whatever the form of discusssion each child should be encouraged to understand four main factors:

1 The role of discussion in problem solving.

2 The right of each child to express ideas without dominating the discussion.

3 The need to listen to others.

4 The logical sequence of thought preceding a discussion in order to seek out the relevant factors effectively.

Through discussion, the teacher can establish a workshop climate conductive to developing a sound relationship between the teacher and child. However it must be remembered that the skills of discussion need to be practised and be recognized as an essential prerequisite for *problem solving* activity. It could be a disaster course for an inexperienced teacher to embark on general discussion with a group of children without first considering an appropriate strategy or identifying the group's previous experience in discussion.

The idea that a child should just sit and listen to the teacher, read books or write essays or just follow instructions hardly goes far enough. The idea of workshop activities based on traditional skills and techniques represents a climate unlikely to develop discussion and child ideas. It is this concept of workshop activities that needs re-assessing and developing in order to include additional learning skills such as discussion.

The concept of a problem can be applied to most things or most situations which require a decision or a course of action to be taken. Whether the course of action is practical in nature or otherwise is irrelevant here. The relevant factor is the need to establish a thinking approach to all practical activities. This entails developing an attitude of mind through a problem solving approach to work.

If a child is to be encouraged to *analyse* then all aspects of work must have the development of analytical skills as an objective.

The interpretation of design education given in Chapter 1 placed some emphasis on the child making progress from child to adult standards during his or her school career. This transition reflects the move from concrete to formal operations where the child becomes aware of gaps in his/her previous knowledge and begins to fill these with hypotheses and to test without manipulating concrete objects. Here the child is in the process of constructing reality and in doing so begins to consider possibilities.

Research on the intellectual development of the child highlights the fact that at each stage of development the child has a characteristic way of viewing the world and explaining it to himself. [5]

This seems to suggest that personal ideas are vital to a child's experience and to developing confidence. The pre-operational period sees a child developing understanding through interplay with the immediate environment.

Then comes the rather more objective view and an awareness that in reality, things work and that personal understanding comes from finding out how they work.

For the teacher this situation represents the challenge of developing an approach to work which will promote analysis, synthesis and evaluation at a level suited to a child's individual needs.

Several courses of action are open to the teacher here.

1 All the work can be pre-determined and carefully directed.

2 A climate of free expression and experiment can be engendered with each child working according to interest.

3 The teacher can offer a starting point for the work and then guide the development of child ideas to a conclusion acceptable to the teacher and child. Care must be taken here to ensure that each child is involved in decision making.

LEARNING
- Analysis
- Thinking
- Discussion
- Problem Solving
- Trial and Error
- Group Activity
- Teacher
- Evaluation
- Methodology
- Communication

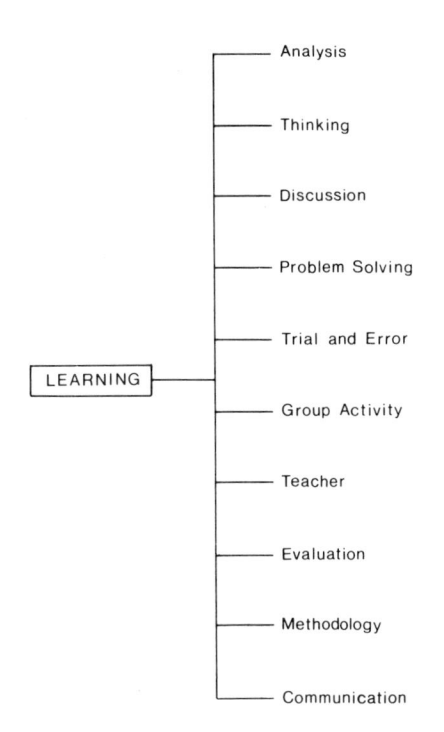

*Figure 14*

4 In an integrated course, the workshop teacher may find the work linked to a pre-determined theme or topic.

A brief comment on each will be helpful here.

1 This represents over-direction and a lack of awareness of a child's needs.

2 There are potential hazards within this approach since a child's work may fail to have any worthwhile structure, especially if the objective is interest based. How a teacher determines what is real interest rather than a passing whim or fancy is open to question here.

3 This approach offers the teacher an opportunity to create a worthwhile structure for a child to work within. At the same time the concept of starting points offers an opportunity to cater for a child's needs. Over direction should be avoided but the teacher's wider experience should be available to the child whenever required.

4 Whilst the approach suggested in 3 above can apply here, there is the added constraint of a theme or topic. Whilst the teacher may have agreed to the theme there may well be constraints that appear during the course which artificially restrict the scope of the work done. The logical development of a piece of work may well be restricted by the theme, thus proving unsatisfactory for both the teacher and the child.

Personal preference here would be for the approach suggested in 3 where the work offers a problem for both the teacher and the child. Here the concept of

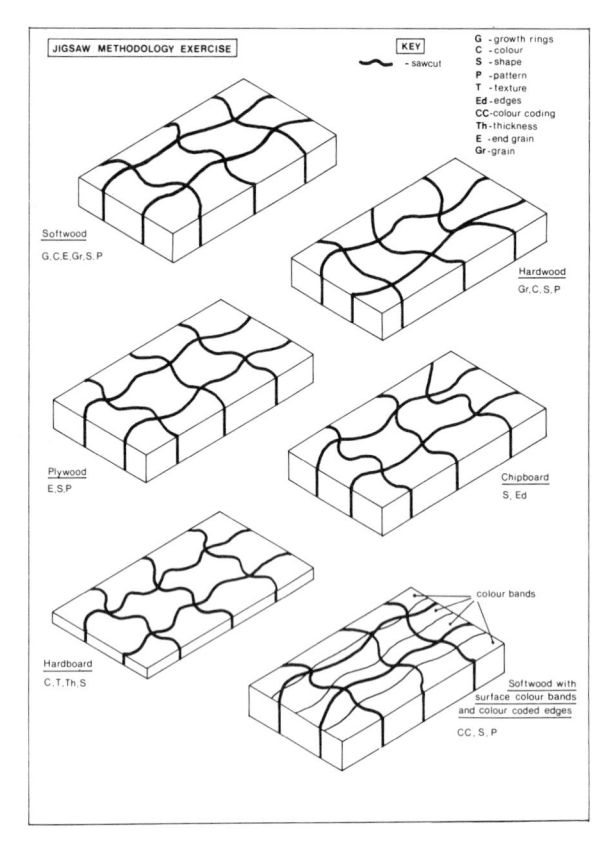

*Figure 15* Jigsaw methodology exercise

the teacher as a co-learner is being introduced. The teacher's position is not totally insecure however since he/she is able to rely on experience and maturity more readily than a child.

For an 11-year-old child the concept of a thought process is difficult to grasp. Therefore there is a need to involve the child in meaningful exercises to develop thinking as a skill.

Figure 15 (Jigsaws) serves as an introductory lesson to emphasize the need for thought when resolving a problem. Here the problem is a familiar one for the child but the emphasis has changed. Attention is being drawn to the methodology of assembling the jigsaw.

Each jigsaw differs in the following ways.

1 Material
2 Direction of cut
3 Natural pattern and colour
4 Applied colour code

Within a workshop this exercise can be carried out as an activity for small groups. Six jigsaws represent six groups and rotation ensures that each child gains the same experience. In addition to the physical properties of the jigsaws the teacher needs to consider the social development of a child within a group. This entails: communication, role playing, decision making, working relationships, organization of work and individual contribution.

The six jigsaws are as follows:

1 Hardwood with a natural finish
2 Softwood with a natural finish
3 Plywood with a natural finish
4 Hardboard with a natural finish
5 Chipboard with a natural finish
6 Soft wood with painted bands of colour and colour-coded edges

The range of materials introduces manufactured boards and natural timbers.

The physical characteristics of each material can be noted and used as part of the methodology to assemble the jigsaw. The introduction of a time factor adds the concept of working within a constraint.

The teacher's role during this exercise is to observe each group and the interaction between children within each group. Discussion must take place during and after group rotation has been completed in order to highlight the following concepts.

1 Group activity
2 Individual roles
3 Organization of work
4 Methodology

Making each member of a group aware that he or she has a role to play is an important aspect of learning. Initially the individual's role may be just to contribute ideas and to discuss an appropriate approach to assembling the jigsaw. The teacher should also raise the relationship problems that exist within a group. This develops the concept of discussion and consensus in order to make decisions. There may well be conflicting ideas but each child should be allowed to contribute since no one can be viewed as an expert within the group.

Successful group activity can only be achieved through a disciplined approach.

Communication between group members must be good. Personal ideas need to be expressed and the teacher's role should be to encourage decision making so that action can take place. A disciplined approach encourages a group to develop methodology. This is an approach to work where each group member is aware of his/her role within an overall strategy determined by discussion prior to commencing action. *Trial* and *error* may well be a feature of group activity and will generally be linked to a confused individual role within a group and a lack of communication.

Methodology promotes the organization of work and this demands an analytical approach to the problem in the first instance.

The visible physical characteristics of the material contribute to the development of a methodology and the pattern, texture, colour and shapes of each jigsaw piece will be significant here.

Finally the teacher can play a significant part in

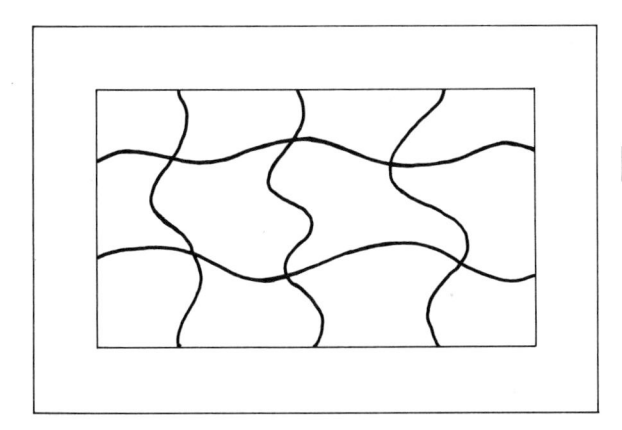

*Figure 16* Solution for assembly based on shapes

evaluating the exercise. The approach may be to make use of the child's experiences during the activity or may be to demonstrate an adult approach to the problem. A skilled teacher can harness both approaches and relate to situations that occur in the children's behavioural patterns during the activity.

As a final problem each group can be given the following brief for discussion.

Without changing the jigsaws in any way, design a methodology for assembly making use of only one characteristic of the pieces.

This promotes further discussion, analysis and a possible solution is indicated in Figure 16. A piece of card showing the assembled jigsaw with each piece correctly placed. Here the child's attention can be focused on one aspect of the problem only — in this instance *shape*.

Each jigsaw requires a different card but this solution is relevant to each one.

A development from the jigsaw exercise is illustrated in Figure 17.

A piece of softwood placed before the eyes of a group of children in the workshop will bring a variety of responses from 11-year-olds.

The initial response to the question: 'What do you see?' will prompt the immediate answer 'A piece of wood.'

Further questioning and encouragement to be more analytical should bring out further responses. These are likely to include

a piece of softwood
a piece of softwood pale straw in colour
a piece of softwood with grain features
a piece of softwood with texture
a piece of softwood with pattern
a piece of softwood with length, width and thickness
a piece of softwood with volume
a piece of softwood with hardness
a piece of softwood which has a source
a piece of softwood which has uses
a piece of softwood which has working properties

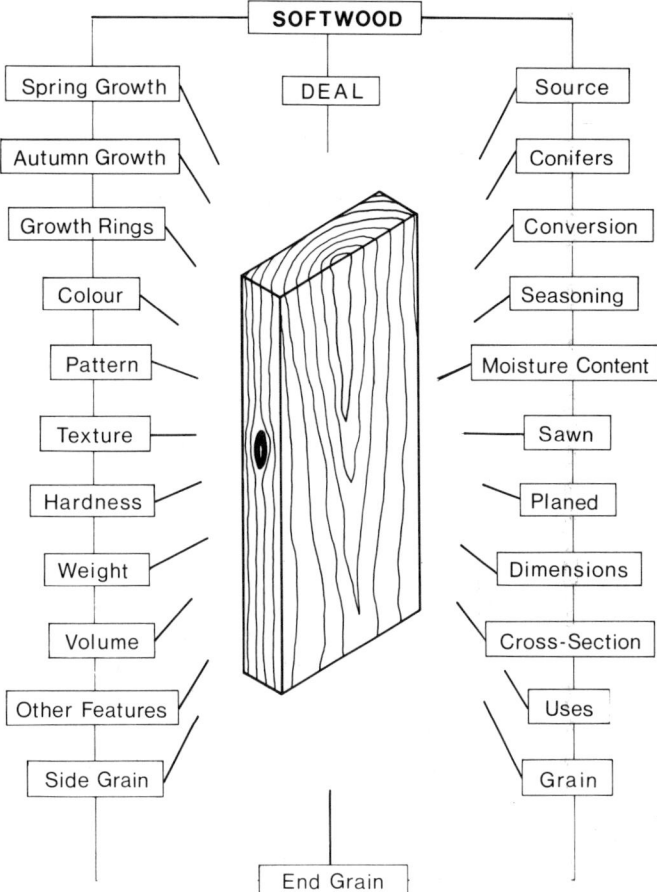

*Figure 17* Softwood analysis

Here the teacher's emphasis is on *analysis* and prompting the children to look and see in depth rather than superficially. The emphasis on clear, precise communication, discussion and individual contribution is high here as in other analytical exercises.

The concept of analysis can be developed further in relation to a product. At a simple level, a child can be encouraged to analyse, synthesize and evaluate a product. The product should be carefully selected from within the child's experience.

A bicycle is a good example of a suitable product.

How the teacher intends to introduce analysis here depends on the individual. There is an opportunity to introduce a *problem solving* situation. The problem itself can be stated in the form of a *design brief*

The Brief could be presented to the child as follows:

You have been given £80 to spend on a new bicycle. Your task is to make the most appropriate use of this money in your purchase.

You should make full use of any information available and be able to give reasons for each decision taken both during and prior to purchase.

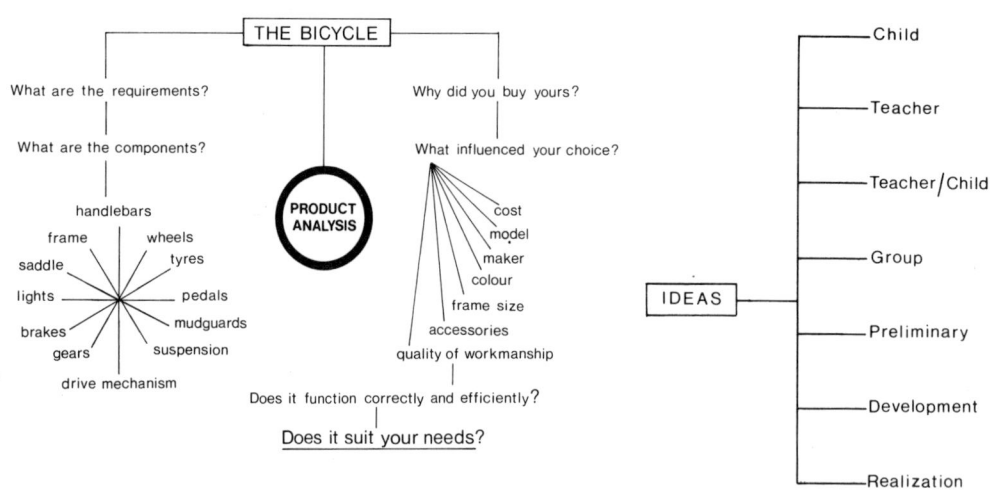

*Figure 18* Product analysis

*Figure 19*

Here the brief can be viewed as incomplete or ill-defined and offers the teacher ample room for discussion in order to promote clarification.

It seems that the child needs to consider four broad issues in order to clarify the brief.

1 Does all the money need to be used?

2 How to determine what 'the most appropriate' decision means in reality.

3 What information is relevant?

4 How to find or become aware of the relevant information.

The basis for analysis here can be based on identifying

1 Basic requirements.

2 Other factors which need to be considered.

Figure 18 offers a framework for discussion with a group of children. The teacher can elect to compile the chart by drawing responses from the children or by offering the major components for discussion in order to focus child attention on details.

The methodology used in this product analysis is to identify major components of the product and then to identify sub-components.

This means encouraging a child to break a problem down into more manageable parts in order to try and conceive the whole more readily.

### Ideas (see Figure 19)

All the work done in workshops represents ideas in two- or three-dimensional form.

For the teacher, ideas represent a decision made during course planning and lesson preparation. For the child, ideas mean developing confidence, work experience, and making progress along the journey from child to adult standards.

Ideas can be teacher based, child based or an amalgamation of both.

Teacher ideas
These can be interpreted in several ways. A teacher can pre-determine the content of each lesson and each piece of work by only using teacher ideas. Here control can be gained over all the work done and each child will be exposed to the same experiences and follow the same instructions.

A teacher can use his/her ideas in order to ensure that each child gains a basic experience of pre-determined techniques as part of a course structure.

The potential of a machine or hand tool can be explored, or the concept of workmanship stressed to a limited extent within a tightly controlled exercise.

There are constraints operating here which can have a marked effect on the range and type of work done. These constraints are generally — facilities, tools and equipment, child ability range, economic factors, range of materials available, time available, importance of future examination course requirements, teacher's personal experience and interests. A child's ideas can be used fully through the problem solving approach advocated in this book. The individual needs of the child can be catered for and supported by the teacher. In reality it is more likely that the amalgamation of teacher/child ideas will occur. The teacher's contribution may well be to offer a starting point and the child's ideas can flourish within the response to that starting point.

Whatever the situation, it is important to realize that ideas are generally a response to a problem. Initially such ideas are preliminary in nature, incomplete and lacking any real detail.

To the individual child or the teacher, ideas represent motivation and the desire to resolve, to work out detail and to achieve realization.

The important role for the teacher here is to encourage the progress from the preliminary stages through development to realization where the idea finally appears in two- or three-dimensional form.

Some kind of structure to the use of ideas is

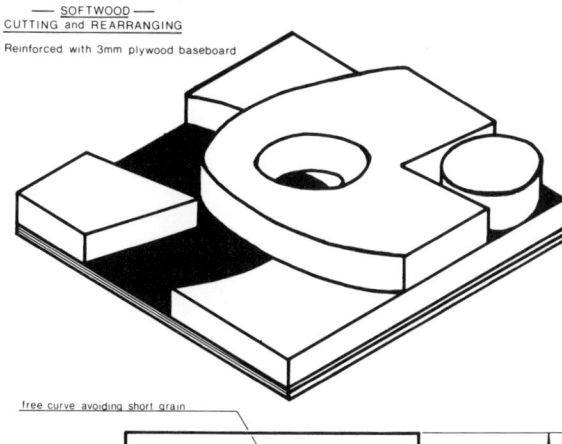

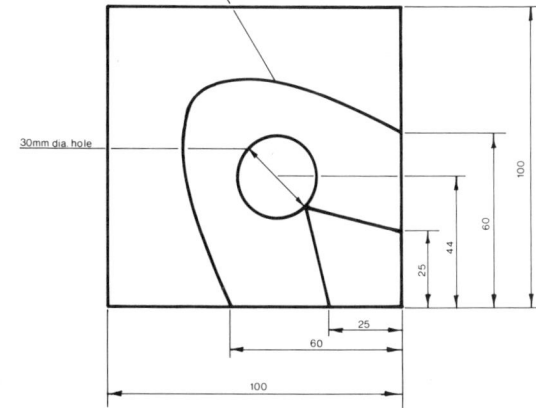

required so that a child can assess personal progress.

Within a craft course, as part of a basic course within a design department, time has become a major constraint on the amount of work that can be achieved. Therefore the teacher's skills are fully tested when determining a project that will cater for basic techniques as well as satisfying the objectives of design education. Figure 20 shows an example of a controlled project making use of wood as the material.

Within this simple project the following objectives can be identified.

**1** Basic understanding of working properties of softwood and plywood.

**2** Use of plane to clean one surface.

**3** Marking out — use of knife and pencil line.

**4** Band saw/jig saw — cutting curves.

**5** Band saw/jig saw — cutting a straight line.

**6** Band saw/jig saw — size of blade in relation to the size of curve cut. Limitations of the machine.

**7** Short grain in softwood.

**8** Plywood used as a strengthening material.

**9** Preparation for finishing.

**10** Applying a finish.

**11** Gluing and Assembly.

These objectives represent quite a comprehensive list that can be demonstrated or discussed formally and reinforced through individual or small group demonstration and discussion during the lesson.

The overall concept here is cutting wood and rearranging the parts into a new, acceptable whole. Decision making here is based on shape, colour, pattern and texture. In this project a simple rule has evolved in order to link each individual piece within a group assembly arrangement. Without a linking factor any arrangement would have shown a lack of awareness on the part of both the teacher and the child. The final product here is suitable for display in the school environment. This approach ensures that a continuous supply of work is available for display. Needless to say, there are many ways of arranging individual pieces into a whole but the final decision must stem from teacher/child discussion and be based on visual awareness.

Child ideas can be used extensively by posing problems in the form of a design brief and allowing each child, with teacher support, to develop preliminary ideas for realization.

Communication is also an important component here. Ideas can be discussed but generally most progress is achieved through sketching and developing the idea on paper. Here the child has to tussle with the task of expressing ideas clearly so that others can understand them. The use of a common language here enables the teacher to contribute to the development of ideas. The form of the communication depends on the teacher. Since the thought process is as important

---

SOFTWOOD —
CUTTING and REARRANGING
Reinforced with 3mm plywood baseboard

free curve avoiding short grain

30mm dia. hole

All dimensions in mm

**Softwood — cutting and rearranging exercise**

The following skills and techniques are included:

Planing
Marking out — pencil and knife lines
Curved cut on band saw or jig saw
Relating free curve shape to the machine's blade width
Short grain
Addition of reinforcing baseboard
Preparation for finishing
Application of finish
Gluing and assembly procedures

*Figure 20* Teacher controlled exercise

*Figure 21* Group response to a brief

as the product, representing the thinking and the making, then the communication must be as explicit as possible.

At basic-course level, the format may be sketches and notes whilst at senior, examination level the requirement will be a comprehensive folio of work.

Group projects
Group projects represent the ideas of a group of children working as a team with the teacher. Viewed another way, the group may well be merely a workforce carrying out the ideas of the teacher. It seems likely that the teacher's role will be to harness all the individual ideas and to provide a structure for decision making so that action can take place.

Figure 21 shows a two-dimensional visual form to be sited in the school environment adjacent to the physical education facilities. The stages of these projects can be indicated as follows:

1 Definition of the brief.

2 Identification of constraints and factors to be considered.

3 Initial ideas from individuals and then from each group.

4 Selection and development of a selected idea.

Within these projects each child accepted the need for discussion, for a structured approach to work and the identification of each individual's role in the making process.

Safety (see Figure 22)

A sound attitude to safety in the workshops is vital and must become part of the workshop routine for both the teacher and the child. The requirements

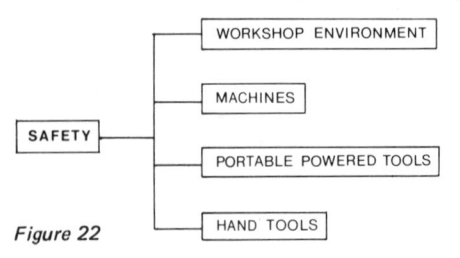

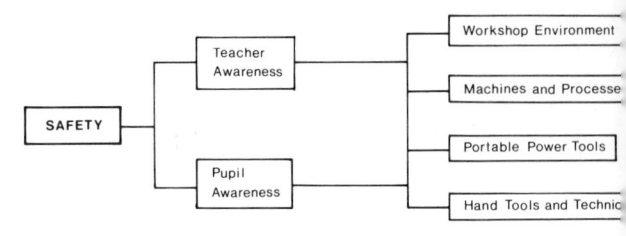

*Figure 22*

*Figure 23* Safety – major components

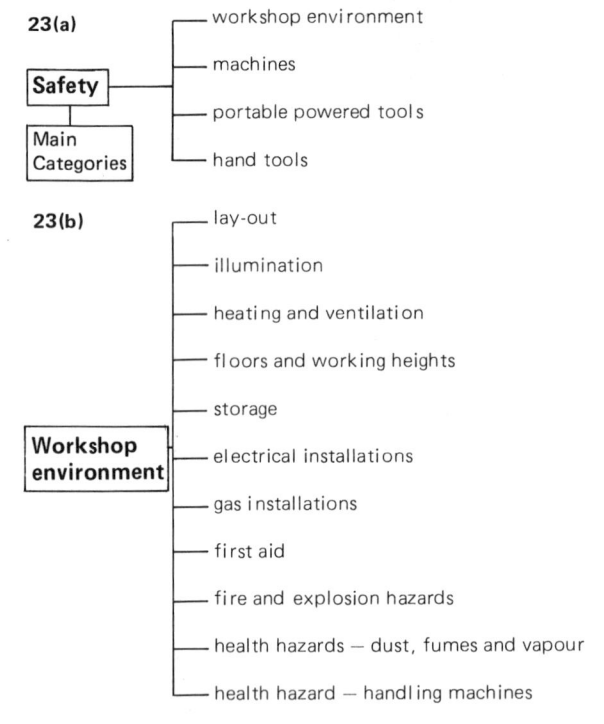

23(a) Safety Main Categories
- workshop environment
- machines
- portable powered tools
- hand tools

23(b) Workshop environment
- lay-out
- illumination
- heating and ventilation
- floors and working heights
- storage
- electrical installations
- gas installations
- first aid
- fire and explosion hazards
- health hazards – dust, fumes and vapour
- health hazard – handling machines

of the Health and Safety Act (1975) make care and attention to the details of safety precautions an essential part of every teacher's role.

Initially, here again, some form of analysis is required of the overall problem of promoting safe working conditions and procedures. The teacher can then:

1 Identify the essential requirements of safety.

2 Relate these requirements to the workshop environment.

3 Promote the development of a child's level of awareness of safety in the workshop.

Safety and the teacher
Figure 23 indicates the major areas of concern for the teacher. From this analysis the teacher needs to identify the detailed content of each area in order to create safe working conditions.

BS 4163 1975, Recommendations for Health and Safety offers the following support for the teacher in the workshop.

**23(c)**

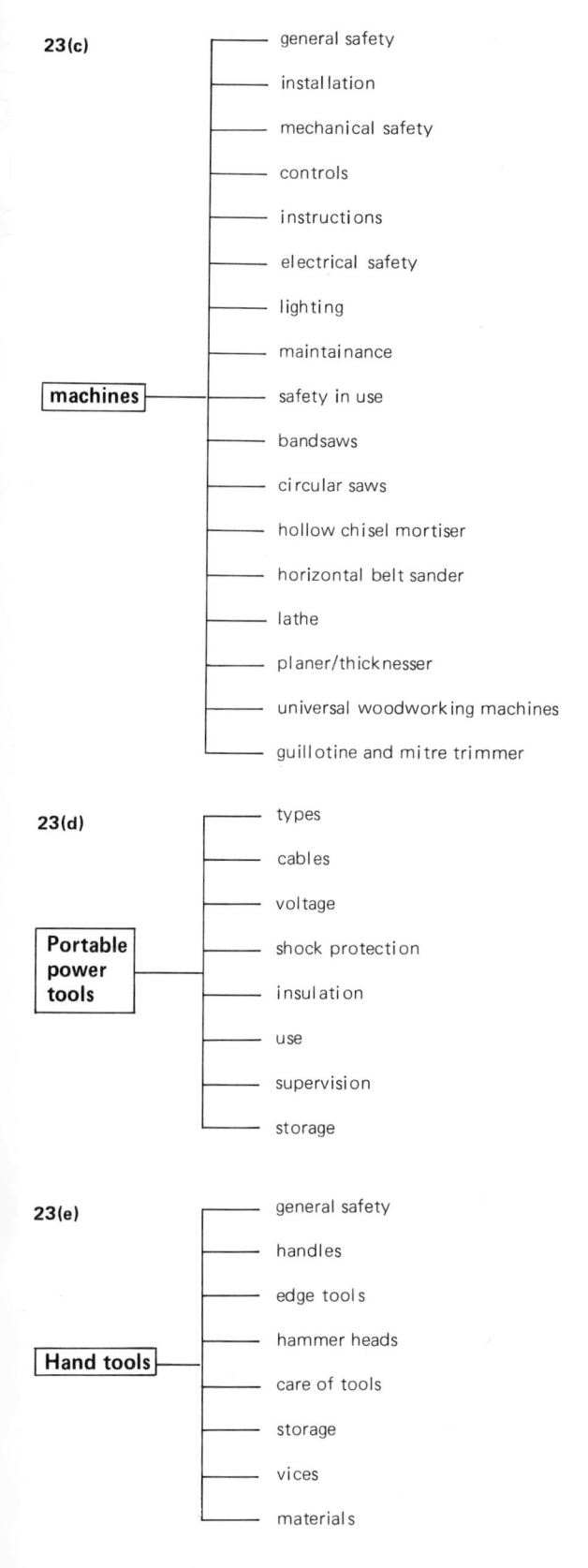

machines
- general safety
- installation
- mechanical safety
- controls
- instructions
- electrical safety
- lighting
- maintainance
- safety in use
- bandsaws
- circular saws
- hollow chisel mortiser
- horizontal belt sander
- lathe
- planer/thicknesser
- universal woodworking machines
- guillotine and mitre trimmer

**23(d)**

Portable power tools
- types
- cables
- voltage
- shock protection
- insulation
- use
- supervision
- storage

**23(e)**

Hand tools
- general safety
- handles
- edge tools
- hammer heads
- care of tools
- storage
- vices
- materials

Teacher awareness of safety must be reflected within the following:

1 Familiarity with the recommendations contained within the act.

2 Familiarity with a course of action to be taken when faults or an emergency arise.

3 Preparation to show pupils, by example, the importance of safety.

4 Preparation to convert these recommendations into a simpler form readily understood by pupils of all abilities.

Figures 23 (a)–(e) illustrate the extent of the problem for the teacher if the content of the Act is to be applied in practice.

In order to comply with 4 stated above the teacher needs to transfer the broader analysis into a more specific course of action to be implemented in the workshop. Furthermore, this course of action leading to a behavioural pattern for children must be quite readily understood by each child.

Here again the teacher can introduce the child to a brief on safety in order to focus attention on possible hazards within a workshop.

'Design a safety poster which illustrates one hazard within the workshop.' (A limit of size, time and content can be imposed as additional constraints within the brief if necessary.)

For each child the problems of safety must relate quite clearly to their workshop experience or at least be an obvious extension of what they have done.

An acceptable analysis for a child could be as follows:

|        | |
|---|---|
| | PUPILS |
| | FLOORS |
| | BENCHES |
| SAFETY | MATERIALS |
| | MACHINES |
| | CUTTING TOOLS |

Each component within this analysis can then be simplified realistically in terms of workshop situations easily recognized by each child.

**SAFETY IN CRAFT WORKSHOPS – INTRODUCTORY PUPIL HANDOUT**

The attitude to safety in any workshop must be the concern of both the teacher and each child, and forms the essential part of workshop routine for everyone.

**Read the following notes carefully, make sure you understand their meaning, then put them into practice.**
*Possible hazard areas in a workshop*

1 PUPILS    3 BENCHES    5 MACHINES
2 FLOORS    4 MATERIALS  6 CUTTING TOOLS

**1 PUPILS**
(a) Always work clear of other pupils so that you are not impeded in any way.

(b) When moving around or through a workshop, avoid hurrying or pushing past others.

(c) During demonstrations by the teacher keep quiet, keep clear and avoid crushing together.

(d) Always wear protective clothing securely tied back and make sure others do the same.

(e) Make sure that talking is never above the level of general work noise in the workshop.

**2 FLOORS**
(a) Notify the teacher if any part of the floor becomes highly polished, wet or slippery in any way.

(b) Avoid dropping scraps of material on to the floor. Use the appropriate waste box or bin.

(c) The floor area around all machines should be clear of any obstruction.

(d) Make sure that there is plenty of floor space around you when handling long lengths of material, eg timber boards, steel rod or tube, plywood sheets, acrylic sheets, etc.

**3 BENCHES**
(a) Open vices use up space and can cause injury. Close the vice when not in use but not tightly.

(b) Cutting tools should never overhang the edge of a bench.

(c) Make sure that you have room to work on a bench top.

(d) Make sure that there is adequate room between benches to allow movement and for work to take place.

(e) Avoid using a bench near a pupil operating a machine.

(f) Never move benches without consulting the teacher.

**4 MATERIALS**
(a) Be aware of the possible dangers when using materials. For example:
  Plastics – take all necessary precautions with resin, glass-fibre.
  Wood – be aware of dust extraction, woodturning hazards.
  Metal – be aware of hazards involving Aluminium Alloy Casting.

(b) Read procedure and process charts or notes very carefully. Ask your teacher if in any doubt.

(c) Take special care when handling and moving long lengths of materials. Is the movement really necessary?

(d) Be aware that dust can be a health hazard in the workshop. Use the dust extraction system provided on the lathe finishing sander.

**5 MACHINES**
(a) Never interfere with a machine when you are not using it.

(b) Never have loose clothing hanging when operating a machine.

(c) Make sure you know how to use the machine or piece of equipment.

(d) Never hold work in your hand, eg when drilling on the pillar drill make use of a jig, machine vice or G-clamp.

(e) Avoid fiddling with machine controls, dials, buttons or levers – they may be set accurately for a purpose.

(f) Keep clear of the operator.

(g) Read any instructions carefully before starting to work.

(h) Avoid talking or distracting others who are operating a machine.

(i) Make sure all is in order before starting a machine.

(j) Switch off in an emergency.

(k) Wear protective goggles.

(l) Never attempt to change speed while the machine is in motion.

(m) Never leave a machine running unattended.

**6 CUTTING TOOLS**
(a) Always carry these edge downwards in the workshop and avoid sudden movements.

(b) Use them in a way that makes the best possible use of their cutting edge.

(c) Keep your hands/fingers behind the cutting edge at all times.

(d) Protect the surface of the bench by using a cutting board.

(e) Always return each tool to its rightful place and report any missing items.

(f) Lay tools safely on the bench when in use.

**Some general points**

1 Never enter a workshop without a craft teacher being present.

2 Movement through a workshop should be at walking pace at all times, without distracting others. Think what others may be doing and avoid breaking your own or someone else's concentration.

3 Wear protective clothing at all times.

4 Avoid loose clothing at all times.

5 Keep talking noise below the level of work noise.

6 Avoid interfering with any equipment which is unfamiliar to you.

7 Do not handle other pupil's work – you may cause damage by accident.

8 Help safety by returning every tool and piece of equipment to its correct place.

9 Remember that Emergency Stop Buttons are for an emergency *only*.

**To sum up**

This may seem a long list but it largely means two words – Common sense, ie
1 Be aware of others.
2 Think before doing anything.
3 Read notices.
4 Act on good advice from a teacher or technician.
5 Whenever in doubt – seek advice.

**Skills and techniques (see Figure 24)**

The methodology described earlier in this book finds further significance here but it is more likely that techniques will be associated with the term *procedure* (sequence of operations) referred to in the Problem Solving Model (Figure 7).

Whatever terminology is used the sequence does represent a deliberate attempt to analyse a task and then to determine an appropriate method of working.

*Figure 24*

```
                    ┌── Preparation of material
                    │
                    ├── Marking out
                    │
                    ├── Cutting/Shaping
                    │
                    ├── Joining
                    │
SKILLS and TECHNIQUES ┼── Surface treatment
                    │
                    ├── Assembly
                    │
                    ├── Volume production
                    │
                    ├── Jigs
                    │
                    └── Templates
```

1. Cut one straight side
Mark
Remove as little waste as possible

*Tools used*
straight edge
trimming knife
cutting board

2. Cut a second straight side at right angles to the first
Mark
Remove as little waste as possible

*Tools used*
try square
trimming knife
cutting board

3. Measure 100mm along one prepared side
Cut to length

*Tools used*
steel rule
try square
trimming knife
cutting board

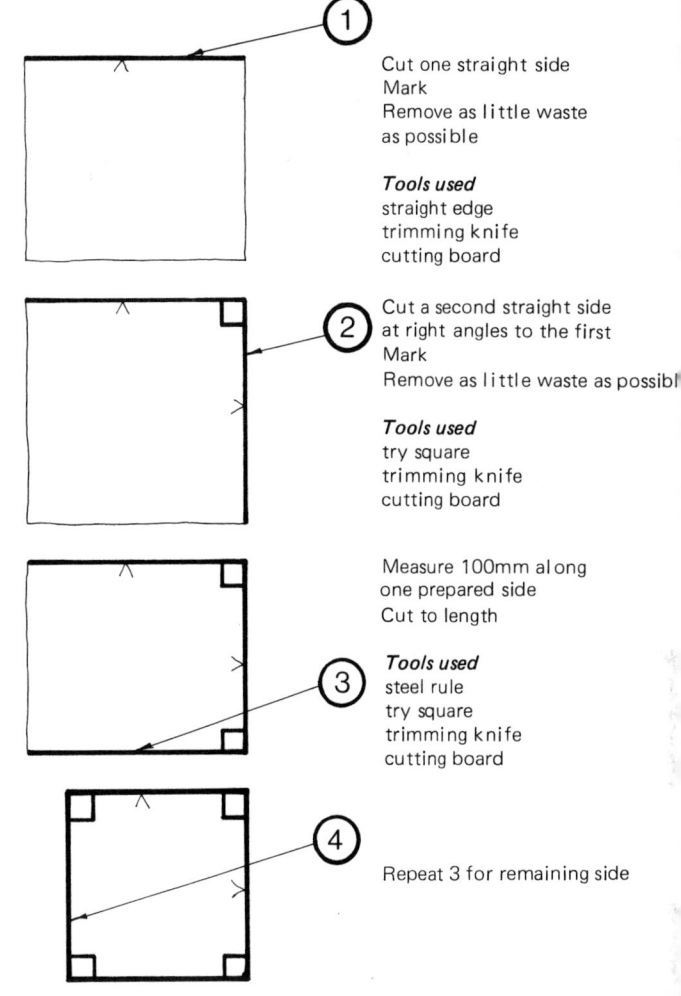

4. Repeat 3 for remaining side

*Figure 25* Preparation to size – basic methodology exercise in card

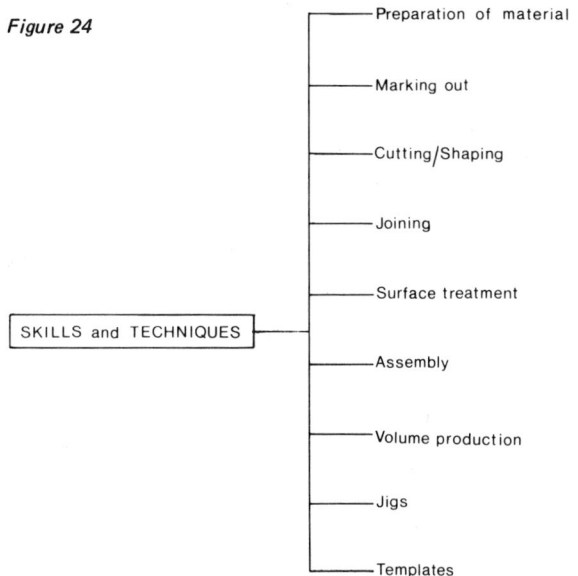

Once the sequence has been established and work commences, it is highly likely that some modifications to the procedure will be required. This represents feedback within the thought process where the operator is constantly having to re-assess in response to any new information that may emerge.

Within skills and techniques there are details to be identified and considered in greater depth. The objective here is to identify and to illustrate aspects of these details which are important in relation to work in the workshop.

Consider first of all *preparation to size*. A basic methodology can be identified which is adaptable to the preparation of any material for a child, the concept of methodology in preparing to size can be simplified initially through the use of softer materials.

Consider the following brief, for example:

'Prepare a piece of thin card, which has ragged edges, to a square shape of 100 mm side. State your method of working step-by-step'.

Here the teacher can either direct the children through a pre-determined sequence or involve the group (or an individual child) in some analytical thinking in order to establish a sound methodology for working. The following question and answer sequence will help to illustrate the objective here and Figure 25 1-4 illustrate each stage.

Q What is the definition of a square?
A A regular geometric figure with four equal, straight sides and four equal internal angles.
Q What is the internal angle?
A 90°.
Q What is the length of side required here?
A 100 mm.
Q What will the first step be in making a square, and why?
A Cut one straight side since that is an essential requirement of a square shape. Leave as little waste as possible for economic reasons and then mark the cut side for easy identification.
Q How can this side be cut?
A With a trimming knife, a straight edge and a cutting board. This gives greater accuracy than a pair of scissors.
Q What will the next stage be?
A Cut a second side at 90° to the first side again with as little waste as possible. This is because a square has straight sides and an internal angle of 90°. Mark the side for easy identification.
Q What will the next stage be?
A Measure 100 mm along the two sides from the point where they meet.
Q What will the next stage be?
A Cut a 90° angle at the 100 mm mark.
Q How can this be done?
A Use a try-square from the accurately cut sides, a trimming knife and a cutting board.

**Preparation of material** — Sequence of operations

| Material | Softwood or hardwood to L x W x TH (up to 100 mm width approx) | Softwood or hardwood to L x W | Manufactured board to L x W |
|---|---|---|---|
| Sequence of operations | 1 Prepare a face side<br>2 Check for flatness<br>3 Mark<br>4 Prepare a face edge<br>5 Test for flatness<br>6 Test for squareness from the face side<br>7 Mark<br>8 Gauge to width from the face edge<br>9 Plane down to gauge line<br>10 Gauge to thickness from the face side<br>11 Plane down to the gauge line<br>12 Square one end using a shooting board or a jig attached to a lathe finishing sander<br>13 Measure and mark from this prepared end<br>14 Mark length with a knife line squared onto all four surfaces<br>15 Saw off the waste and shoot to the line | 1<br>2 Select a face side and mark<br>3<br>4<br>5 Select a face edge and mark<br>6<br>7<br>8 Gauge to width from the face edge<br>9 Plane down to gauge line<br>10 Not applicable<br>11<br>12 As for previous example<br>13<br>14<br>15 | 1 Prepare one edge<br>2 Test for flatness<br>3 Mark<br>4 Prepare an adjacent edge<br>5 Test for flatness<br>6 Test for squareness from the first edge<br>7 Mark<br>8 Measure and mark out width<br>9 Remove waste and plane to the line<br>10 Measure and mark out length<br>11 Remove waste and plane to the line<br>NB With this material the technique will vary according to the size of the material |

*Figure 26* Preparation of material – sequence of operations in chart

The visible outcome of this exercise should be a square piece of card with 100 mm sides. The teacher's task here has been to try and illustrate to a child why a sequence of operations is essential. Each stage has been carried out for a specific reason and this has been an essential requirement of a square. The dialogue between the teacher and child will have many deviations *en route* but understanding can be developed this way, since together they have analysed a problem. The success or failure of the sequence of operations they adopt is the result of their collective, considered thoughts.

If the nature of the problem is changed and related to pieces of other materials, then the need for a methodology remains but the starting point depends on the material.
Consider for example:

1 A piece of softwood to be prepared to length, width and thickness.

2 A piece of softwood to be prepared to length and width where the thickness has already been planed.

3 A piece of manufactured board (plywood) which needs to be prepared to length and width since the thickness is constant and cannot be planed.

The table in Figure 26 indicates a typical sequence and the different starting points for each material.

Here is the basis for a teaching aid and a source of reference readily available for children in the workshops.

A child's understanding of techniques can be developed by analysing the relationship between hand and tool in several simple operations. Consider the following for example:

| | |
|---|---|
| use of a pencil | use of a marking gauge |
| use of a marking knife | use of a tenon saw |
| use of a try square | use of a jack plane |

The location of the thumb, forefinger and the other three fingers in each case suggests that control can be achieved with this arrangement. Figure 27 (a)–(f) illustrate these tools in use.

Marking out

If we consider the function of marking out then we are concerned with accuracy, workmanship and control. *Accuracy* stems from the type of line used and the tool used to make the mark. *Workmanship* stems from the clarity and suitability of the line. *Control* stems from the combination of accuracy and workmanship.

Marking out generally uses the following types of line: pencil line, knife line and gauge line.

In broader terms these fall into two categories:

Lines for guidance which are temporary in nature.

**27(a)**      **27(b)**      **27(c)**

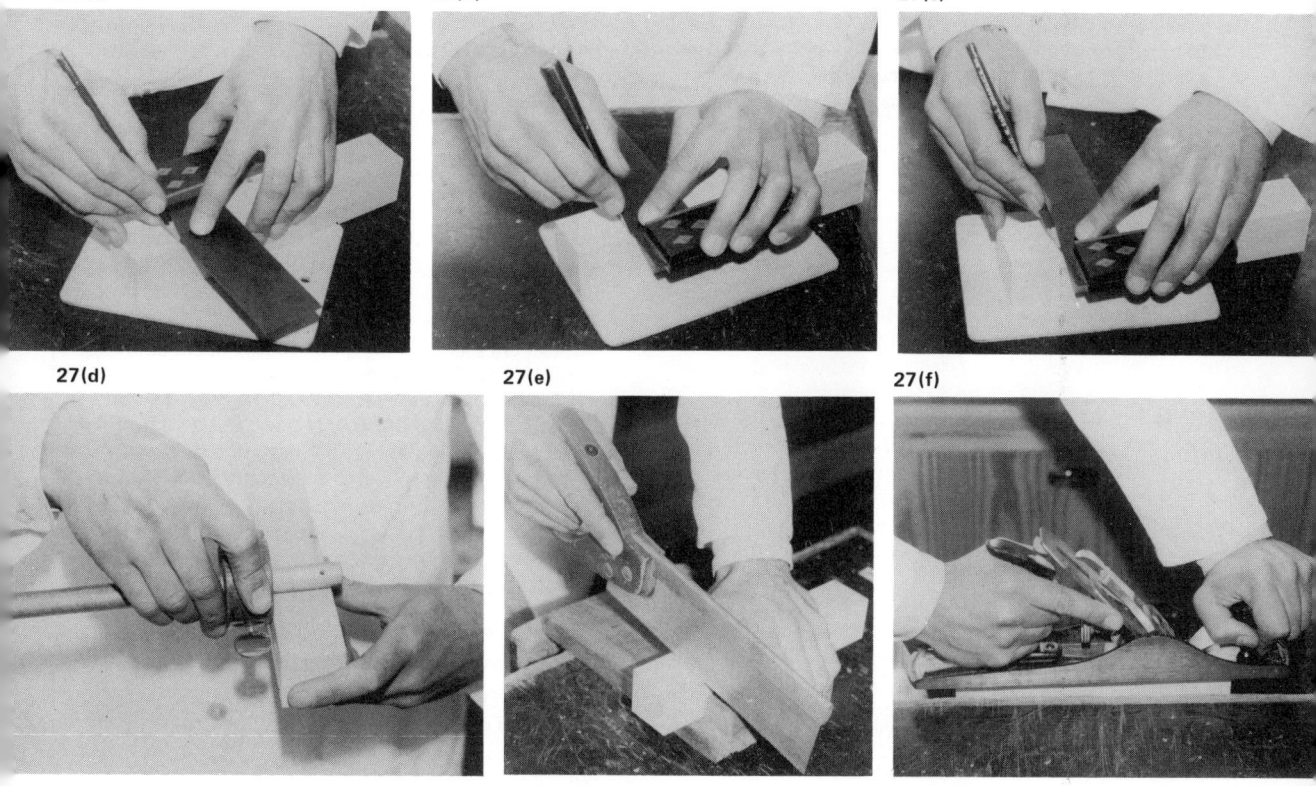

**27(d)**      **27(e)**      **27(f)**

*Figure 27* The relationship between the hand, tool and the work
(a) pencil   (b) marking knife   (c) try square   (d) marking gauge   (e) tenon saw   (f) jack plane

Lines for indicating as precisely as possible where material is to be cut accurately.

**Pencil line** – A mark on the surface of material. Generally used for guidance where an accurate edge is not required. Often used in shaping where a template has been made as an aid to marking out. Can be used along and across the grain.

**Knife line** – A mark cut into the surface of material. Generally used across the grain wherever accuracy is required. When used along the grain the knife will tend to follow the grain, giving an undesirable result. Used whenever wood is to be cut away and a precise edge is required.

**Gauge line** – A mark cut into the surface of material using a marking, mortice, or a cutting gauge. A gauge is used from a face edge, face side or a prepared end whenever a parallel line (or lines) is required. The task of using a marking gauge can prove difficult for a child but the problem can be eased by inclining the spur.

Having identified the basic types of line and possible applications, the teacher's role must be to encourage each child to determine the most appropriate application of each type as the need arises.

Questions arise when any marking out problem is encountered:

What is the marking problem?

Is the shape to be cut accurately to fit another part? eg joint shoulder line.

Is the mark to be made along or across the grain?

Is the line to be parallel to an edge, side or prepared end of a piece of wood?

A continuous dialogue of this nature can take place in many learning situations, whether during a teacher's demonstration, a group discussion or an individual child's problem. Discussion must not only resolve the type of line that is most appropriate but must also direct attention to the marking or cutting action of the tool itself. Generally a child ignores the details of a tool unless attention is focused on its function.

The pencil line is a good example, since a child will assume that any pencil will be satisfactory for marking. There will also be the assumption that a pencil point is always in good order in the same way as a cutting edge should be in good order. Experience suggests that a sharp point on a pencil gives a more precise line and improved workmanship as a result. It is also sound to assume that an HB and 2H pencil will cover most of the requirements as long as they are kept in a sharpened state. Here the teacher can quite readily demonstrate the effects of a thick, heavy black line in comparison with a sharp more precise line.

When considering a cut line, the technique of using the knife comes into focus. If a child can be encouraged to identify a well executed cut line then any deviation from that standard should raise questions:

Why is the cut line ragged?
Am I using the correct part of the cutting edge?
Is the cutting edge sharp?
Is the material particularly difficult to work?
How can I improve the lines?

A good example of the importance of technique can be seen when marking out a circle which is to be cut out. Here a pencil line is inappropriate and a knife or gauge line is impossible to execute. The solution lies in a pair of dividers or wing compass which have been sharpened to give a point and a cutting edge. Since the problem involves marking across and along the grain the technique of inclining the cutting edge is most vital here if a well executed line is to be achieved.

Cutting and shaping
Cutting and shaping wood covers the range of work from fabrication to sculpture.

Although considered here in isolation, cutting cannot be divorced from the preparatory activity of marking out. However, if a child is to be encouraged to analyse the problem of cutting then attention must be focused on this task alone. Take, for example, a simple hand-tool operation — sawing to a line at a bench.

Tools and equipment required

Tenon saw            Holding device
Sawing board         Working surface

Questions arise immediately:

Why has the Tenon saw been selected?
Why is a sawing board necessary?
Why is a holding device required?
Where is the most appropriate place to carry out the task?

Answers to these questions focus attention on the following:

1 Size and weight of the saw.
2 Shape and cutting action of the teeth.
3 Back saws.
4 Protection for the workbench.
5 The sawing board as a holding aid.
6 The vice as a holding device.
7 Value of having adequate working space on a bench.

It is highly likely that early attempts at sawing to a line will be inadequate by adult standards. The teacher is concerned here with technique. However the objective should not be just to ensure a carbon copy performance from a child but to stress the need for understanding why technique is important and how it can be improved.

For a child there are many potential difficulties when sawing. These include:

Starting the cut         Considering the angle
Guiding the saw          of cut.
Observing the line       Body balance
Weighting the cutting    Arm movement
action                   Holding the saw

Most adults will have experienced the complexity of learning to drive a car. Perhaps the memory fades but the complexity of that task is gradually unravelled through practice.

Games coaches often use the technique of 'coaching within the game' during coaching sessions where the game is frozen and a technique pointed out or emphasized so that improvement can be encouraged. In the workshop, the complexity of a technique can be gradually unravelled for a child by freezing a lesson in order to focus attention on a problem and to develop a child's analytical approach to work.
Similarly the complexity of a technique on the bandsaw can be simplified.

Is the bandsaw the appropriate machine for the task?

Is the blade width suitable, especially if the cut is curved?

Is the blade guard set at the correct height?

Is there a need for using the fence?

What rate of feed should be used when cutting?

Is the dust extraction system operating?

It seems that only a consistent analytical approach by the teacher will eventually engender a similar approach from a child.

Consider *shaping* in a similar way. What are the different ways and means of shaping material. With wood, the teacher can cope with the wide range of possibilities but has the task of introducing them to a child as confidence grows and as the need arises. The implication here is that techniques should be introduced as a need arises rather than just for the purpose of teaching techniques alone. The skilled teacher can satisfy both these needs through careful preparation and course planning.

Shaping can be achieved with the following tools:

planes         surform              file
saws           gauges (carving)     boring tools
spokeshave     rasp                 abrasives

Each tool demands a different technique which varies again in relation to the material. A course structure can readily make use of a small number of shaping techniques in order to introduce a child to work that he/she can comprehend.

Joining
The techniques of joining wood have expanded considerably as a result of technological advance and the introduction of new fastenings. Development has

partly been due to new ideas but mainly in response to the increased use of manufactured boards. Traditional joining methods often prove unsatisfactory since their efficiency as a joint depended very much on the structure of wood grain.

However the basic principles of joining wood have not changed. Today there is a wider range of possibilities to consider when resolving a joining problem but a child needs to understand the basic principles before contemplating the range of joints available.

In simple terms, a child should find the following questions pertinent when considering a joining problem and should be encouraged to raise questions in discussion.

What does the strength of a joint depend upon?

What properties of the material need to be considered when making a joint?

What type of fastening can be used and why?

What type of adhesive can be used and why?

Where is the information about joining methods stored in the workshop?

Do the surfaces to be joined need any special preparation?

How important is workmanship when joining surfaces together and why?

Does the joint require cramping if an adhesive is used?

Are any special techniques required to make the joint?

This analytical approach can be used by the teacher as a basis for discussion. Whatever the project may be there will always be an alternative means of joining. With more able children the problem can be resolved through discussion. With other children, especially the less able, there will be the need to see examples and to visualize the joint itself. Careful teacher participation here can encourage some analytical thought at an appropriate level.

Adequate resources must be available as a source of reference for all children and as aids for the teacher. These can include:

Information cards or sheets.
Practical three-dimensional examples.
Reference text books.
Manufacturer's sample board of fastenings.
Teacher demonstration.
Slides or filmstrips.

If the range of resource material is extensive then this can cause organization problems for the teacher. However a carefully organized resources area can readily cater for the needs of a well structured course. In a purpose built department, the resource area can be a central feature. In a single workshop the resource area may revolve around a single filing cabinet and open shelves. Whatever the circumstances, it will always be the teacher's task to ally the resources to the needs of each child.

Finishing

The Problem Solving Model (Chapter 1 Figure 7) refers to surface treatment rather than finishing. This extends the context to include texturing.

In terms of skills and techniques, the intention is to make a brief analysis of finishing as applied to the surface of wood.

For a child, the meaning needs to be clarified and distinguished from the generally accepted lay meaning of the word.

A relevant question and answer sequence with a child could be as follows:

Q What is the function of a wood finish?
A To protect, improve appearance and facilitate easy cleaning.

Q What types of finishes are available?
A Many types, for example, oils, stains, dyes, polishes, varnishes, lacquers, paints.

Q What are the visual effects of these finishes?
A To add colour, a sheen to the surfaces or to enhance the natural grain features of wood.

Q How are these finishes applied to wood?
A There are various methods such as cloth application, polishing pad, immersion, brushing or spraying.

Q Is there any special surface preparation needed?
A Surfaces must be dry and free from grease, blemishes and dust. A surface finish gained from normal finishing preparation and a final rub with 00 glasspaper is usually acceptable.

Q Are there any special precautions to note, safety perhaps?
A Each finish has its own properties. Some require more careful handling than others. In practice the user must check on the details specified by the manufacturer to ensure safe application.

Q Is there a sequence of operations needed to ensure the successful application of a finish?
A Here again each finish has its own particular needs. Technical notes plus practical experience offer the best sources of information.

Within this dialogue the teacher can make use of resources available in the workshop. If the only resource is to be the teacher's own practical knowledge then the outcome will be unsatisfactory.

Resources can include the following:

Teacher's demonstration.
Samples of wood finishes.
Technical notes for each product.
Procedure sheet — general surface preparation.
Procedure sheets — specific for each finish.
References to examples of finishes on products eg furniture, exterior furniture, boats.

Figure 28 suggests a sample resource sheet which could be developed further by the teacher to suit a particular need.

**RESOURCE SHEET** — **Surface finishing**

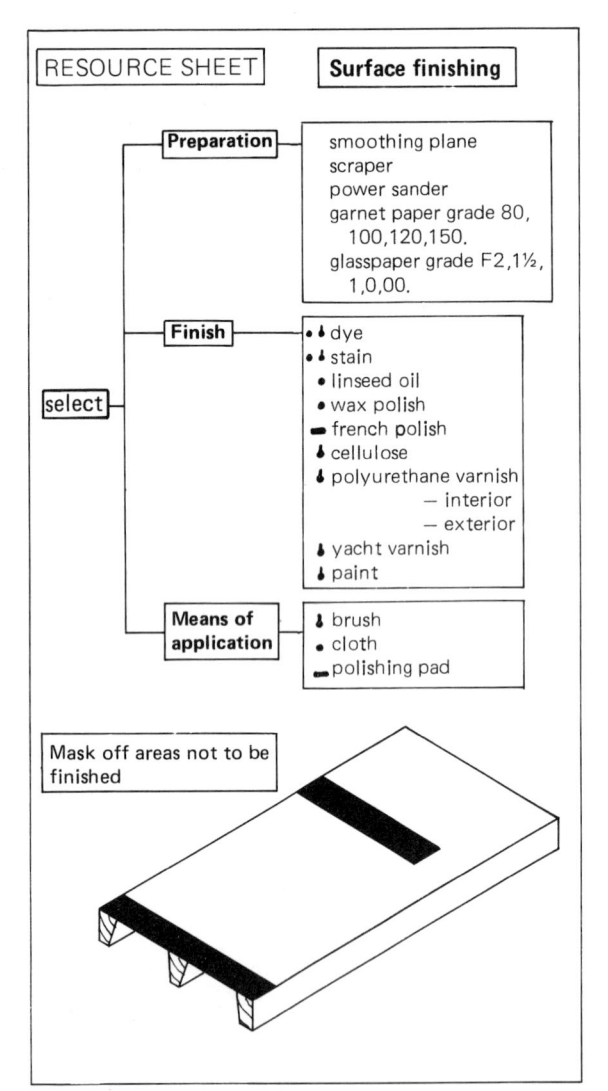

select
- **Preparation**: smoothing plane, scraper, power sander, garnet paper grade 80, 100, 120, 150. glasspaper grade F2, 1½, 1, 0, 00.
- **Finish**:
  - • ♦ dye
  - • ♦ stain
  - • linseed oil
  - • wax polish
  - – french polish
  - ♦ cellulose
  - ♦ polyurethane varnish
      – interior
      – exterior
  - ♦ yacht varnish
  - ♦ paint
- **Means of application**:
  - ♦ brush
  - • cloth
  - – polishing pad

Mask off areas not to be finished

*Figure 28* Wood finishing – sample resource sheet

**RESOURCE SHEET** — **Assembly**

Waste removed after gluing when preparing outer surfaces for finishing

**Sequence of operations**

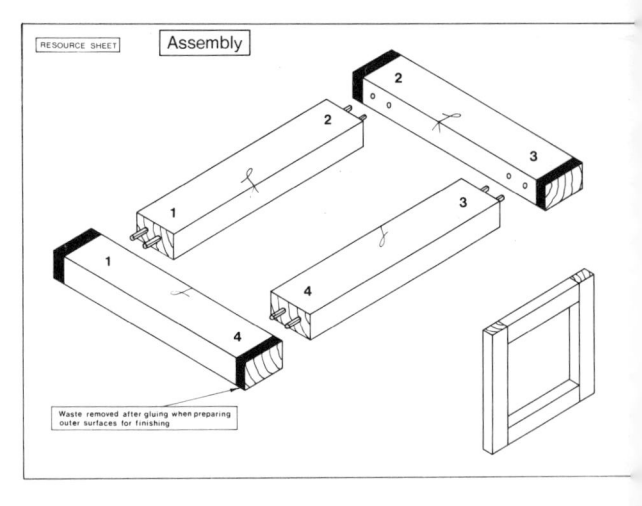

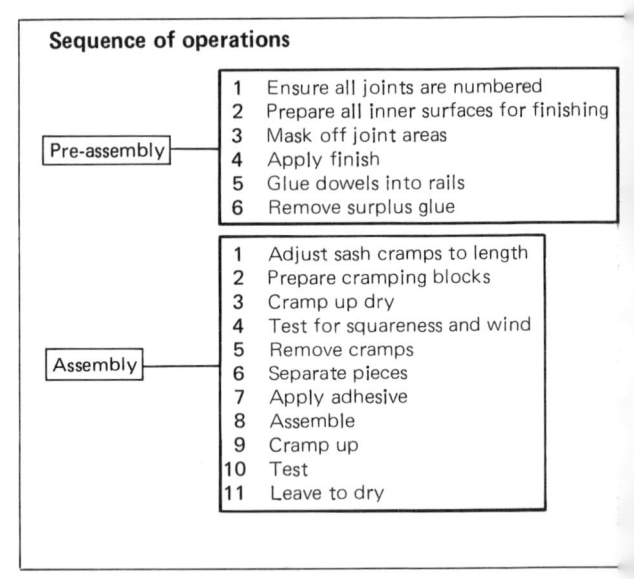

Pre-assembly
1. Ensure all joints are numbered
2. Prepare all inner surfaces for finishing
3. Mask off joint areas
4. Apply finish
5. Glue dowels into rails
6. Remove surplus glue

Assembly
1. Adjust sash cramps to length
2. Prepare cramping blocks
3. Cramp up dry
4. Test for squareness and wind
5. Remove cramps
6. Separate pieces
7. Apply adhesive
8. Assemble
9. Cramp up
10. Test
11. Leave to dry

*Figure 29* Aseembly – sample resource sheet

## Assembly

This component is closely linked to joining and finishing. Analysis will indicate that joining and finishing are part of a sequence of operations leading to final assembly.

Final assembly means what it suggests, but some preliminary assembly generally takes place during the early stages of construction. Similar problems will emerge at these preliminary stages.

Generally, assembly implies joining pieces together finally, and where little or no additional treatment or processes need to be carried out beyond this stage.

Figure 29 shows one example of an assembly problem facing a child.

Each part has been carefully numbered for reference, so that a sequence can be determined and the reasons for that choice carefully considered. Once again reference to an earlier chapter and the jigsaws exercise is relevant here. Assembly is no more than a jigsaw puzzle which is complicated by the need for relevant technical knowledge to be considered eg joining, shaping and finishing.

However, this does not imply that a child should evade the task and rely on direction from the teacher. The teacher's task is to organize resources and to develop an approach to learning which encourages a child to seek out the relevant information required to cope with the problem in hand.

## Volume production

The general concept of production in the school workshop is based on hand and machine processes catering for the needs of individual and group projects.

Volume production involves a different organization of work where children form the work force.

The sequence of operations mentioned earlier still applies here except that the need for a clear analyis of the total project is essential at the outset.

Consider the following example of a volume production line involving a group of children. Although the product involves wood and other materials, the methodology of volume production is the relevant factor to be considered here. The teacher's task was not just to set up a production line but rather to involve children in the task of organizing work for themselves as a group. At the same time they would become aware of the problems involved in volume production in terms of:

| | |
|---|---|
| the product itself | the organization of work |
| the supply of components | management and worker roles |

The need stemmed from a real problem existing within the school. A batch of stools with cracked polypropelene seats was gradually accumulating in the furniture store area. The tubular steel underframe was still sound but the cost of replacing the seats at the manufacturers was prohibitive. The underframes were therefore potentially scrap material after a very short life span. The problem facing the group was to design and make new seats for the stools and to refurbish the total item for further use within the craft workshops.

Problem analysis made use of the model illustrated in Chapter 1.

### Basic requirements
Each stool required a structurally sound underframe.
Each stool required a new seat.
A means of joining the seat to the underframe was required.

*Factors to be considered:*
the time available
the expertise available
material for the seat
a suitable construction
a suitable finish for both the seat and the underframe
the organization of work
the organization of the workforce
how to simulate a production line
how to utilize fully the workshop resources available
cost
number of stools required

These factors were considered through small group discussion. Each group in turn was asked to discuss, resolve and report their conclusions. The most appropriate ideas were selected and a final choice of idea for development emerged from a consensus of opinion. The final idea was adopted democratically as a result of a collective effort by the children.

The teacher's major contributions were required in the following areas:

selection of materials
size and shape of the seat
construction
lay-out of the production line

Here again, small group discussions set out to resolve the problems posed by these four categories. Further teacher support was given by recording the details that emerged from group discussion at each stage. This ensured continuity between the weekly sessions during problem analysis. The organization of work, the work force and the graphic representation of workshop lay-out was carried out initially by a group of children. The final model for the production line was drafted by a child who had a keen interest in graphic work.

### Responses from group discussion during problem analysis

*Time available* — Design was timetabled for two one-hour sessions on a Friday afternoon each week. The group felt unable to predict the number of sessions required. A period of six weeks was available if required.

*The expertise involved* — Fourth-year boys and girls with varied experiences comprised the workforce. The adequacy of their skills depended on the complexity of the processes involved. The workshop technician and two craft teachers were available.

*Materials for the seat* — A manufactured board (birch plywood 12 mm thickness) was selected for its strength, stability and working properties. The board size was readily cut to give a maximum number of seat blanks with little waste.

*Construction* — This was determined mainly by the original seat fastening positions. The holes already drilled in the underframe were used for part of the new construction. A jig was made for drilling additional holes and for matching holes in the seat blanks.

*A suitable finish for the seat and the underframe* — A painted finish was preferred and black Hammerite paint selected for the underframe. The preparation required was to key the original painted surface. The smooth, sanded seat shape was to be colourized with a polyurethane colourizer varnish to give a contrasting colour to the underframe. This also offered adequate protection for general workshop use.

*The organization of work* — Discussion identified the processes to be carried out on the production line. From this list the organization of work and the workforce was determined.

*The organization of the workforce* — Since the total number of stools was only 40, then the workforce could not be deployed on a permanent basis. Weekly changes would be required as the stocks of seats and underframes were established as key points on the production line. Children carried out the roles of personnel, time and motion and quality control officers. Staff adopted management roles and weekly meetings were held to re-deploy the workforce so that production could continue.

It became apparent that some means of ensuring standardization was necessary, especially for the seat shape, the hole positions and depth of counter-

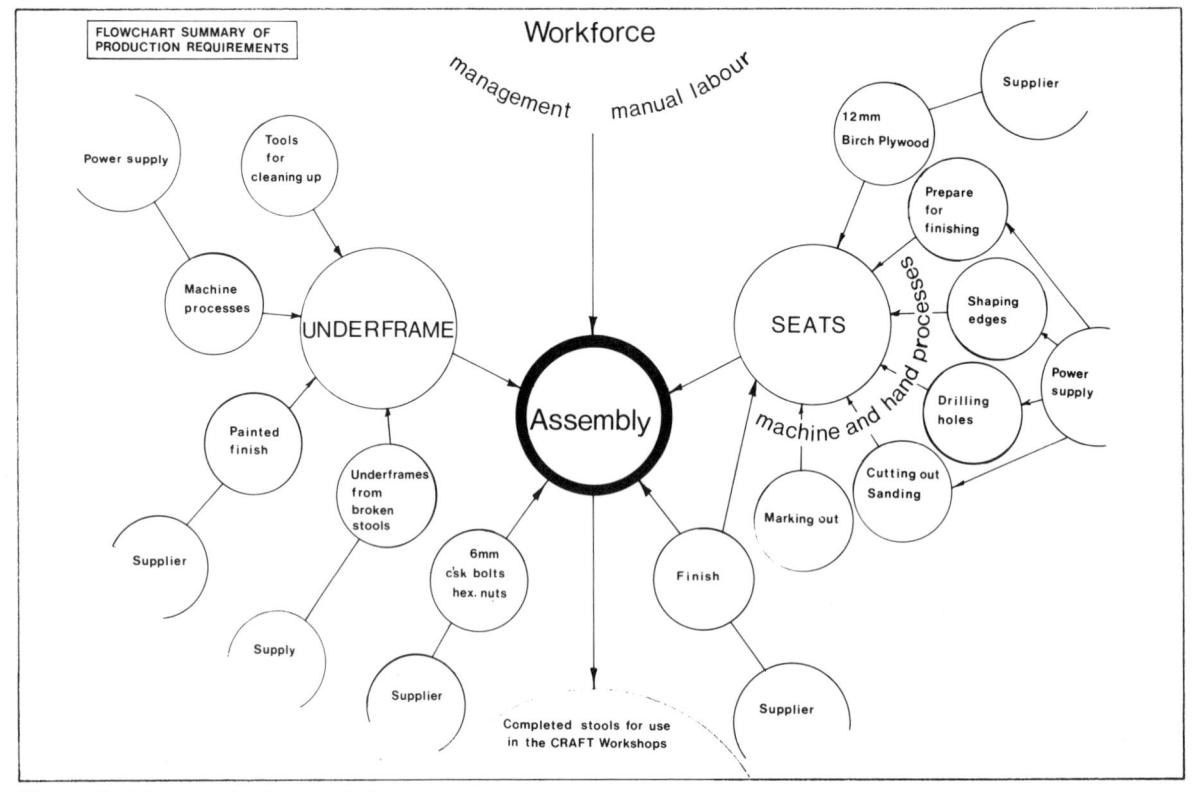

*Figure 30* Volume production – analysis

*Figure 31* Production line layout

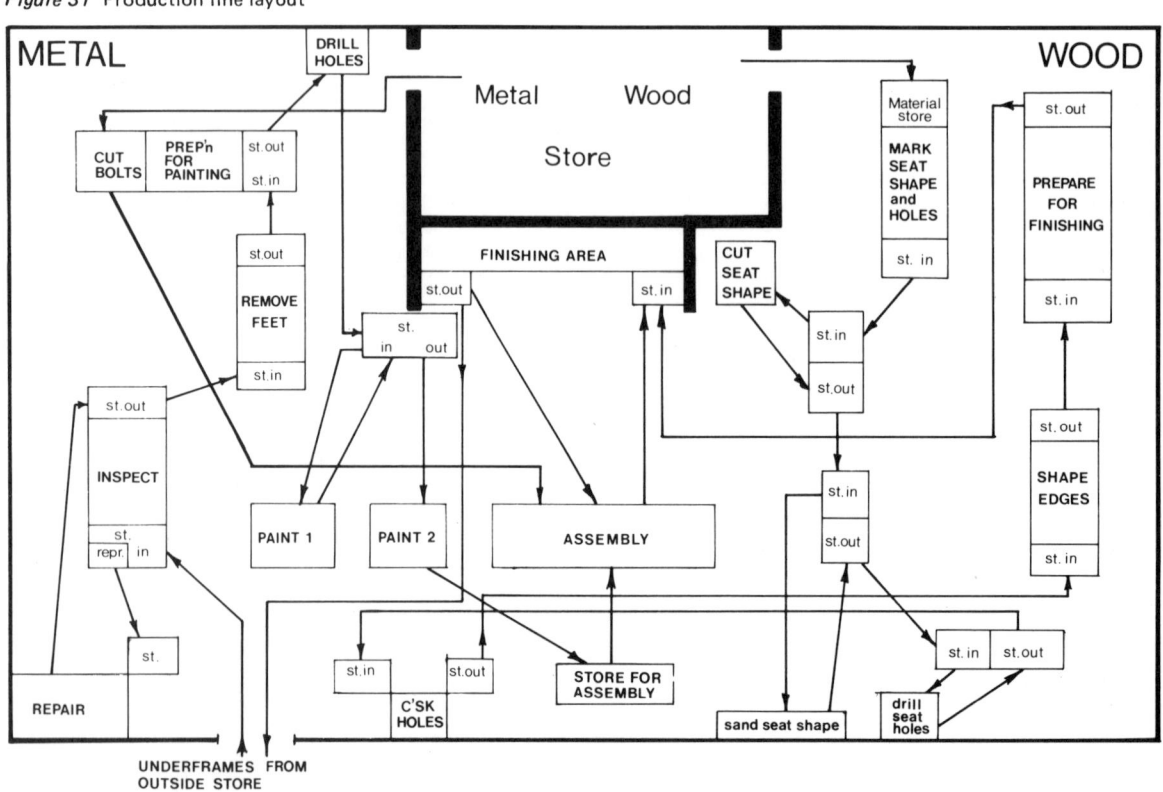

| Production line operations | Work force |
|---|---|
| **Seats** | |
| 1  Mark out seat shape and hole positions | 1 |
| 2  Cut out seat shape on the bandsaw | 1 |
| 3  Sand to final shape | 1 |
| 4  Drill 6.5mm dia. holes | 2 |
| 5  Countersink depth (fixed depth) | 2 |
| 6  Shape seat edges | 3 |
| 7  Glasspaper, prepare for finishing | 3 |
| 8  Apply first finishing coat | 1 |
| 9  Apply final coat after assembly | 1 |
| **Underframe** | |
| 1  Inspect and repair if necessary | 1 |
| 2  Remove feet | 1 |
| 3  Emery in preparation for painting | 2 |
| 4  Drill holes using jig | 2 |
| 5  Apply first coat of paint | 2 |
| 6  Apply second coat of paint | 2 |
| 7  Insert new feet | 1 |
| **Assembly** | |
| 1  Cut bolts to required length | 2 |
| 2  Match seat to underframe | 1 |
| 3  Cut bolts to required length | 1 |
| 4  Insert bolts and nuts hand tight | 2 |
| 5  Tighten nuts finally | 1 |
| 6  Return to finishing bay for final coat | |
| Transfer of work | 3 |
| Personnel officer | 2 |
| Work study engineer | 2 |
| Quality control | 2 |
| Safety officer | 1 |

*Figure 32* Allocation of workforce

sinking. Appropriate templates and jigs were produced to ensure standardization.

*Cost* — The cost of refurbishing the stools was based on the following factors:

the cost of material for the seats
the cost of paint for the underframe
the cost of bolts for joining
the cost of varnish for the seats

Labour costs were discussed but no acceptable means of implementing this could be determined for such a small production run.

At this stage the teachers felt that the most important aspect of the work was the decision making demanded from the children to organize a production run.

Figures 30, 31, 32 indicate the final form of the list of processes, production line layout and the workforce in action.

Completion of this short production run enabled the children to appraise their experience critically. The issues raised as part of their critical analysis were as follows:

control of quality of workmanship

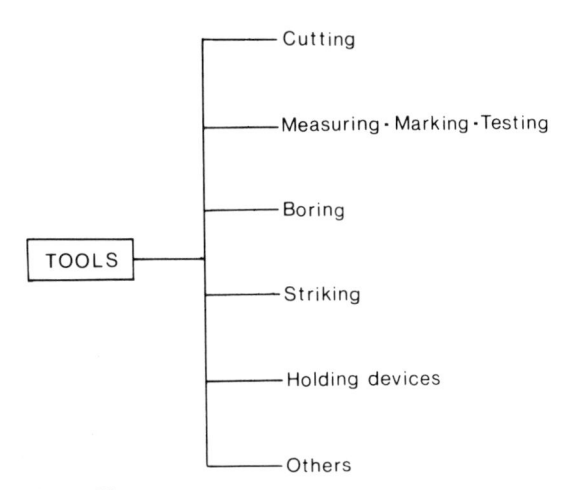

*Figure 33* — TOOLS
- Cutting
- Measuring · Marking · Testing
- Boring
- Striking
- Holding devices
- Others

working conditions, especially dust and paint odour
monotony
repetition
relationships with officers and management
tea-break
working environment, a request for background music in particular
interpersonal problems where workers were paired or grouped together
safety generally and especially on machines
clothing — special protection and safety requirements eg face masks, goggles
lack of identity with the finished product
self-criticism of workmanship
initial enthusiasm followed by some apathy as weeks passed by
some criticism of the production line lay-out

From the teacher's viewpoint, the exercise had succeeded in encouraging children to participate in decision making and to experience the consequences of those decisions.

## Tools (see Figure 33)

For a child in the workshop there will seem to be a bewildering array of tools available for use. For the 11-year-old child just beginning to experience working with tools in a formal situation, the introduction will need to be gradual and a considerable period of time will be required for familiarity to develop.

However, tools must be considered as an essential part of the workshop environment. They are generally carefully stored in racks in order to maintain safety and to keep them in good working order. The enlightened teacher will also show initiative in developing well organized, carefully labelled storage systems which will promote both safe keeping and tool identification. The need to focus attention on the technical language of the workshop can be developed here, and further analysis can then relate each tool to its function.

**34(a)**

- cutting tools
  - saws
    - hand
    - back
    - bow
    - coping
    - pad
    - fret
  - planes
    - jointer
    - fore
    - jack
    - smoothing
    - router
    - plough
    - rebate
    - shoulder
    - bull nose
    - spokeshave
  - chisels
    - bevel edge
    - firmer
    - mortice
  - gouges
    - firmer
    - scribing
    - woodcarving
  - surform
    - file
    - plane
  - files
    - flat
    - half round
  - knife
    - trimming

**34(b)**

- measuring marking testing
  - gauges
    - straight edge
    - metre rule
    - 300mm rule
    - flexible rule
    - winding strips
    - marking knife
    - marking
    - mortice
    - cutting
  - squares
    - try
    - mitre
    - adjustable
  - trammel heads
  - wing compass

**34(c)**

- boring tools
  - drills
  - bits
    - carpenter's brace
    - hand drill
    - twist
    - screw centre
    - twist
    - forstner
    - expansive
    - auger
    - rose countersunk
    - screwdriver
    - dowel bit
    - machine centre
    - machine flat
    - hole saws
  - bradawl
  - gimlet

**34(d)**

- holding devices
  - cramps
    - bench vice
    - G
    - sash
    - rack
    - deep throat
  - others
    - bench holdfast
    - corner cramps
    - bench hook
    - shuting board
    - mitre box
    - dowelling jig

**34(e)**

- striking tools
  - hammers
    - warrington
    - pin
    - adze head
    - claw
  - mallets
    - bench
    - woodcarvers

**34(f)**

- unclassified
  - screwdrivers
    - cabinet
    - posidriv
    - phillips
    - ratchet
    - spiral ratchet
  - pincers
  - scrapers
    - hand
    - plane
  - saw set
  - nail punch

*Figure 34* Classification of tools

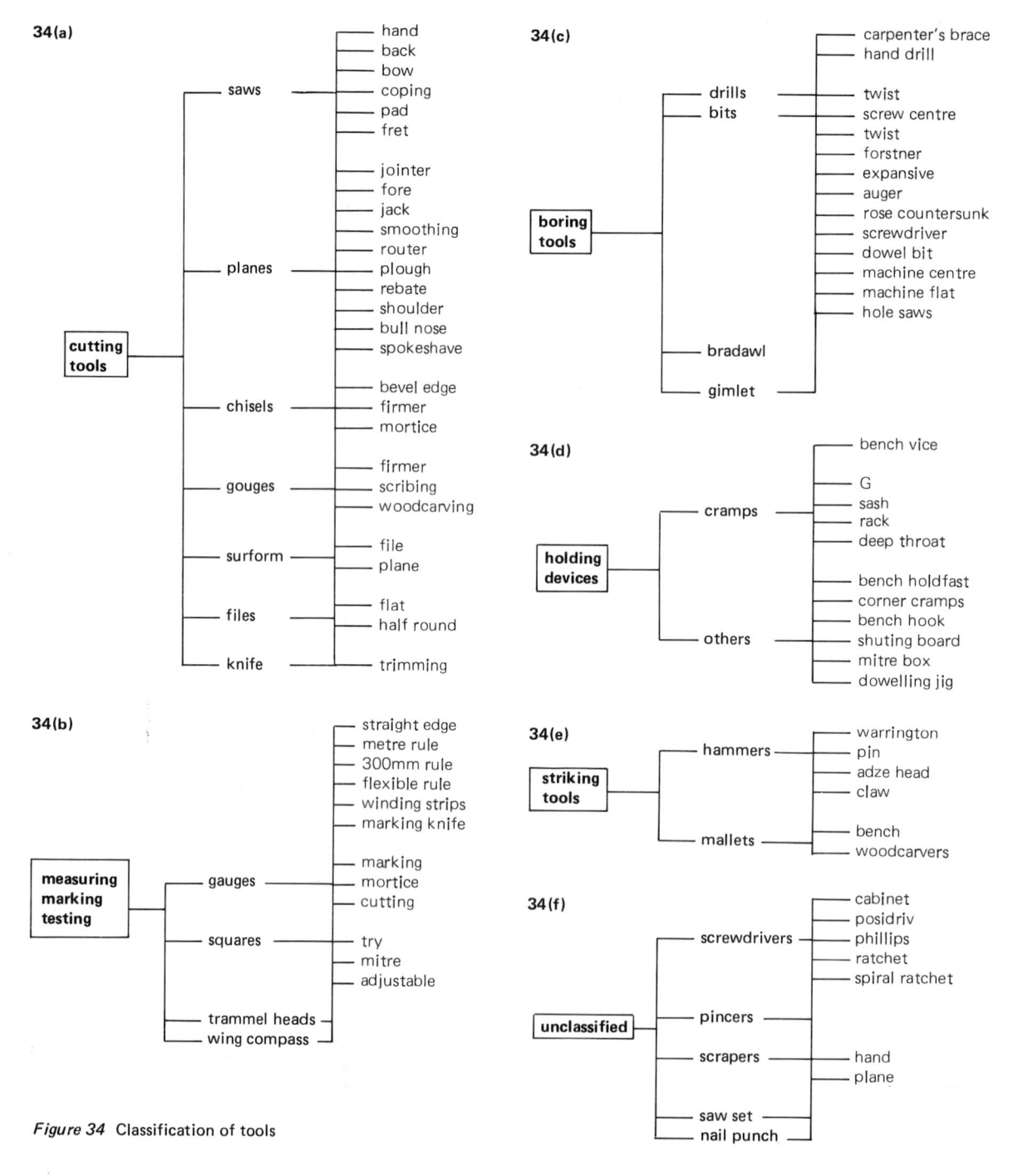

Consider the following groups of tools classified according to function:

cutting tools  
measuring, marking and testing tools  
boring tools  
striking tools  
holding devices  
unclassified group

The problem facing a child seems to contain three major factors.

1 The terminology – names of tools.
2 The uses of each tool.
3 Personal experience of developing techniques with a range of tools.

The terminology problem can be lessened through constant exposure in the workshop, supported by a teacher insistent upon the use of correct terminology as part of the workshop dialogue.

38

Figure 34 indicates a suggested classification of tools.

Figure 35 suggests a possible development from a list of tools, to a more individual, and more memorable, form for workshop display.

Overall it seems likely that a child will only develop a personal awareness of tools if the workshop environment itself promotes analytical thought and if the teacher attaches importance to the need for learning technical detail.

### Machines and portable powered tools (see Figure 36)

Machines and portable powered tools have added a new dimension to working with wood. A wider range of shapes can be cut, joining techniques have improved, drilling can be more precise and finishing can be completed more speedily without as much physical effort.

Whilst the range of work has expanded so has the range of potential safety hazards. Here the objective is to analyse the potential and the limitations of machines in the workshop. In this way a child can be encouraged to become aware of the range of work that can be carried out safely and efficiently on machines.

#### Sawing

The band saw and the jig saw are the major contributers here. All the necessary safety precautions according to BS 4163 should be observed. Each child should be given sufficient instruction in the use of each machine and only responsible pupils allowed to use the bandsaw under the direct supervision of the teacher.

#### Bandsaw

This machine has the potential to cut curved shapes continuously and accurately, thus cutting down the amount of hand finishing required.

In conjunction with their teacher, children should become aware of the form of the blade, and understand the reason for delay between pressing the stop button and the end of the blade's movement. The machine's full potential can only be utilized if the following factors are stressed.

1 The importance of selecting the most suitable width of blade for the type of cut to be made.

2 The importance of tensioning the blade to suit its width.

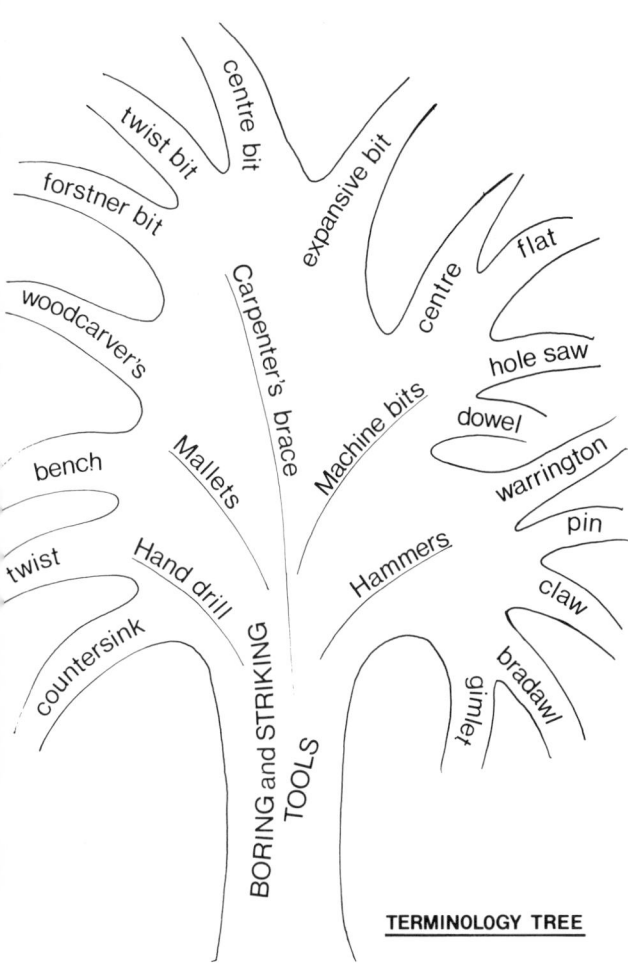

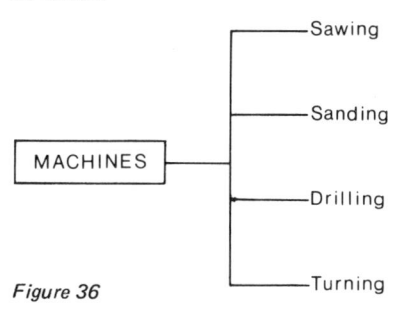

*Figure 35* Terminology tree for workshop display

The problem of identifying each tool's function can be supported by providing information adjacent to tool racks as a means of easy reference for all children. This aspect can then be developed further through a child's personal practical experience of using tools with materials. The teacher's role here must be to grasp every opportunity possible to develop the child's level of awareness with tools.

Visually, workshops can be dull and drab but some relevant charts and diagrams can quite readily bring change and a more purposeful environment. Consider the following as possible learning aids in relation to tools:

charts and diagrams

carefully labelled tool racks or cupboard storage systems

relevant information posted alongside tool storage

teacher demonstrations of the use of tools

technical data leaflets and wallcharts available for reference

filmstrip of processes eg planing, indicating the most appropriate use of the tool

*Figure 36*

3 The importance of keeping the blade sharp and correctly set.

4 The importance of the rate of feed when cutting.

5 The importance of allowing sufficient working space around the machine.

6 The use of a fence for straight cuts.

7 The dangers of attempting to remove waste from the area around the blade whilst the machine is still running.

8 The importance of planning the approach to a cut before commencing, so that any potential difficulties are anticipated.

9 Awareness of the machine's depth of throat.

10 The importance of setting the guard at the appropriate working height.

11 The importance of having adequate lighting.

The importance of the above factors emphasizes the need for a responsible attitude on the part of a child using this machine.

The width of the blade is most important since it must be appropriate for the thickness of material and the radius of the curve to be cut.

Unnecessary twisting of the blade to follow a tight curve must be avoided since this affects the working life of a blade and constitutes a safety hazard for a child.

The bandsaw should be locked when not in use and the following standard procedure carried out daily by the teacher or technician in order to ensure its safe use.

1 Unlock.
2 Check the blade width for the day's general needs.
3 Check the sharpness and set of the blade.
4 Set correct tension.
5 Cut a sample of wood to check blade efficiency.
6 Check work space around the machine.
7 Leave mains isolator switch off until the machine is required for use.

Care must be taken when marking out large shapes to ensure that the blade can cater for the need and that the throat depth gives adequate clearance. In some instances marking out will need to be repeated on the reverse side of work and cutting planned in two or more stages. A further, often ill-considered hazard is the point of balance in a length of material. This applies especially when the material is lengthy and difficult to keep flat on the working surface of the bandsaw table.

It is hoped that a dialogue about the problems of using a bandsaw will take place between the teacher and child as the former carries out work for the latter. It would be sad if each child was relegated to the role of an onlooker without being encouraged to develop any understanding of the use of this machine. Experience also suggests that there are many pupils who are responsible enough to use this machine if the instruction has been extensive and thorough in nature. If cuts are simple a child can cope. Then the teacher's role relates mainly to the more complex cutting operations on the bandsaw.

### Jigsaw

Whenever cuts with a small radius are required then the jigsaw is a more appropriate machine for the task. Once again adequate instruction must be given to ensure safe and efficient use.

The cutting action here differs from the bandsaw and there is a danger of the work lifting with the blade's motion unless the foot is set at the correct height and the work firmly held down onto the table.

Here again the teacher's demonstration should aim at reaching beyond a memorized list of instruction. The reasons why should be stressed and a child encouraged to consider carefully the potential difficulties of cutting with a jigsaw. In practice the teacher can readily hear the sound of a jigsaw being abused.

Further reinforcement for the use of the jigsaw can appear as clear instructions alongside the machine. These should be precise and easily understood by children and include all necessary aspects of safety that need to be observed.

If a general pattern exists within a workshop where instructions, information and safety precautions are clearly displayed, then the child's attention must be focused on these details. A child's level of awareness can only be improved through practice. The use of sawing machines demand that a child is aware of both safe use, techniques and the potential safety hazards.

### Sanding

Most workshops today have realized the potential and consequences of operating a finishing sander, whether disc or belt type, in the workshop.

For a child this machine can represent the solution to every problem unless the appropriate use of the sander is clearly discussed at the outset. As the term 'finishing sander' implies, the disc sander is a disc of abrasive paper, glued to a plywood disc attached to the lathe faceplate and used for finishing a shape in wood.

The teacher's approach to the use of a finishing sander raises many questions. These relate to effective use, limitations, the size of work and safety. Here, once again, is a basis for a dialogue and a child should be encouraged to become aware of the following in particular:

The potential and limitations of the machine.

The potential in terms of the shapes and sizes that can be sanded and the limitations in terms of table size and the direction of rotation of the disc.

The relationship between speed, grade of abrasive, size of work and the amount of waste to be removed.

The potential safety hazards.

The need for adequate workspace around the machine.

One major hazard from the finishing sander is the dust emitted. Some workshops may be equipped with an extractor system, others use their own expertise to alleviate the problem. The next chapter refers to a system designed and made by a school workshop technician coupling a disc and roller sander, a bandsaw and a circular saw to a vacuum extraction system.

Children quite readily become aware of the need for such a system when the potential health hazard from dust is indicated to them.

Drilling

The pillar drill offers a child the opportunity to drill holes accurately, a series of holes in alignment and holes to a pre-determined depth. The use of a fence, jigs and holding devices and a wide range of drills and bits add to the range of uses.

The potential of this machine for a child depends on the range of equipment available in the workshop. The following represents a range:

| | |
|---|---|
| twist drills | countersink bit |
| machine centre bits | forstner bit |
| flat bits | brad point |
| hole saws | |

This range also represents complexity so that the teacher must develop a child's experience on the pillar drill through a carefully structured approach. One limitation for the teacher is the number of machines available. The quota per workshop may be one machine, in which case there will be a greater need to structure work in order to allow each child to experience a range of drilling techniques.

In some ways the above constraint can promote the effective organization of work. If the work required has been introduced to a child then the organization of work should be part of the learning activity and not just an afterthought.

In many schools resources may be more generous or adjacent workshops may provide an added drilling facility.

Turning

Although the woodturning lathe offers more general use today through its function as a finishing sander, the woodturning facility is still in demand.

For a child the techniques required here are more specialized but they can still be placed into two categories.

1 Turning between centres.
2 Face-plate work.

The techniques of woodturning are not readily mastered by a large number of children since time and practice are required to gain competence.

The 11-year-old child can be made aware of the potential of the wood turning lathe. The machine is a response to the need to produce round sections in wood. The application of round sections of wood can be found quite readily in furniture, door handles and banister rails.

At a later stage, where examination courses allow individual responses to a design brief to include turned solutions, then the potential of the woodturning lathe can be explored further. At that stage a child should have developed a greater degree of control and an improved understanding of the cutting action of woodturning tools.

### Material (see Figure 37)

This simple analysis serves to illustrate those areas that should concern the teacher when developing a child's overall concept of the potential of wood as a material. A similar analysis can be done quite readily for other materials available in school workshops today, eg metals, plastics, concrete.

The range of wood materials available today has increased with technological advance yet the two main categories still remain unchanged. Materials can be broadly classsified into natural and manufactured.

The visual appearance of wood materials differs sufficiently to allow a child to identify a range quite readily. This can be encouraged through early

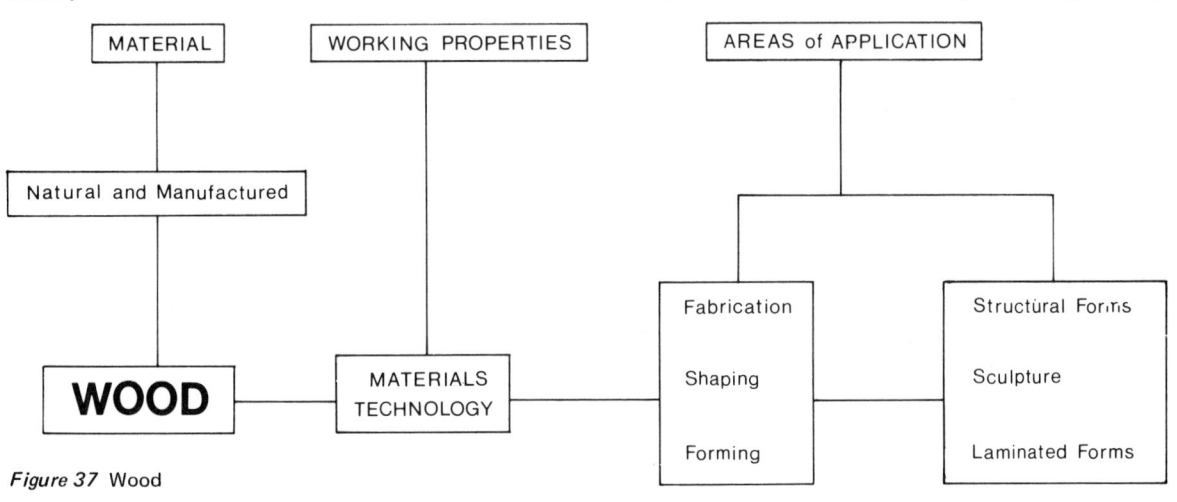

*Figure 37* Wood

experiences with materials and can include the following:

| | | |
|---|---|---|
| hardwood | blockboard | dowel rod |
| softwood | chipboard | beading |
| plywood | veneered chipboard | framing |
| hardboard | | |

Within each material named there exists a range based on the variety of wood used or the special properties built into the manufactured boards. For example plywood may be:

| | |
|---|---|
| birch | mahogany faced |
| gaboon | interior, exterior, aircraft |
| sapele | or marine quality |
| oak faced | |

Further technical data on grades of plywood could add to this complexity for a child. Familiarity with a range of this nature comes from experience. One stage further takes the work into materials technology.

Whilst a working knowledge is most useful a great deal of time and experience is required by a child in order to build up this resource. It is important for a child to realize that the selection of wood for a particular function may depend on properties that may not be visually apparent.

Consider the following:

| | |
|---|---|
| weight | toughness |
| hardness | strength |
| elasticity/rigidity | |

Whilst these properties may not be relevant on each occasion they represent a spectrum of properties worthy of consideration.

Value judgements are made constantly on the properties of wood in relation to function. This may be adequate for a large portion of the work and will cater for the intellectual needs of many children. In a mixed ability teaching group there will be abler children who will be motivated by other means of determining the properties of wood. These means should be made available and demonstrated to all children so that those who are motivated are able to respond.

Questions arise here:

How else can the properties of wood be determined? Can laboratory bench tests play a part in comparative hardness tests of different materials of the same section?

If so, what value will these hold for a child?

The answer to the last question relates to practical work and to learning in a broader sense. A test may usefully confirm a judgement based on working experience or conversely may question a judgement. It may also help a child to make a decision, to choose between materials.

In a broader sense testing can open a child's eyes to the possibilities of materials testing, and not with wood alone. The value of information gained can then be usefully applied in designing and making.

Further design considerations relate to : working properties, joining methods, surface finishing and cost.

Overall, a child's attention must be drawn to all the important aspects of working with wood. The teacher's task, once again, is to simplify the problem and provide more manageable parts for a child to cope with complexity.

A child will generally relate wood to its uses in the man-made world. If attention has to be directed specifically to the task of extending the known range of uses then a child's level of awareness is being extended.

Consider some possible applications of wood:

| | |
|---|---|
| laminated roof structures | fishing rods |
| boat hulls, decks and fittings | furniture building |
| sea defences | exterior construction work |

A child can compile such a list quite readily from resources made available in the workshop.

The areas of application for wood can be simplified further so that a child may be able to cope with a long unmanageable list of uses. Three major categories can be identified and uses classified into these or combinations of these categories: fabrication (joining), shaping (reducing) and forming (bending). Attention can now be focused quite deliberately on one category and examples listed. For example:

Fabrication — any structure where sections of wood have been joined together.

| | |
|---|---|
| furniture | carpentry and joinery work |
| building | shelving |
| packing cases | portable buildings |
| garden fences, gates | |

Shaping — where wood has been reduced from its original shape for visual or functional reasons.

| | |
|---|---|
| parts of furniture eg table legs, drawer handles, shaped table tops and edges | lamp base fruit bowl napkin ring sculptural form |

Forming — where wood has been used in thin, flat sections and glued together to produce a new, generally curved form.

| | | |
|---|---|---|
| rocking chair | surfboard | crossbow |
| rocking horse | chair back | parts of furniture |
| water skis | archery bow | roof beams |

A child's analytical skills can only be developed if learning is taken beyond the needs of making.

A child can compile a useful folio of personally researched information in response to the teacher's course structure requirements. Chapter 3 will deal with some aspects of the problem of establishing a worthwhile course structure.

# 3 Organization and management in a workshop

In this chapter the interpretation of organization and management is as follows:

**Organization** — implies giving an orderly structure
**Management** — implies some form of control

The organization and management of learning activities for children in a workshop relates quite readily to the interpretation of design education given in Chapter 1 (Model 6). Figure 38 suggests how these components can be re-arranged in relation to the needs of this chapter.

The management of children in a workshop cannot be separated from the physical organization of the workshop and the management skills of the teacher within that workshop. Each must complement the other. Both will be personal to the teacher concerned but there are likely to be common elements in all forms of organization and management, largely due to safety requirements, economic and educational needs.

In shared workshops, the task of achieving an agreed consensus of opinion about organization and management may prove difficult. However, if the teacher is prepared to analyse and identify the essential requirements of the problem, then a model can be formed as a basis for action. Figure 38 can be viewed as a model for action, and the outcome of problem analysis (Figure 7 Chapter 1). The essential requirements are: order and control.

*Factors which influence* are:

| Organization | Management |
|---|---|
| environment | problem solving |
| resources | methodology |
| materials | pupil ideas |
| tools and equipment | skills and techniques |
| | communication |

*Awareness* serves as a linking component equally important to both teacher and child.
The design brief for *organization* could be:
   'To provide the facilities for children to work safely with materials'.
For *management* the brief could be:
   'To provide a structure for learning with materials in order that a child may achieve his or her full potential'.
Considered together these statements could be viewed as broad educational aims. Preference here is given to viewing them as a brief and a starting point for problem analysis.

## Organization

Consider now the 'factors which influence' in some depth:

### Environment

The workshop environment is created to a large extent by the nature of the equipment contained within it. Workbenches, tool cupboards, machines and storage space all help to create an environment which can be quite readily described as rather barren.

The nature of the building itself generally is hardly conducive to developing a lively working environment. However, these are the real issues facing the teacher and therefore a great deal of initiative is required in order to overcome such limiting factors.

*Figure 38* Organization and management – major components

## Wood workshop – LAYOUT and ORGANIZATION

*Figures 39 and 39a* Workshop organization and layout

**Wood workshop — Layout and organization**

Key

**Machines**
1. circular sawbench
2. tool grinder
3. woodturning lathe
4. pillar drill
5. woodturning lathe with sander
6. bandsaw

**Storage**
7. sidebench cupboards
8. workbench cupboards
9. tool cupboards 1 and 2
10. sash cramps
11. hand saws
12. G cramps and sash cramps
13. glasspaper rack
14. woodturning tools and equipment trolley
15. stools
16. bandsaw equipment
17. circular saw equipment
18. tools and small equipment stock cupboard
19. woodscrews
20. painting equipment

**Services**
21. dust extractor
22. water and sink unit
23. gas point
24. mains electricity isolator box
25. first aid

demonstration and/or discussion areas

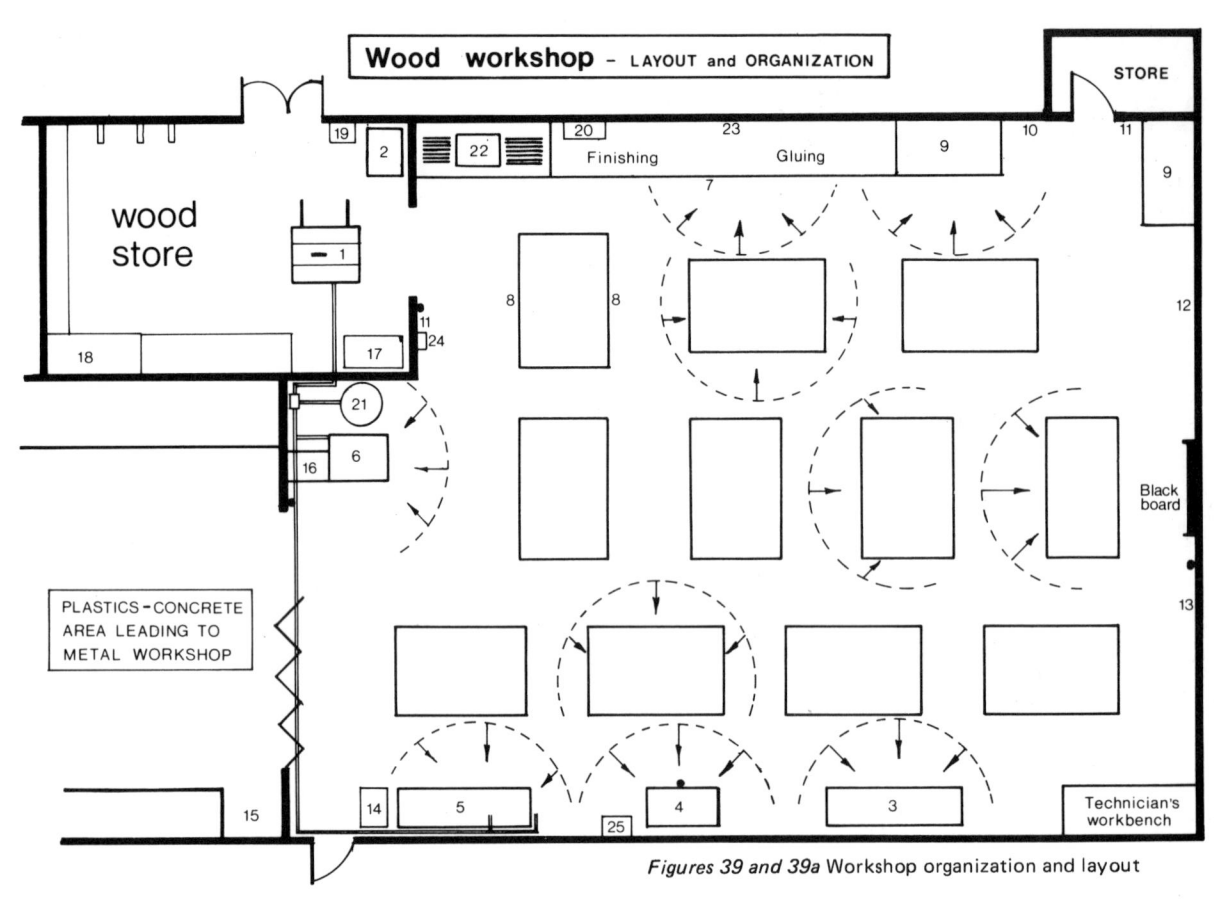

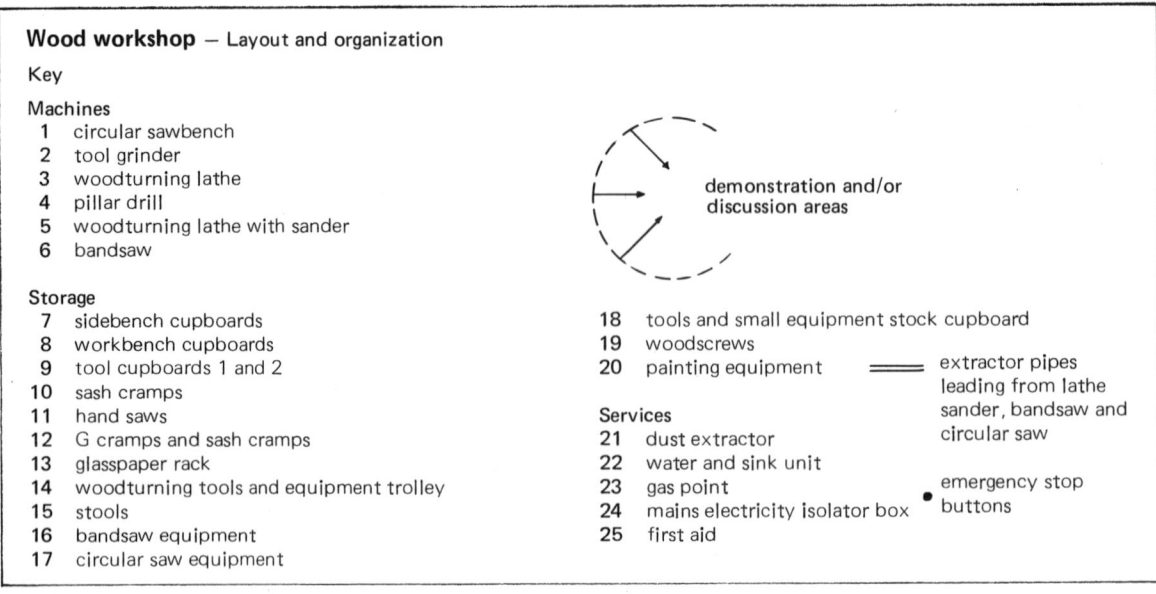

===== extractor pipes leading from lathe sander, bandsaw and circular saw

• emergency stop buttons

    Figures 39 and 39a indicate a basic workshop layout, typical perhaps of many wood workshops. The content is easily identified as workbenches, tool cupboards, storage areas, blackboard and machines.

    There is a degree of flexibility for the teacher in determining the layout of these features. Whilst such flexibility is possible it is highly likely that a basic layout will emerge which suits general needs. Flexibility will be required when undertaking large project work, volume production or small group activities which demand larger working areas or surfaces.

    Where workshop display space is available then a

great deal can be added to the environment through the display of children's work. This can provide a stimulus for further work and motivate other pupils to raise their level of performance.

Storage also makes a valuable contribution to organization, but not only in terms of orderliness. Where only open shelving is available an uninteresting array of identical products will hardly stimulate onlookers. A range of products representing child ideas offers variety and excitement.

In many workshops the wallspace available only allows for the display of two-dimensional work. Many more temporary display spaces can be created without restricting the normal working needs of a workshop. Window ledges, side benches and display stands can be utilized fully if the teacher considers that the outcome will have beneficial effects. The point to note here is that a child's work needs to be made important both within the workshop and the school environment generally.

Drawing and communication work, allied to making in design and craft, require an organized working area. In many workshops this takes place on side benches or by converting woodworking benches into drawing surfaces. Some more fortunate schools are able to make use of a specially equipped drawing area, part of a design department complex or adjacent to the workshop. Whichever is the case the need for order in preparing this environment is vital if a high standard of drawing and communication work is to be achieved.

A child senses a purposeful atmosphere within an environment. Hence, the need is to ensure that an 11-year-old child's first impression of workshop activity is one of order and purpose.

Teachers from other curriculum areas can be encouraged to become aware of workshop activities through work displayed around the school. Craft, design and technology requires a shop window in order to promote its educational value as part of a core curriculum in schools.

Resources
Generally the term resources can apply to tools and equipment as well as other materials and information used in the workshop. Here attention is drawn to the latter and the task of ensuring that the approach to its organization is both educationally sound and economically viable.

The advent of open-plan teaching areas, especially within design faculties, seemed to advocate a more flexible and freer approach to organization. Experience indicates quite clearly that the need for sound organization is greater under these circumstances. The reasons are both economic and human in nature. The key factors here are:

| | |
|---|---|
| storage | initial and replacement cost |
| accessibility | space available |
| distribution | stock checking system |
| the range available | |

Resources exert a major influence on the starting point of any learning activity. The type of work the teacher wishes to pursue with a child is determined by the type and quantity of resources available, their location and mobility. However it must be remembered that these resources represent the range of work that the teacher is prepared to conceive as part of workshop activities.

Resources may be available as follows:

**(a)** Directly from the teacher by demonstration.

**(b)** In text book form.

**(c)** In a pre-packaged form where work may be categorized into specific aspects eg woodturning, construction, laminating, jewellery.

**(d)** In some form around the workshop, adjacent to tools, equipment and processes.

**(e)** In a form readily available for homework to support work done during a lesson eg typed handout.

**(f)** In a central departmental resource area.

**(g)** In a school central resource area and issued on a loan service.

**(h)** In any combination of (a)–(g).

The range of resource material is extensive and is likely to reflect some capitation expenditure, some school-produced information, extracts from useful texts and a great deal of teacher initiative, time and expertise in packaging these together to suit the need. Here the school reprographic facilities can produce resource material for individual, small group and year group use. The range of work can extend from banda sheets or roneo-duplicated typed work to high quality photocopied or off-set litho work.

Whatever the process, it must be remembered that the resources produced for the workshop environment must reflect the high level of professionalism that all other aspects of work are trying to maintain.

Materials
These can be considered as part of resources but they do demand a large portion of the workshop storage space.

In economic terms materials need careful organization. In methodological terms the order established for their storage should reflect the teacher's approach to workshop activities generally.

In terms of wood materials, new boards, short ends and the range of off-cuts generally accumulated from various sources, should be readily accessible. This can avoid wastage in the use of wood.

Materials should not necessarily be freely available to children. In reality a designer would need to take advice, order and await delivery of materials. A child can accept a similar sequence, with the teacher acting as a consultant and distributor of material. The order can be placed quite effectively on an appropriate cutting list.

Smaller items such as wood screws should be kept within a lockable storage system. Information should

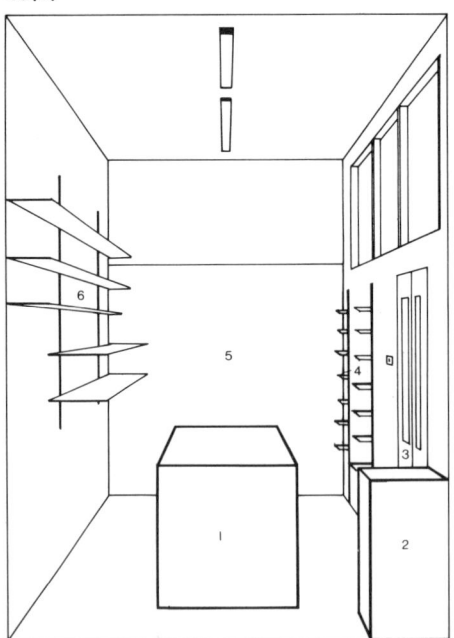

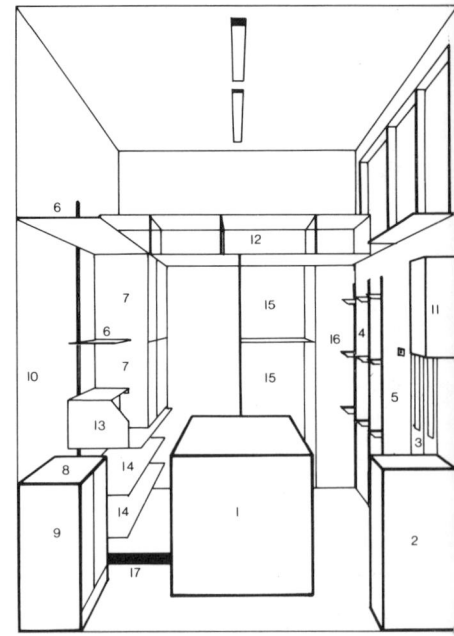

*Figure 40* (a) Typical woodstore in use (b) Initial layout and organization (c) Modified layout and organization

**Wood store** – Initial layout and organization  40(d)

Key

1. circular sawbench
2. tool grinder
3. exterior door
4. timber storage – horizontal stacking
5. area for manufactured boards
6. open shelving – adjustable

**Wood store** – Modified layout and organization

Key

1. circular sawbench
2. tool grinder
3. exterior door
4. timber storage – vertical bays with safety ropes
5. area for manufactured boards
6. shelving
7. main stock cupboard for tools and small equipment – lockable
8. bench surface for oilstones
9. cupboard for circular saw equipment
10. wall space for safety notices
11. lockable storage cupboard – woodscrews
12. open shelving
13. shelving for short ends – softwood and small pieces of plywood
14. shelving for short ends of hardwoods
15. shelving for short ends of manufactured boards
    – small above
    – large below
16. storage for small quantities of long hardwood sections and reclaimed timber
17. dust extractor pipe leading to vacuum drum in the workshop

be available about the screws in stock but these items should only be issued on demand.

Painting facilities can also be a real headache within a workshop due to the natural human tendency to abhor the task of cleaning brushes, replacing lids on paint tins and organizing the task of painting methodically.

Order in the use and storage of materials can only be achieved through a careful analysis of the problem they pose in each individual workshop.

What is needed is a real sense of commitment by the teacher to determine an appropriate form of organization and translate that into action. Figures 40 (a)–(d) illustrate a typical store room for a craft teacher in a wood workshop and an attempt to resolve the problem.

Tools and equipment

A major contribution to workshop organization is made here. Whether the tools and equipment are static machinery or part of the wide range of consumable items stocked, some form of organization is required to make them available.

Where a head of department holds overall responsibility for the workshops the role of the individual teacher depends a great deal on departmental policy. However, the individual teacher should not develop a negative attitude in such a situation. He/she has the responsibility to define the need for policy changes to be made if necessary and to present a carefully documented case to the head of department. If conflict exists between the individual teacher and departmental policy, insurmountable problems can sometimes occur. In such instances the professionalism of both the individual teacher and the head of department should ensure that the final decision is made in the educational interest of children.

For all craft teachers, whether working in isolation or as part of a team of staff in a suite of workshops, the organization of tools and equipment must be soundly based and clearly defined. Whilst it may be argued that a child should be exposed to a variety of systems, it would be foolish for teachers to adopt a wide range within a department and permit inconsistency of standards to prevail as a consequence. This would prove counter-productive generally since children respect a consistent standard and their confidence and relationship with the teacher can stem from this source.

If communication is good within a department, then what really matters is not that all hand saws are racked in exactly the same way, but that a logical storage system does exist for all hand saws. It would seem equally logical to display relevant information about the use of these saws adjacent to the storage point. This information should be clearly presented, precise, and of value to a child about to use a hand saw.

Such information can perform several functions:

1 Assist a child in decision making.
2 Develop a child's terminology.
3 Form a ready source of relevant information.
4 Encourage a child to look and to read relevant infomation.
5 Develop the methodology required if workshop organization is to be of value to both the teacher and the child.

Each child needs to be encouraged to be aware of the range of tools and equipment available. Workshop organization should include the objective to develop a child's vocabulary in this respect. Unless encouraged to look and to see, a child will generally become aware of the minimum required to serve immediate needs. Unless encouraged to look and to see the methodology applied by the teacher, a child will not actively participate in either monitoring the system or in becoming familiar with its content.

The teacher can gain support for design methodology through displaying the same qualities personally in workshop organization.

The child's contribution to workshop organization should be to support it, by learning appropriate usage, rather than being allowed to abuse it. Here the teacher must accept that developing a child's level of awareness is a worthwhile objective.

Figure 41 illustrates a workshop-built tool cupboard for a combined workshop where a range of materials are to be worked. Each tool has a specific compartment and as far as humanly possible, slots, hanging spaces and recesses have been made to accept the correct tool in one way only.

Here the child's attention is being focused on the

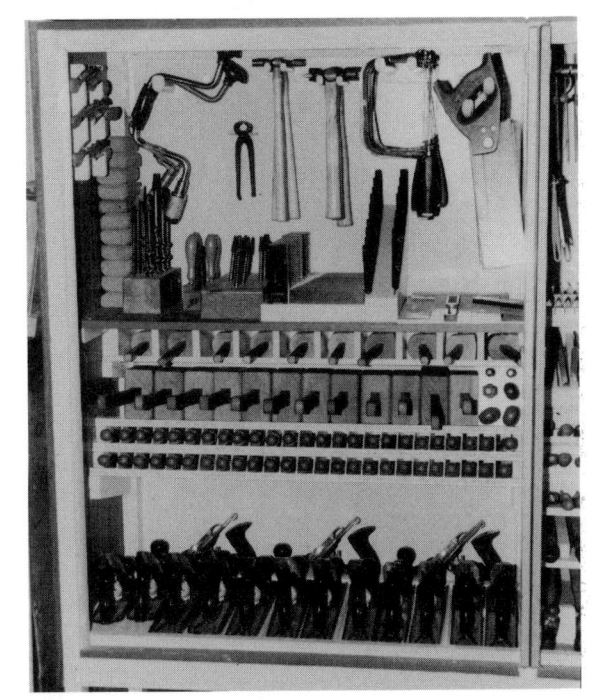

*Figure 41* Workshop built tool cupboard designed for a mixed materials workshop

need for sound methodology in order to ensure that all the tools can be stored safely at all times. This can be achieved if each child recognizes the need for methodology. Overall the cupboard indicates that tools warrant special care and should not be abused or misplaced according to individual whim or fancy.

Each child can make a contribution here through using the tools and ensuring that they are all in place at the start and end of each session. The teacher must also play a consistent part in checking each cupboard at the beginning and end of each session. Gradually, a child's behavioural pattern within the workshop will be influenced. The *why* and *how* of workshop learning activities will be developed. This understanding cannot be viewed as the content of a lesson at the start of a course but rather more like an attitude of mind that is being carefully cultivated over a period of time. In mixed ability groups the rate of growth will depend a great deal on the teacher's management skills. Control over the type, quantity and quality of work depends on management skills and utilizing fully the potential of workshop organization. It is to be hoped that the craft teacher has by now realized the interrelated nature of these two components.

## Management

The categories identified here for achieving effective control of workshop activities, relate to the following components within design education (Model 6 Chapter 1)

## Problem solving

If the teacher is to adopt this approach to learning as the basis for teaching method in the workshop, then it is vital that all children are able to develop their understanding of what this approach implies.

Chapter 1 has suggested, quite strongly, the need for developing models of thought within problem solving. This can be developed during the course of a child's experience in the workshop. The approach should be consistent in its attempt to establish and maintain a dialogue between the teacher and child in relation to work.

If a model is presented for problem solving then the teacher can focus a child's attention to any one part of that model at any time. This places the responsibility on the child to ensure that design folio work is methodical and available for discussion at any time. If the work is not being done then the teacher can pinpoint a specific aspect for a child's attention immediately. In this way effective control can be achieved, but only if the child is aware of the requirements.

## Methodology

This component is reflected generally in all aspects of workshop activities. The process of designing implies the methodical analysis of a problem, the organization and application of knowledge, and the use of an appropriate sequence of operations in order to realize the product effectively.

It should also be reflected in encouraging a child to make decisions, form opinions, organize and select a preferred idea during the process of designing.

## Pupil ideas

Closely allied to problem solving, this component is the response from a child to the problem. Since problem solving demands that each child explores ideas as possible solutions the teacher has effective control over the child's work.

Once again the child must be fully aware of what is required and this can be achieved within the problem solving models advocated in this book. (Chapter 4 suggests a means of making a model clear to a child at examination level.)

## Skills and techniques

Pre-determined by the teacher, skills and techniques can offer a most effective means of controlling a project. Viewed as limitations within a design brief, they can confine the work into manageable proportions for the teacher.

Alternatively, a basic number of skills and techniques can be identified and demonstrated to a group of children. Any additional techniques beyond these can be dealt with quite adequately as the need arises. Attempting to deal with *all* techniques as the need arises would be an effective way of losing control of workshop activities.

## Communication

This component deals with all aspects of workshop activities which require ideas to be discussed and decisions made. The teacher has several means of controlling this aspect of work. Techniques can vary as follows:

1 Communication during a demonstration to the total group.

2 Communication with a sub-group involved with similar problems.

3 Individual discussions with a child.

4 Discussion groups.

5 Prepared resource sheets and work cards used with work sheets.

6 Incidental discussion digressing from a workshop problem.

Several other situations could be specified. The need here is to establish a dialogue between the teacher and the child. The latter can then gradually be encouraged to adjust or select the appropriate technique for communication, to suit a particular situation.

More formal communication techniques apply within the design folio and offer a positive form of control for the teacher.

## Awareness

If *order* and *control* are to co-exist then some effective means of linking them must be identified. Within design education this component is *awareness*.

Relevant for both the teacher and the child awareness needs time for its development. In its broadest sense the context encompasses teacher and pupil needs within the relationship they try and establish within the workshop learning situation.

The text so far has stressed the need for teacher commitment and initiative in order to create the environment, to organize tools and equipment, to provide resources, to vary teaching methods and to emphasize the need for methodology. The response from the child has been implied as learning to see and to accept the responsibilities afforded by a learning situation in the workshop. This situation and its organization, is there to benefit every child who participates. Irresponsible actions taken by any child can be viewed as harmful to the rights of other children. If the teacher's involvement in developing the workshop environment is personally meaningful, then the child's contribution should have a similar objective.

## Standards

A linking factor relevant to all the other components identified here. In terms of a child's school career, standards gradually progress from child to adult level. The teacher's role is to exercise control along this journey.

A teacher's personal qualities can play a significant part in developing relationships. For the experienced teacher, personal qualities will be used to advantage whilst the inexperienced teacher could well be swayed by the popularity image amongst children.

The teacher can make a valuable contribution to a child's development consistently, through degrees of success and failure in order to build up confidence. Similarly, it is the manner in which standards are maintained consistently that matters in the workshop situation. Our roles as adults mean that we must make value judgements on certain issues.

In the workshop the following questions seem pertinent in relation to a child's behaviour pattern:

1 In what manner does a child enter the workshop?

2 What factors influence behaviour patterns in the workshop?

3 What is considered to be appropriate dress in the workshop?

4 What is the objection to having a child's personal baggage in the workshop?

5 How should a group be arranged for a demonstration?

6 How important is the organization of work?

7 How should tools and equipment be used on a bench?

8 Should a child record progress personally?

9 What special requirements are there for workshop organization at the beginning and end of a session?

10 In what manner should children leave the workshop?

Many other questions can be raised but the important factor remains that each teacher should feel the need to ask such questions.

If children are in disarray upon entering the workshop environment, if the environment itself lacks purpose, then it is highly likely that the children's attitude will lack purpose.

Experience suggests that children respect a workshop which has a lively purposeful environment and where dress and behaviour patterns are well defined. This concept is equally relevant for the teacher. If personal standards are maintained consistently at a high level then the children will accept such a norm or strive to reach an improved standard themselves. It must be the teacher's role to encourage them to become aware of the need for personal standards. If the teacher wears clean, functional, protective clothing at all times then it is easier to request the same from each child. An effective form of control can be gained this way.

Similarly, communication requires a consistent standard. Awareness within design education suggests looking and seeing more than face value. If a child is to be encouraged to analyse and resolve problems, then the efficient use of language must be encouraged during communication.

If the teacher demands good, precise language consistently, then gradually a child will respond.

Furthermore the teacher's own language must reflect the same qualities.

Teacher/pupil relationship

Consideration of organization and management in a workshop cannot exclude the area of teacher/pupil relationships. The teaching/learning situation stems from the relationship established between the teacher and the child.

As suggested in Chapter 1, the traditional concept in the workshop was one of the master craftsman and the apprentice. A preferred analysis here is that of the teacher and child as co-learners but with the former able to be seen as a more experienced learner, able to lead the child towards a means of resolving a problem.

Teaching to-day in the workshop centres on teacher/pupil relationships and this chapter so far can be viewed diagrammatically as follows:

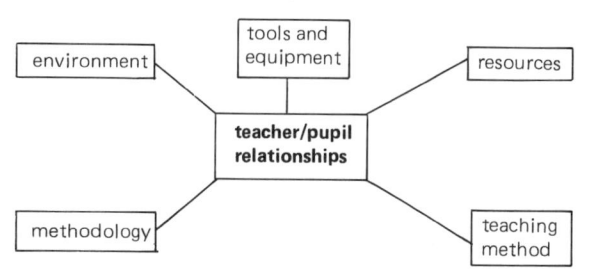

*Figure 42*

The text, so far, has been quite explicit in stating the need for commitment and initiative in order to create the environment, to organize tools and equipment, to provide suitable resources, to vary teaching methods and to emphasize the need for methodology.

The response from the child has been implied as one of learning to see and to accept the responsibilities afforded by a system established in the workshop. This system is intended to benefit every child who participates in workshop activities so that irresponsible actions taken by any child can be viewed as harmful to the rights of other children.

If the teacher's involvement in developing the workshop environment is personally meaningful then the child's participation in that workshop should be meaningful. Here the teacher's responsibility must be towards developing a child's understanding of the need for such an organized environment.

Figure 43 expresses the key issues in teacher/pupil relationships bearing in mind that each component has been isolated in order to simplify the whole.

Teacher/pupil relationships in the workshop have changed quite considerably since the scene illustrated in Figure 1 (Chapter 1).

Evaluation

Used in a limited sense in terms of group management, evaluation can be a terminal exercise where the

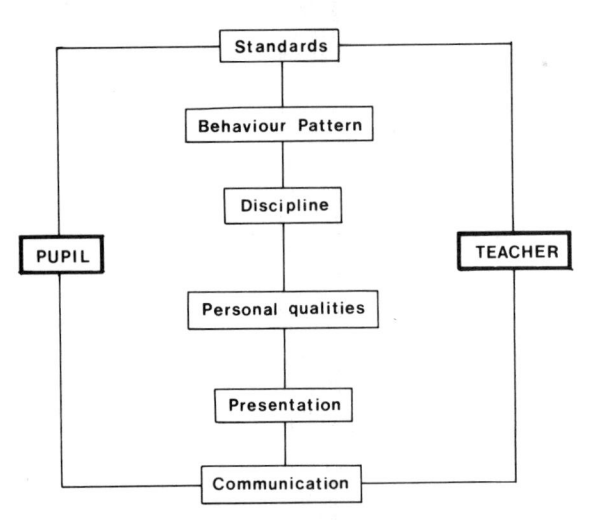

*Figure 43* Teacher/pupil relationship – major components

teacher makes a value judgement based upon a set of criteria deemed to be suitable for that purpose. What form the evaluation takes depends entirely on the teacher's level of perception and performance in the field of evaluation. The Schools Council's policy on evaluation has always been aware of the teacher's role. This has led to emphasis on the formative evaluation of new materials and teaching methods so that any material published will have been tested in trial schools.

It seems that the major problem facing a teacher is one of evaluating in the affective domain. In the cognitive domain some form of objective tests can be carried out and scores gained. In the affective domain, where only sets of criteria can be established as a basis for evaluation, the teacher's problem is far more complex.

Working alone, a teacher has difficulty in making judgements which are not influenced by a personal vested interest in the course and the children.

A distinction can be made between two forms of evaluation which will prove useful in the workshops:

*Formative evaluation* takes place during the project lifespan and is aimed at improving the work being done. It can be argued that this is the only form relevant to design education because its on-going nature ensures that change takes place when change is really needed.

*Summative evaluation* tends to come after the project has been completed and attempts to establish whether the outcome fits the original intention. In practice it is likely that both forms of evaluation are relevant and necessary.

The behavioural objectives model of evaluation is another form available. This model can be restricting in nature since it does not allow for the covert changes not prescribed in the initial objectives. In this respect the Schools Council has supplemented the objective testing with information gathering techniques, interviews with teachers, classroom observation and attempts at rating attitudes. The outcome is *illuminative evaluation* which accepts objective tests where appropriate but also attempts to identify the key issues and to evalute them in the most fitting way possible.

Examinations are a traditional part of evaluation at secondary school level. Workshop activities have experienced examination at G.C.E. 'O' and 'A' level, C.S.E., Modes 1, 2 and 3, 16+ systems of examination. More recently at 'O' and 'A' levels, design examinations make use of the potential of the workshop more widely than previous woodwork courses.

Whatever form the examination takes there will inevitably be a range of relevant factors to be considered by the teacher.

Basically, the aim should be to ensure that the examination serves the needs of the curriculum wherever possible. In this respect many questions have been raised regarding Mode 3 schemes and their reliability in terms of national standards. Here the responsibility for standards lies with the examination board and its acceptance of the criteria for assessment submitted for each course. The subjective element in all workshop courses makes agreement on standards more difficult, but not impossible. This does not mean that this form of evaluation is less reliable but that the appropriateness of previous techniques may be questionable.

In conclusion, the organization and management of a workshop cannot be divorced entirely from the teacher's role within the school's structure. It is highly likely that a teacher who is aware of the school's organization and management structure will adopt a more critical approach to the workshop situation.

The brief reference made in Chapter 1 (Models 3 and 4) to this aspect of a teacher's role at school and departmental level, suggests the normal, dual role of a teacher to-day. Both the academic and pastoral aspects should be used to advantage in terms of organization and management.

# 4 The range of work – a chapter of ideas

The range of work within a craft workshop represents the collective efforts of both teacher and child in communicating, developing and realizing individual ideas. This suggests a departure from the idea of a prescribed scheme of work where every child performs the same task and produces pre-conceived artefacts.

*Figure 44* Teacher support material A

Where the teacher is part of a team within a department structure then a like-minded approach to work is desirable; this cannot be achieved through prescription but can be encouraged through discussion.

Consider the following:

## The approach to craft in years 1 and 2

Teaching craft within the design department must be seen clearly as part of a complete design concept. Since design education cannot be defined precisely, then the course within design must reflect the teacher's own interpretation. However, to ensure continuity and a core element of common experience for pupils, this interpretation must take place within a structure.

The aims of Design Education can be stated as follows:

(a) To use constructively all that is relevant from the past.
(b) To exploit the present.
(c) To be ready and able to anticipate change.

This adds up to the development of the whole being in physical, perceptual and conceptual terms. Broadly speaking these aims are relevant as a basis for all craft work.

*Consider the following as a basic structure.*

### 1 Safety

This is one aspect of the workshop environment that cannot be ignored. The wide range of materials, tools and equipment offer many possibilities for accidents to occur. The initial lesson should include discussion on safety based on the department's hand-out.

It is the teacher's responsibility to make sure that pupils are aware of possible hazard areas, and to continue with the application of the precautions necessary in all aspects of work.

The starting point here must be for all pupils to wear protective clothing and girls especially to tie their hair back safely.

The teacher's example must be unquestionably sound, and this entails ample forethought and preparation of information sheets for use within the workshop eg information charts for machines, notes on the correct and safe use of materials etc.

*Note*
Safety should be developed as a 'common sense' attitude in the workshop, and this does not differ from the attitude that should exist in the everyday environment.

### 2 Materials

A wide range of materials is available – paper, card, clay, plaster, paint, metal, plastics, enamels, concrete, etc.

The aim should be to develop an understanding of the materials as follows:

(a) Source and manufacture (briefly) for natural and man-made materials.
(b) Forms of the material eg wire, rod, sheet, board. The material's properties influence the forms available.
(c) Strength/weakness in relation to scale. Increasing the strength of weak materials.
(d) Selection and use in two- and three-dimensional forms.
(e) Application – uses in the man-made environment.
(f) Machines in relation to the materials.
(g) Materials in relation to the machines.
(h) Safety precautions essential to the materials.
(i) Size and measurement.
(j) Tools in relation to the material.
(k) Tools in relation to each other and the user.
(l) Joining materials.

Pupils should be visually aware and be able to recognize and distinguish the following:

(a) Softwood
(b) Hardwood
(c) Manufactured boards
(d) Wood in laminated form
(e) Metals – ferrous and non-ferrous
(f) Plastics – thermoplastics, thermosetting

These materials can be introduced by the use of simple jig-saws. This also facilitates the introduction of the methodology of design.

### Materials in the environment

A collection of items by pupils and an appropriate display within the workshop in the form of a discovery area or similar.

### 3 Terminology and methodology

Design involves communication which requires a language. A basic terminology must be developed from the concepts of line, space, form, shape, pattern, texture, colour/tone, structure.

Since design is a total process, it is unrealistic to isolate these concepts completely. However, emphasis may be laid on specific concepts where necessary, for teaching purposes.

Design demands an analytical approach, so a methodology becomes vital. This should stem from a total awareness of the problem involved. At this level methodology can evolve from a teacher working systematically through a problem and making pupils aware of each stage.

**4 Aesthetics and function**
Craft lends itself well to the aesthetics of design, and the materials offer a wide range of possibilities which can be exploited without undue repetition. The aim should be to offer a starting point so that work may develop:

(a) In a pre-determined manner.
(b) In a manner determined by a group.
(c) In a manner determined by the pupil.

In each case, the discussion involved is aimed at developing design terminology as a sound basis for future design work. A starting point may be offered using a source of inspiration gained from: mathematical forms, 2D or 3D forms, natural forms, problems involving pattern, shape or texture.
Function offers a complex problem in the following sense:

1  Physical capabilities of pupils at this age.
2  Limitations of facilities.
3  Limitations of space in the workshop.
4  Limitation of working time available.
5  Extent of the desire to produce functional artefacts.
6  Choice of suitable material.

However, the problem can be tackled as follows:

(a) Introduction of problems involving an equal element of function and aesthetic value. The need for a study of simple ergonomics to be emphasized, laminated wood kitchen utensil — spoon, spatula; acrylic paper knife.
(b) Use of essentially functional problems based on: elastic powered vehicles in flight or simple vehicles.
(c) By analysis of a known item, through discussing or sketching its function eg bicycle, motor car, town, village.
(d) By collecting and analysing natural and man-made forms.

The work done involving function is of importance even in its limited form for accuracy, in terms of measurement, will become increasingly important in years 3,4 and 5.

**5 Sketching**
The development of ideas and the wide range of possibilities within one idea is essential to the process of designing. To this end sketching must be included at all relevant stages.

(a) To develop the design methodology.
(b) To develop an awareness of the range of possibilities within one idea.
(c) To develop the self confidence needed to communicate ideas to oneself on paper.
(d) To communicate ideas to others.
(e) To communicate ideas, select one and develop where practicable.

**The quality and clarity of sketches should be as high as possible within the bounds of:**

time  
working conditions  
needs of the problem in hand  
ability of the pupil  
resources available

**6 General**
The teacher has a specific responsibility as follows:

(a) To prepare adequately.
(b) To set a high standard in both thought and application.
(c) To attach importance to discussion at all stages.
(d) To mount and display work in a professional manner bearing in mind that standards are always important.
(e) To use a range of teaching methods according to the problem in hand.
(f) To provide a stimulating but organized working environment and to maintain it that way.
(g) To tackle the work with pupils as if it had never been done before.
(h) To develop the skill of using pupil ideas as a starting point for future work.
(i) To realize that pupils cannot provide ideas without an adequate amount of stimulation.
(j) To use film strips and slides to illustrate the use of materials, and examples of designing in the man-made environment.
(k) To illustrate the wealth of inspiration available from natural forms and to be prepared to analyse in simple terms.
(l) The course work should provide a sound, balanced approach to craft with the development of the child's imaginative and inventive qualities constantly in mind.

**Written work**
(a) Worksheets
(b) Crossword
(c) Sketches for project work
(d) Homework set when relevant

**Conclusion**
The thought process relevant to design/craft activities does not differ from the process of living. With this basic philosophy in mind, our work in the workshop must be relevant to a child's development. We have the facilities and consequently the responsibility to make our work relevant to a child's future needs.

---

Here the emphasis is placed on developing the teacher's ability to analyse, synthesize, evaluate and translate into work for children. The work of years 1 and 2 (11 and 12-year-old children) forms a basic course where imaginative and inventive work needs to be fostered and not suppressed by an imposed rigid scheme of work. However, within this approach there must be some guidance to course content so that each child gains a common experience but also gains from the teacher's individual interpretation and specialist expertise.

Figure 45 Teacher support material for Year 3 suggests the need to prepare a child more specifically for the demands of examination courses in years 4 and 5.
The content of a third-year course within a design department structure can be shown as suggested in Figure 46, to include aspects of work to be covered in terms of time available.

*Figure 45 Opposite*  Teacher support material B

## The approach to craft in year 3

Third year work must be seen as a logical extension of the work done in years 1 and 2. If a sound foundation has been laid, then the time should now be ripe to pursue problem solving more specifically.

The outcome of work in years 1 and 2 can be summarized as follows:

(a) Pupils have been encouraged to think away from preconceived ideas. The selected solution to a problem has been one from several possibilities.
(b) The ability of pupils to discuss and evaluate ideas both individually and in groups has been encouraged extensively.
(c) The approach to materials has been broadly based with some experience gained in the qualities, properties and uses of a limited range of materials.
(d) The need for skills and techniques has been made apparent for the successful use of materials.
(e) The aesthetic values have been dealt with and a parallel understanding of function has been gained.
(f) The concept of design as a thought process has been applied to 2D and 3D work using a range of materials.

### Safety

The attitude to safety developed in years 1 and 2 should be continued as rigorously during the third year.

### Project work

Third year work demands a greater element of function. This means the application of the design process to functional problems.

This entails a design brief which can be determined by: the pupil, a group or the teacher.

In each case the constraint of time will need to be considered.

### Problem solving

This is to be seen as a logical, analytical approach to resolving practical problems. The analysis entails breaking the problem into parts and assessing each. However, it must be stressed that considering parts in isolation from the whole is quite unrealistic, so the whole problem must be seen as being made up of parts which are simpler units for a child to conceive.

Although teachers can agree on the fundamental approach to designing, their interpretation in the teaching situation must allow for individuality.

The aim should be to encourage pupils to pose the questions and record the answers when resolving a problem. The problem solving model should be seen as a model to guide a child's thoughts to ask relevant questions.

This can be achieved as follows: (a) as a complete process before commencing practical work (b) as a progression during the course of working (c) at the conclusion of work as a summary of all the work done previously in the form of freehand sketches and notes.

**The method adopted must be suited to the child concerned**

### Problem solving and communication

Resolving problems in the workshop demands the need to communicate ideas to oneself and to others.

Initially the means must be sketching, preferably freehand, which must be taught and not be allowed to occur haphazardly. All pupils tend to be reluctant to sketch freehand. This is largely due to their own pre-conceived ideas about lines being straight at all times.

The basic skills can be taught:

(a) Choice and use of pencil. Type and use of line.
(b) Use of paper — movement, layout.
(c) Sketching to convey as much information as possible.
(d) Analytical sketches — start with set exercises for a common experience.
(e) Drawing as an international/national means of communication.
(f) Sketching may be strictly controlled or free — the latter will be more difficult to control and not suited to all pupils. The use of both forms during the course would be ideal.
(g) All ideas should be sketched — several possible ideas before one is selected for development.
(h) All sketches should be retained.
(i) Drawing may be introduced allied to a controlled piece of 3D work.
(j) Audio-visual material/equipment should be used to illustrate and stimulate as resource material in the workshop.

### Materials

Although the experience gained already has been broadly based, this should be sufficient for a child to be able to select a material in consultation with the teacher.

The aim should be to consolidate the work done in years 1 and 2 and to:

(a) ensure suitable selection and good use of material.
(b) Ensure development of the understanding of the working properties of materials.
(c) Be aware of the relationship between the pupils, the tool and the material.
(d) Relate scale to material.
(e) Realize the need for suitable surface finishes.
(f) Ensure that all pupils understand the need for a logical process for preparing materials to the sizes required.

A range of materials will be used within the workshop, but every pupil will not necessarily use a wide range. Each child must be encouraged to look at other work and other problems.

### Workshop environment

Since this forms the base for activity, staff should make a real effort to create a stimulating working environment. This will pay dividends in terms of pupil response.

Visual material should be both stimulating and relevant, and should not stagnate. Ideally, visual material should be individual to the teacher concerned. Gradually a wealth of aids should become available for use by all staff.

The need for communication within the workshop is essential ie information sheets for machines, processes, safety, tool identification.

### In conclusion

Although this information is aimed specifically at the third year, the general content of the document for years 1 and 2 is still relevant.

The success of the work done by pupils in the workshops depends on the staff working as a team, pooling ideas and resources. The outcome will be stimulating work from both teachers and pupils.

**Design department**        Third year courses

**Craft**

*Time allocation* — 19 weeks x 3 hours per week

*Areas of work to be covered*

**Communication skills and techniques**
discussion
sketches and notes
drawing — orthographic
            — isometric
            — perspective

**Skills and techniques with materials**
preparation to size
marking out
cutting out
preparation for finishing

**Technology of materials**
source
identification
uses
working properties

**Identification of tools**
cutting tools
marking out tools
testing tools
boring tools
striking tools
holding devices
unclassified

**Problem solving**
problem
design brief
initial ideas
development
construction
finish

**Design folio**
logical presentation of idea resolving the problem set out in brief

**Imaginative work**

*Course organization* — approximate time allocation
Communication skills — 12hrs
Basic skills — materials — 12hrs
Problem solving — 21hrs
Design folio — 6hrs
Technology — 6hrs

*Presentation of work*
Individual folio of work working within the prescribed guidelines given on the following:
use of communication skills
content
format
individuality

*Figure 46* Third year course content

## Communication

A vital part of any learning situation and the essential skills here relate to:

discussion        formal drawings
written language     models
sketching

Communication is part of designing. Initially a child has the need to communicate ideas to him or herself. Then the ideas require clarification for others to understand them. Further development enables someone else to make them from detailed working drawings or sketches.

Since most ideas evolve and change at several stages of development, the whole range of communication skills listed are relevant. Figure 47 shows group discussion and individual communication within workshop activity.

Sketching as a means of communication is often undervalued and poorly executed in the workshop. It seems that the domination by formal working drawings has inhibited the skills and techniques of many craft teachers. There is a need for teachers to develop their own sketching skills and techniques. This can be achieved through in-service courses or on a self-help basis. Within a department structure the expertise of teachers can be used to advantage in order to develop the skills of other teachers.

If sketching skills and techniques are to be developed in children then a structured approach is needed. This can allow a teacher to present sketching as a structured course, and also allow children with a natural flair to develop further as individuals.

A child can use the folio as a shop window for his/her skills, to show care and attention to detail to show initiative and the ability to generate ideas when resolving a problem.

For examination purposes, where assessment may be a year or more hence, the folio acts as an effective means of recording a child's thoughts at a particular moment in time.

## Resources

Resources here refer to the body of knowledge retained in a form readily available for children. These can be related to both practical activity and design folio work. Resource packs and worksheets are prepared for mixed ability teaching groups. The worksheets cater for three levels of ability, (high, mid and low) and are colour coded accordingly.

In order to link a child's research work from these resource packs with practical activity, design briefs are prepared for the same ability levels for each material. In this way a child can identify the following quite readily:

the structure of the course
the work required from each resource unit
the progress made in relation to ability
the organization of resources

Each child can work at an appropriate level which can be adjusted if necessary as the course progresses.

The teacher can establish resources to encourage the development of a child's work in:

a rational manner
a manner based on observation
an intuitive manner

The final form of these resources represents the ideas of that particular teacher. In the workshop the influence of major research projects will be both helpful and apparent in this context.

Realistically resources can take many forms, for example:

| | |
|---|---|
| materials | interest corner |
| tools and equipment | natural forms |
| text books | man-made forms |
| films, filmstrips, slides | process information |
| information sheets | cards |
| work sheets | safety precautions |
| design briefs | design — past, present |
| wall charts | and future |

*Figure 47* Discussion as part of designing

How the teacher uses the potential resource material listed here is determined by individual initiative within the constraints of a particular situation. Resources are an essential part of organization and management in the workshop. The environment itself is not conducive to written material being used or produced. However, this problem can be overcome and research sessions can become part of the workshop routine.

**Pupil ideas**

Ideas can be generated in response to a rational, empirical or intuitive approach to workshop activities. It is highly likely that the final forms produced will reflect an amalgamation of these approaches.
Consider the following examples:

Figure 48 illustrates a response to the following design brief:
*'Design a desk unit to contain essential writing equipment, suitable for use by a young executive'.*

Figure 49 illustrates a group project in response to the following brief:
*'Design and make a two-dimensional wall panel to enhance the environment in that area of the school adjacent to the physical education facilties'.*

Figure 50 illustrates group responses to the following brief:
*'Design and make three dimensional sculptural forms within the following constraints:*
*Size — maximum board size available.*
*Material — 16 mm chipboard.*
*Joining — halving and built-up forms only.'*

*Figure 48* A response to a specific brief

*Figure 49* Assembly of work done by five sub-groups

*Figure 50* A response to a specific brief

Teacher directed work can be used to control:
1 the material used
2 the techniques used
3 the tools and equipment used
4 the skills developed

*Figure 51* Design folio guidance notes for a child at fourth and fifth year level

## Applying the problem solving model

It would seem logical to suggest that some more specific guidance is necessary if a child is expected to use a model as a basis for folio work at examination level. Figure 51 suggests how guidance notes can assist a child in problem solving activity. Figure 52 suggests how these notes can be developed to suit the needs of more advanced courses.

---

**Problem solving model**
An explanatory sheet for a child, to be used as a basis for folio work in problem solving activity at fourth and fifth year, examination level.

### Design brief
This is a statement saying what the problem is. It is a response to a need. It also states the limitations that you need to consider eg a maximum size, a maximum cost, age of person, etc.

### Basic (essential) requirements
Here the essential requirements are identified as understood from the brief.

eg   A table is a solution to a problem.
     What are the essential requirements of a table?
     A *surface* and a *support* for that surface.
     Does a table necessarily need four legs since legs are really only one example of a *support*.

### Factors which influence the design
Here you are concerned with specific questions that need to be answered at this stage, or a list of things to be considered in detail later

eg   Who is to use the product?
     Where will the product be used?
     How and how often will it be used?
     The age of the user?
     The disability of the user?

### Factors to be considered in detail later
material              finish
construction          cost
shape and size        sequence of operation
appearance            (production)

### Ideas sketched and discussed
Here initial/preliminary ideas need to be sketched. Use each sheet of sketching paper fully so that there are as many ideas as possible on each sheet. Add notes to the sketches to explain your ideas eg thoughts on construction, material, strength, stability.

Consult your teacher about the idea to be developed. Select one idea and develop fully to the stage of a working sketch or drawing.

Developing an idea does not mean just drawing it again. Sketch and modify extensively until you are satisfied with the form it should take. Then, following consultation with your teacher, produce good clear, dimensioned drawings and sketches with construction details and a materials cutting list. Present your drawings using the techniques used earlier in the course.

### Appearance
Here you must be concerned with how the product looks. This means that the shape of each part must look as if it belongs to the whole ie shapes must be related to each other or intended as a contrast. Shape may also be influenced by the function of the product. Also included are colour, texture and pattern which can be used to improve the product's overall appearance.

### Materials
Here you must consider all the materials suitable for making your selected idea. This means giving examples of possible materials and reasons for their suitability. Details should include notes on the following:

Strenght of the material
sections available
ease or difficulty of working
possible cost
construction problems

### Shape and size
Shape and size are related here to the function of the item as well as to its appearance eg the sizes of material used, the height of a seat, the size and shape of a table top.

The size of each part needs to be suitable for the purpose for which it is designed.

### Construction
What are the essential requirements of any structure?

What is meant by a joint?
How can satisfactory joints be made between materials?

Your ideas should be shown in the form of sketches and notes. Consider as many ideas as you can and then suggest the most suitable, giving reasons for your choice.

**Use the resources available to find the range of constructions available**

### Finish
This refers to the surface treatment of the materials you have used.

Why is a finish necessary for your piece of work?
Consider the types available for the materials you have used. Select the most suitable giving reasons for your choice.

### Procedure (sequence of operations)
Your folio should also include your planned organization of work.

Every part of your work needs to be carried out in a logical order to ensure a satisfactory end result.

State the order in which you are going to carry out the practical operations required.

State why you have selected this order and show any modifications made whilst working on your project.

**Appraisal (Critical analysis)**
Having completed the making process, look at the finished product and then at the design brief.
How well have you succeeded in satisfying the requirements of the problem that you identified?
Express your thoughts and give reasons.
How could you improve your solution to this problem?

**Folio presentation**
Your design folio must be presented for assessment with your realized product (if the product has been realized).
Your presentation must be viewed as a shop window in which you have the opportunity to show the following:

(a) Graphic skills
(b) Range of ideas
(c) Extent of personal research
(d) Logical sequence
(e) Care and attention to detail
(f) Sufficient information for someone else to follow your thoughts and to be able to make your product

*Figure 52* Guidance notes for 'A' level design folio work

## 'A' Level design

**Design folio** — guidance notes.
The process of designing can be seen to include the three essentials of:

*analysis   synthesis   evaluation*

These can be described in simple words as 'breaking the problem into pieces', 'putting the pieces together in a new way', and 'testing to discover the consequences of putting the new arrangement into practice'. Most design theorists agree that it is usual to cycle many times through this sequence and some suggest that each cycle is progressively less general and more detailed than the one before it. These three stages do not necessarily fit together to form a universal strategy composed of ever more detailed cycles. They are more elementary than that, being merely categories into which the many loose ends of design theory, as it now exists, can be discussed at the inexact, or fanciful, level that our partial knowledge and partial ignorance permit.

The three stages can be named divergence, transformation and convergence. These terms are meant to refer more to the new problems of system designing than to the traditional procedures of architecture and of engineering design.[1]

Whilst a professional designer would not be too eager to view these stages as separate items, such separation is necessary in order to consider the methodology needed to produce a process that works.

At 'A' level the design folio represents each student's effort to analyse, synthesize and evaluate and the final from of the product should be greatly influenced by these three stages. However, these stages form the underlying theory of designing and evidence of their presence will be reflected in the problem solving process that all students have been encouraged to use as the basis for their folio.

**Design brief**
This represents a need and generally requires clarification so that the nature of the problem is clearly understood by the designer. Clarification may be required as follows:

*Definition of terms used*
*definition or identification of constraints*
*redefinition of the brief if considered inadequate*

It must be remembered that the brief represents the terms of reference to which the designer elects to work. In some instances the brief is given, other times the designer is shown the need and is then responsible for compiling the brief on behalf of the client.

Coursework at 'A' Level Design generally has prescribed briefs. The major project requires the student to compile the brief in response to a perceived need.

**Basic requirements**
Here the essential parts of the problem are identified so that they are not overlooked as potential solutions emerge. It is also essential to identify these requirements in order to generate new thinking on the problem. We generally relate problems to our previous experiences as a means of identifying the nature of the problem for our own peace of mind. However this does tend to reinforce preconceived notions rather than encourage new thoughts. In these terms the essential requirements of a table can be viewed as a surface and a support rather than a top and legs.

**Factors which influence**
Here we are concerned with specific questions that need to be answered. These also include questions which will be dealt with in detail later. This part of the folio represents the analysis of the problem.

Who, how, where, why, how often, type of use and user, location or environment, materials, shape, size, aesthetic qualities, construction, weight, finish, cost, maintenance, procedure for making, etc. are all relevant factors to be considered in depth according to the needs of the particular problem.

**Ideas — sketched and or discussed**
Ideas can be generated in a variety of ways. Each individual will need to develop an approach which proves to be most fruitful and suited to his/her needs but, at the same time, satisfying the needs of the course. The following sequence provides a guide:

Preliminary sketches, incomplete ideas offering images of possible solutions but expressing an eagerness to explore new ideas. At this stage all ideas may not be practical but this should not deter the designer from trying to work outside his/her own limited experience. The total composition here should represent a wide range of possible starting points which could be developed in detail later.

Discussion around sketched ideas can generate new ideas and develop existing ones. Discussion can also cast a different perspective on one aspect of the problem in hand and change direction of thought.

A brain-storming session can also be useful. Here a group of students can pool ideas at random in order to stimulate thought when the ground has become rather barren. A team of designers can use this approach in order to establish an acceptable common approach to a problem.

[1] J.C. Jones   *Design Methods: Seeds of Human Futures* p. 47.

A flash of insight may also occur. Here a seemingly insoluble problem can suddenly be seen in a new and clear perspective.

The folio must be seen as the only tangible means of communication available at the end of a project or the course. Therefore, it must represent as accurately and as comprehensively as possible, the thoughts and ideas generated by each student within the constraints imposed by a specific brief.

### Aesthetic qualities

A term used in preference to appearance since students are expected to make reference here to basic design language and to try and relate the theory of the latter to their own work. Simple analytical sketches may be required to isolate certain concepts from the total idea in order to explain fully.

Reference to line, shape, pattern, colour, texture, form, mass, space, etc. should be used freely here.

### Materials

The selection of materials from a range is part of the decision making process here. Ideas generated may lend themselves to more than one material. Some basis for making a decision must be established here eg working properties, weight, production problems, construction problems, aesthetic judgement, etc. bearing in mind the following general facts about materials:

Five major categories exist when working with materials:

casting, forming, wasting, fabricating, surface treatment.

Into these categories the following processes will be classified:

alloy casting, resin casting, concrete moulding, acrylic forming, wood and plastic laminating, wood turning, preparing material to size, shaping, joining, finishing, etching, enamelling, plastic coating, painting, etc.

Some text references should be used to support decisions wherever possible.

### Shape and size

These relate to the function of the item as well as to the overall appearance. Whilst basic design requirements influence relationships between forms and space, functional and economic requirements demand detailed decisions in terms of measurements. Both aspects need to be satisfied here.

### Construction

What are the essential requirements of any construction?

How is an appropriate means of joining selected?

How can satisfactory joints be made between either the same or different materials?

Possible constructional ideas must be shown as sketches and notes.

Preliminary decisions are as important as final decisions about construction, and these need to be shown.

The final decision for construction needs to be shown in order to explain detail for making.

This requires either sketches to an appropriate scale or conventional drawings showing three or more views using an appropriate scale.

Models should also be included if they have been part of the decision making process and are the most appropriate means of communication.

### Surface treatment

This refers to the surface decoration and/or finish used.

Why is a finish necessary?
What were the alternatives considered?
What were the constraints imposed here and why?
Suggest and select the most appropriate giving your reasons.

### Procedure

This refers to the planned organization of work. Some degree of methodology is required here in order to conceive the total process of making in advance. The basic procedure adopted will inevitably be modified as work progresses. The procedure given in the folio should indicate such changes and the reasons for change. The procedure can be quite effectively illustrated by a flow diagram showing the essential information only and the sequence.

### Appraisal

An appraisal of the final form produced should also be included. This appraisal should consider the solution offered in relation to the brief. Such an appraisal will be subjective but should aim at giving some reasons for making each value judgement.

It should be noted here that an appraisal should not be confused with evaluation, since the latter is very much part of the decision making within the total process of designing.

### Presentation

This can, and should, reflect the individuality of students but the overall aim must always be to communicate ideas and relevant information in relation to a particular problem. In real terms the visiting examiner needs to be convinced of the quality of thought, standard of work, presentation achieved by each candidate during and at the end of the course.

---

## Examination courses

Traditional courses have placed the emphasis on the quality of workmanship. Change has placed increasing emphasis on the need to be concerned with developing a child's learning process through designing and making.

Consider the example illustrated in Figure 53, where the responsibility for course work is placed with the teacher. The scheme for this examination is based on educational aims and objectives which can be realized within workshop activity.

The implications of such a scheme can only be fully conceived if placed alongside a more prescriptive examination syllabus where the concern is with a body of knowledge rather than the process of learning.

The dangers inherent within such a scheme cannot be ignored but the professional competence of the teacher is being fully tested here.

This design and craft examination comprised of coursework which was assessed by the teacher and validated by the examination boards. Additionally, examination papers were set and marked by the examination boards to cover the following aspects of the scheme:

Paper 1 Design and realization of design.
Paper 2 Design and communication.

It must also be emphasized that a great deal of communication was essential during this 16+ examination feasibility study, between the examination boards and participating schools. This took the form of discussions, standardizing meetings and agreement trials.

Whilst the study was terminated in 1979 it provided invaluable experience for the participating bodies and has influenced many subsequent schemes.

The intention here has been to illustrate an approach to design and craft rather than to give precise details of a specific examination.

**Project work**

Figures 54(a)–(g) illustrate the starting point and the end product of the minibus project mentioned in Chapter 3.

One important feature within this project was to relate the finished product to the initial problem analysis. This focused attention on the changes that were necessary as new problems became apparent as the project developed. This example also serves as a useful example of designing and making, seen as an essential part of the school's extra-curriculum programme for several years. Each child who participated has the opportunity to identify with a part of the final form as well as to enjoy the facility offered by the bus functioning effectively.

Technology
For the 11-12 year-old child technology must include information which can be substantiated through practical experience. Figures 55(a)–(c) illustrate an approach to basic technology through the use of information sheets, worksheets, etc.

Evaluation
In relation to a *product*, evaluation requires the teacher to exercise value judgement on a child's work.

In relation to *learning*, evaluation requires some understanding of a child's growth and development.

In relation to *designing*, evaluation involves the constant feedback of information, implementing change where necessary and recognizing that a child's cognitive skills are being developed.

At examination level, Figure 56 illustrates how criteria for assessment can be set out in relation to: the design folio, the making process and the finished product. Figure 57 suggests an approach to assessing a child's attainment, potential ability and individual attitudes. Here the craft teacher cannot be divorced from the school's function of assessing a child's progress and development within the educational system.

---

**Aims and objectives of the examination**

Aims:
To foster a degree of understanding and expertise in those areas of creative thinking which can be expressed and developed through planning and working with materials.

To provide situations which encourage pupils to use their practical and intellectual skills in design experiences, operating through a process of analysis, synthesis and realization in a variety of materials.

To promote the development of initiative, ingenuity, resourcefulness, self-involvement, co-operation, social responsibility and the ability to communicate.

To encourage students to relate the course to their personal interests and thereby create opportunities to study, experiment and carry out research into the nature of the world in which they live.

Objectives:
To provide candidates with the opportunity to demonstrate their abilities in the following.

*Group A:* To recognize a need.
To identify, analyse and evaluate a problem.
To identify and record relevant information.
To apply their knowledge and experience to the solution of a problem.
To formulate a number of ideas for the solution of a problem and examine the feasibility of each.
To develop the most feasible of a number of ideas to a solution.
To be aware of the qualities of and inter-relationships between line, form space, colour, texture, in the context of their design work where appropriate.
To communicate ideas in an appropriate manner.

*Group B:* To assess and evaluate a finished product.
To suggest possible modifications to a product.
To design a part to fit a particular situation.
To discriminate between different existing solutions to the same problem.

*Group C:* To plan the production of a job.
To use skills and techniques appropriate to the material.
To decide when holding devices should be used.
To use jigs, patterns, formers or moulds to assist operations.
To decide the kind of finish and standard of accuracy necessary for a particular piece of work.
To be critical of personal standards of work.
To use equipment and materials with care and safety, and be aware of the social responsibilities involved.
To anticipate dangers and take appropriate action.

*Figure 53* Design and craft 16+. Aims and objectives for the examination. Reproduced with permission of the West Yorkshire and Lindsey Regional Examining Board and the Associated Examining Board

It is generally beneficial for each child to be aware that evaluation takes place and of the criteria involved. This can apply quite readily in a specialist area and form a useful basis for a dialogue between the teacher and the child.

A chapter of ideas cannot be totally comprehensive. However, the intention here has been to suggest how a child's ideas can be used within a structured course, to ensure that valuable learning experiences can occur for a child involved with designing and making.

*Figure 54* Minibus project – main components. (a) to (e) Specific job sheets based on the major components given in Figure 54. (f) Bus – original state (g) Bus–end product

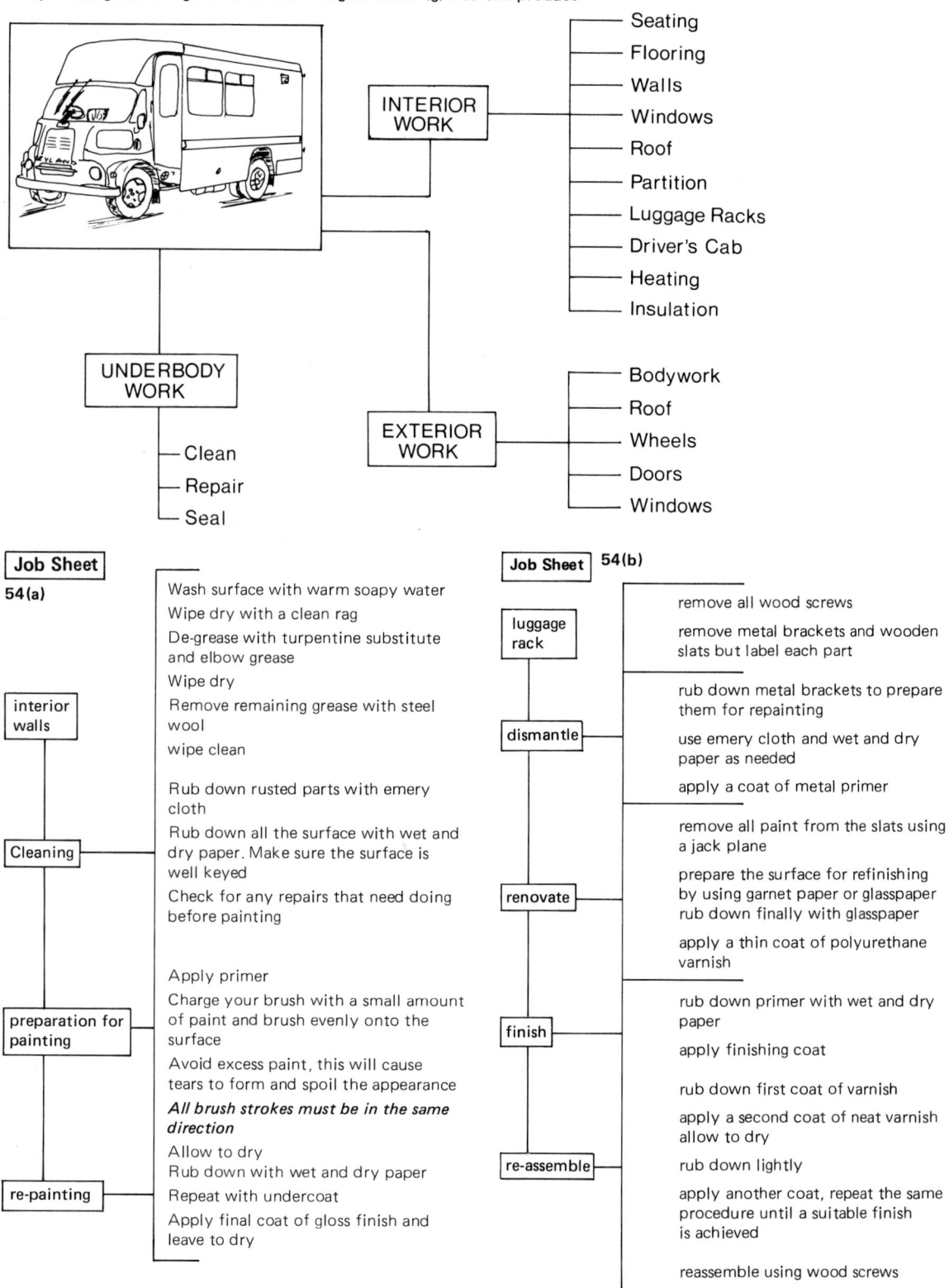

**INTERIOR WORK**
- Seating
- Flooring
- Walls
- Windows
- Roof
- Partition
- Luggage Racks
- Driver's Cab
- Heating
- Insulation

**UNDERBODY WORK**
- Clean
- Repair
- Seal

**EXTERIOR WORK**
- Bodywork
- Roof
- Wheels
- Doors
- Windows

**Job Sheet 54(a)**

*interior walls*

- Wash surface with warm soapy water
- Wipe dry with a clean rag
- De-grease with turpentine substitute and elbow grease
- Wipe dry
- Remove remaining grease with steel wool
- wipe clean

*Cleaning*
- Rub down rusted parts with emery cloth
- Rub down all the surface with wet and dry paper. Make sure the surface is well keyed
- Check for any repairs that need doing before painting

*preparation for painting*
- Apply primer
- Charge your brush with a small amount of paint and brush evenly onto the surface
- Avoid excess paint, this will cause tears to form and spoil the appearance
- **All brush strokes must be in the same direction**
- Allow to dry
- Rub down with wet and dry paper

*re-painting*
- Repeat with undercoat
- Apply final coat of gloss finish and leave to dry

**Job Sheet 54(b)**

*luggage rack*

*dismantle*
- remove all wood screws
- remove metal brackets and wooden slats but label each part
- rub down metal brackets to prepare them for repainting
- use emery cloth and wet and dry paper as needed
- apply a coat of metal primer

*renovate*
- remove all paint from the slats using a jack plane
- prepare the surface for refinishing by using garnet paper or glasspaper rub down finally with glasspaper
- apply a thin coat of polyurethane varnish

*finish*
- rub down primer with wet and dry paper
- apply finishing coat
- rub down first coat of varnish
- apply a second coat of neat varnish allow to dry

*re-assemble*
- rub down lightly
- apply another coat, repeat the same procedure until a suitable finish is achieved
- reassemble using wood screws

61

**54(c)**

- **wheels**
  - remove all loose dirt from both sides of the hub use the scraping tools provided
  - rub down rusted parts until the best possible surface is achieved ready for painting

- **hub**
  - apply a coat of metal primer, evenly
  - allow to dry
  - rub down
  - apply undercoat and finishing coat with the same care pay attention to the instructions given with any paint used

- **tyre**
  - all tyres must have 3mm depth of tread on them
  - remove any stones from the tread
  - note any faults in the tyres
  - apply one coat of black tyre paint

**Job sheet**

**54(d)**

- **bodywork**
  - remove detatchable parts
  - remove all loose paintwork
  - scrape badly rusted parts
  - rub down rusted parts using emery cloth, wet and dry paper as required until an even surface is achieved
  - apply anti-rust solution
  - apply cellulose primer
  - rub down lightly with 500 grade wet and dry paper
  - mask off ready for re-spray
  - mask off — roof
    - windows
    - lights
    - remove wing mirrors
  - respray undercoat all over
  - respray truck yellow section and allow to dry
  - mask off all truck yellow
  - respray middle brown section
  - remove masking
  - replace accessories

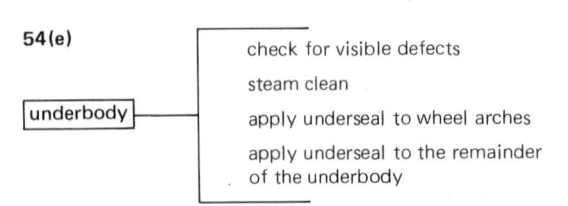

**54(e)**

- **underbody**
  - check for visible defects
  - steam clean
  - apply underseal to wheel arches
  - apply underseal to the remainder of the underbody

**54(f)**

**54(g)**

62

## DESIGN – CRAFT – INFORMATION SHEET NO.1

### Softwoods

**Definition**
The terms 'hardwood' and 'softwood' can be misleading because hardwoods are softer than many softwoods, and *vice versa*. The difference between them is a botanical one based on the way the cells or fibres are arranged. These fibres form the grain and the way they lie gives us the direction of the grain.

**Source**
Coniferous Trees. These trees grow thin needle-shaped leaves which do not fall in the autumn. They are found in the forest belts which stretch across northern Canada, Scandinavia and northern Russia, where a very cold climate is experienced. Conifers are also found in regions with much warmer climates but only where the land is so high above sea level that the climate becomes similar to that of the colder regions. A coniferous tree matures in about a quarter of the time taken by a hardwood tree.

**Identification**
Softwoods are quite easy to identify because of:

their distinct growth rings
their light colour
they are usually lighter in weight
they are easier to work than most hardwoods

**Examples**
The trees found in coniferous forests are numerous and include all types of Pine trees, Spruce, Firs, Yew, Western Red Cedar and the giant Redwood or Sequoia.

**Uses**
*Outdoor* – buildings – structural work, carpentry, sheds, fencing, gates.
*Indoor* – carpentry, furniture, cupboards, shelves, floors.

Spruce is especially used for producing wood pulp, paper and hardboard.

## DESIGN – CRAFT – INFORMATION SHEET NO. 2

### Hardwoods

**Definition**
A botanical classification based on the way the cells or fibres are arranged. The bulk of the fibres are needed to support the tree and other pores serve the purpose of carrying sap from the roots to the leaves.

In tropical hardwoods the interlocking grain is caused by the cells growing in spiral fashion throughout the length of the trunk.

**Source**
These timbers come from the broad leaved deciduous trees found in temperate and tropical climates. Their source may therefore be European, Far-Eastern, American or West African. There are hundreds of different types and only a few find their use in school.

As supplies become short so the type will change — especially the West African timbers. These trees take a long time to mature.

**Identification**
Darker and more varied in colour than softwood.
Harder than softwood } with the exception of balsa
Heavier than softwood
More difficult to work
More expensive and can be in short supply

**Examples**
*European (Temperate) Hardwoods*
Ash, Elm, Beech, Birch, Lime, Oak, Sycamore, Walnut.

*West African (Tropical) Hardwoods*
Agba, Gaboon, Limba, Mahogany, Sapele, Mansonia, Meranti, Utile, African Walnut, African Mahogany.

*Others from Far-Eastern Sources*
Japanese Elm, Japanese Oak, Burma Teak.

**Uses**
*Outdoor* – seats, building, garden furniture, cricket bats and stumps, marine plywood.
*Indoor* – furniture, toys, veneers, carving, domestic woodware.

## DESIGN – CRAFT INFORMATION SHEET NO. 3

### Plywood/Multiply

**Definition**
This is a manufactured board made up of an odd number of wood veneers (not less than three) with the grain of alternate layers at right-angles to each other. This combination of layers and a large gluing area gives plywood exceptional strength and stability.

**Source**
*Manufactured.* Veneers (thin sheets of wood) are cut, dried and graded according to their quality. These layers are glued together, pressed and the final product is a sheet of plywood or multiply (more than three layers) trimmed to the standard size of 2440 mm x 1220 mm.

Each sheet has a grade.

*Interior grade* – made with animal glue, casein glue or similar non-waterproof adhesive.

*Exterior grade* – made using a resin glue such as Aerolite.

*Marine quality* – weatherproof and boilproof, made using a resin glue – usually Aerodux (Aerolite and Aerodux are made by the CIBA company).

**Identification**
A layered structure with the grain of each layer at 90° to the adjacent layer.

*White* – this is made from Birch imported from Scandinavia and the USSR.

*Red* – mainly from the Gaboon.

Other timbers such as Beech and Limba are used and facings of more expensive timbers are placed on one side. eg Teak, Oak, Walnut, Rosewood.

**Examples**
Birch plywood
Gaboon plywood
Faced plywood eg oak faced; teak faced

**Uses**
*Interior* – used very extensively in furniture as well as building, shopfittings, wall panels, interior walls.
*Exterior* – building, temporarily also for concrete shutterings and portable buildings, marine work ranging from canoes to cruisers.

## DESIGN – CRAFT – INFORMATION SHEET NO. 4

### Blockboard, chipboard

**Definition**
A manufactured board designed to replace thick multiply which is expensive.

**Blockboard**
Made by gluing a number of strips of solid timber side by side to form a core. This core is then sandwiched between two facings with the grain at 90° to the core.

**Laminboard**
Similar to blockboard except that the core strips are narrower and it is a better quality base for veneering.

**Uses**
Furniture especially as groundwork for veneering.

**Chipboard**
A new material used in mass produced furniture. It is made from fine wood particles compressed and bonded together with a synthetic resin adhesive (Aerolite).
  The board can take the form of a single layer, a sandwich construction or be veneered with wood or plastic on both faces. A well known brand is Conti-plas and Contiboard.

*New materials need new forms of joining so conventional joints cannot be used.*

## DESIGN – CRAFT – INFORMATION SHEET NO. 5

### Hardboard

**Definition**
A board of even thickness and colour, without a grain structure, manufactured to give one smooth surface.

**Source – manufactured**
Made by subjecting a mixture of wood pulp and resin to heat and pressure. The resulting board has one very smooth surface that can be veneered with wood or plastic. An improved board can be achieved with a high pressure and treating the surface with oil. The reverse side has a rectangular pattern as a result of the manufacturing process where a fine mesh forms the lower pressing surface.

**Identification**
Dark brown colour, one surface smooth. Thickness of a sheet can vary from 0.6 mm to 6 mm.

**Uses**
Ideal for use where strength is not required.
Can be veneered with wood or plastic for use in furniture.
Used extensively as backs for cheap cabinets.
Can be used to face softwood frames for interior doors.

**55(a)**

## Year 1 Craft worksheet – Wood

Using the information sheets provided, complete the following questions.

1 _____ trees give us softwoods. They are recognized by their _____ shaped leaves.

2 _____ trees give us hardwoods. They are recognized by their _____ leaves.

3 Describe how you would recognize a piece of planed softwood.

4 Describe how you would recognize a piece of hardwood.

5 Softwoods have many uses. Name two uses for each of the following
Outdoor _____
Indoor _____

6 Hardwoods have many uses. Name two uses for each of the following
Outdoor _____
Indoor _____

7 Underline the softwoods in the following:
Pine, Oak, Ash, Beech, Fir, Yew, Cedar, Spruce.

8 Underline the hardwoods in the following:
Oak, Elm, Sycamore, Fir, Birch, Ash, Spruce, Mahogany, Teak, Walnut.

9 Describe how plywood can be recognized.

10 Why is plywood a strong material?

11 What is chipboard?

12 'A board of even thickness and colour, without a grain structure, manufactured to give one smooth surface'
To which material does this description apply?

## Year 2 Craft worksheet – Wood

Using the information sheets provided, complete the following questions.

1 Coniferous trees give us _____ woods.

2 Deciduous trees give us _____ woods.

3 Canada, Scandinavia, Northern Russia have a very cold winter climate. Which kind of tree does this climate suit?

4 Which parts of the world supply us with hardwoods?

5 Describe briefly a piece of softwood (Deal).

6 Choose one hardwood and describe it briefly.

7 Which material would you suggest for building the following?
Garden gate _____
Park bench/seat _____
Household furniture _____
Shelves _____

8 How is paper made? Describe the process briefly.

9 List the following as hardwoods or softwoods.
Ash, Pine, Birch, Lime, Willow, Larch, Walnut, Mahogany, Beech, Cedar, Fir, Teak, Sapele, Yew.
Hardwoods _____
Softwoods _____

10 Describe the structure of plywood.

11 'Wooden particles compressed and bonded together with a resin adhesive'
Name this material _____

12 Hardboard. Describe this material.

## Design department

Third year craft worksheet
Before starting this worksheet, walk around the workshop and use your eyes, not just to avoid the furniture and other pupils, but to see what is around you. Look carefully since you will need this information to complete the questions in this worksheet.

Hand tools
You will all have used many hand tools. They are usually classified as follows:

1 *Cutting tools*
2 *Marking and measuring tools*
3 *Testing tools*
4 *Boring tools*
5 *Striking tools*
6 *Unclassified tools* ie those not included in the above categories.

Take an example from each class, 1-6, and make a clear sketch showing the main parts. Give your reasons why these tools are shaped as they are.

Power tools
What is a power tool? Give as many examples as you can and state their uses. (You may have some examples from home as well.)

Machines
Wood can be cut and shaped by machine quite easily.

1 Name the machines which can be used with wood. List the processes that you can carry out with these machines.
2 Make a sketch of one part of any machine.
 (a) Name the machine
 (b) Name the part
 (c) Make sure that your sketch shows the shape clearly, each part and how it would be used

How do machines work?
Many machines are driven by a belt running on pulley wheels attached to the spindle of an electric motor.
What do we mean by a machine that is 'belt-driven'? To answer this question make a sketch to explain clearly what it means to you. Explain how we get different speeds. List the speeds of the machine and say why you think these speeds are needed.

Safety
Safety is most important in all areas of the workshop, but machines in particular can give us problems if we are careless.

*Select one machine*

1 Name the accidents that can happen on that machine.
2 What advice would you give to someone using that machine to lessen the possibility of an accident happening?

Sketching
Sketching is the language that we use to pass on information clearly to others. Imagine that you are describing the wood workshop to a stranger. Make a sketch or sketches which would show this person as clearly as possible what the workshop looks like.

Presentation of work
All your sketches and notes must be done clearly and neatly. You have been taught how to sketch, shade, and colour wash. Use these techniques to produce a booklet containing your answers to all parts of this worksheet.
 The overall appearance can include your own ideas for the cover piece, bearing in mind that a cover usually indicates what a book contains.
 The aim should be to present the information in a way which will be interesting to yourself, other pupils, teachers and anyone who reads the booklet.
**Only your care and thought can produce this.**

*Materials required*

A4 drawing paper
A4 lined paper
HB pencil for sketching
crayons for colour
colour wash materials
spray adhesive for mounting
card for the cover piece
some form of fastening

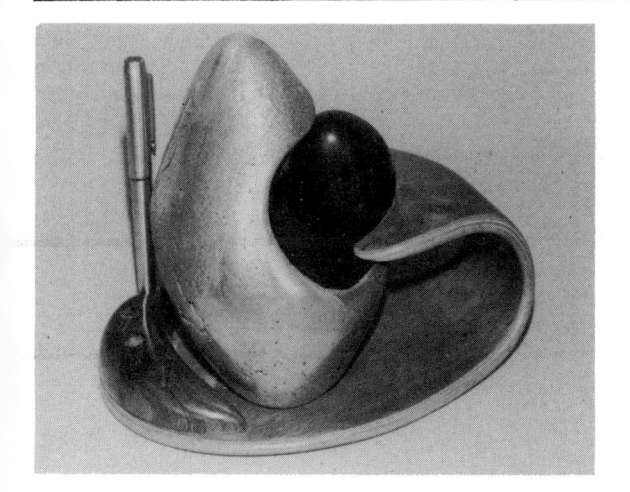

55(c)

**Design** and **Craft**  **year 1**

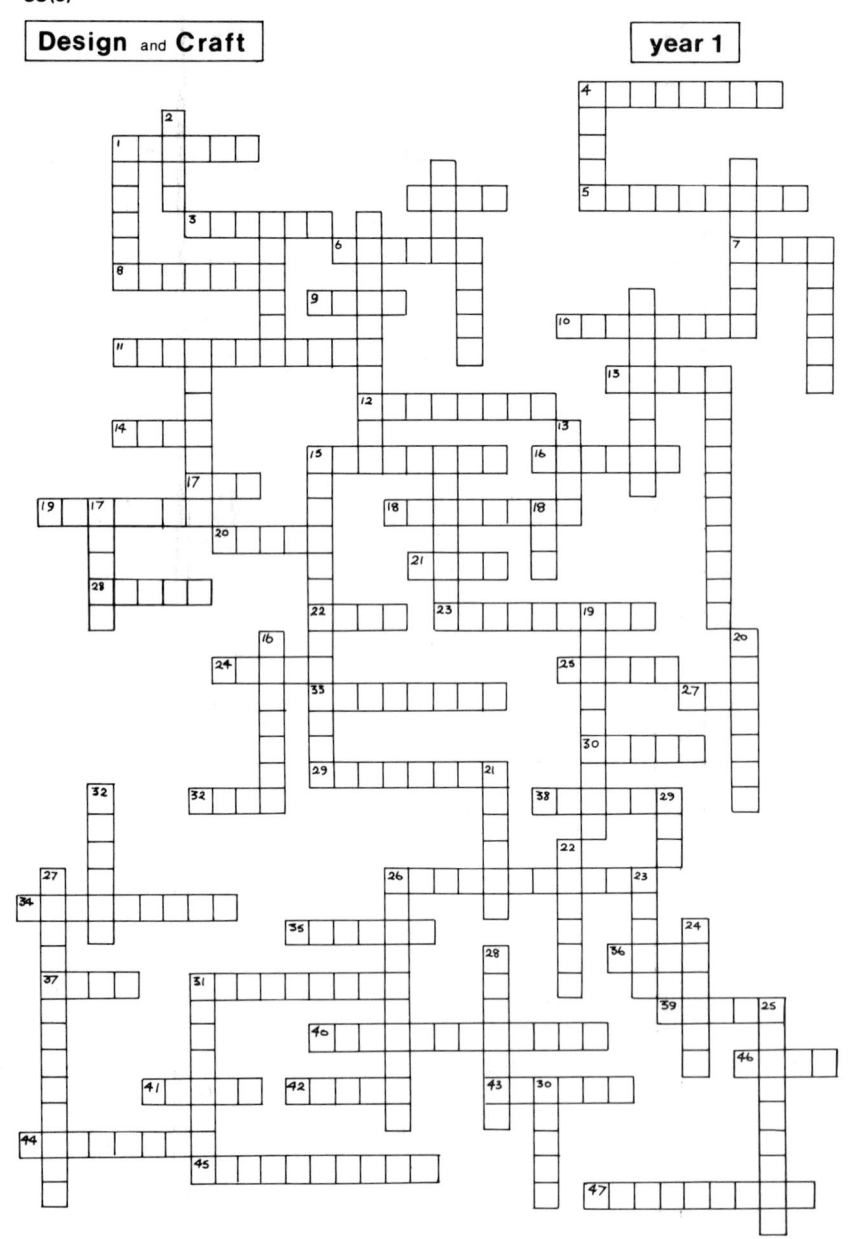

## Design and craft

**Clues across**
1. Iron and ___ give us steel
2. A tool for metal really
3. Wood and acrylic can be held in one of these to produce a form
4. A means of transferring from a drawing onto material
5. Tool for checking a 90° angle
6. Animals may be described this way
7. A section of metal, light in weight and with four equal sides
8. Shapes which belong together are
9. A term used when describing any object
10. A term used when an object serves a purpose
11. Shapes not related are
12. Something difficult to describe using words
13. Needs to be understood in wood
14. Needed for forming acrylic
15. Sheet metal with a difference
16. Coarser than glasspaper
17. A section of mild steel, easy to work
18. Timber from a deciduous tree
19. Acrylic when cold is ___ and breaks easily
20. A type of drilling machine
21. A means of joining two pieces of wood together
22. An example of a coniferous tree
23. A hand tool for cutting curves in wood
24. A type of wood — light, soft, brittle from South America
25. Leaves on a deciduous tree can be described this way

66

| | | | |
|---|---|---|---|
| 26 | Can be seen quite clearly in softwood | 6 | Balsa is used a lot for this purpose |
| 27 | Polyvinyl Acetate Emulsion glue in brief | 7 | This should be avoided in wood |
| 28 | Combine metals together to form a new metal | 8 | Must be pleasing to the eye |
| 29 | Softwood comes from these trees | 9 | A finish which can be used to advantage on softwood |
| 30 | A saw for cutting wood accurately by hand | 10 | Metals which contain iron |
| 21 | These trees give us hardwoods | 11 | A surface can be described this way |
| 32 | When drilling on a pillar drill, work should not be held in this | 12 | A thermoplastic |
| | | 13 | Useful for making models |
| 33 | Timber from a coniferous tree | 14 | Metals which do not contain iron |
| 34 | A quick means of joining wood | 15 | Acrylic is one |
| 35 | The largest drilling machine in the workshop | 16 | Thin layers of wood with grain of each layer at $90°$ to the adjoining layer |
| 36 | For holding work | | |
| 37 | A low temperature kind of soldering | 17 | We need these when working with materials |
| 38 | For holding work on a bench perhaps | 18 | A well known deciduous tree |
| 39 | For scorching wood | 19 | Pieces of wood, metal or plastic joined together can form one of these |
| 40 | For marking long edges over 300mm long | | |
| 41 | Mild steel – a flat section | 20 | Hard soldering |
| 42 | For cutting straight edges on card | 21 | Most important in any workshop |
| 43 | The leaves of coniferous trees are shaped like this | 22 | For cutting curves accurately in wood |
| 44 | Used for cutting sheet steel | 23 | A type of heater used with acrylic |
| 45 | The process of firing powdered glass on metal | 24 | Acrylic has one |
| 46 | Needed when soldering | 25 | This file is not completely flat |
| 47 | Used to communicate ideas | 26 | For a smooth surface before polishing wood |
| | | 27 | Brazing is an example of this |
| | | 28 | A tenon saw, jig saw, chisel, plane, knife all have a sharp edge |

**Clues down**

| | | | |
|---|---|---|---|
| 1 | Adds something to any piece of work | 29 | A type of hammer |
| 2 | _____ and carbon give us steel | 30 | For cleaning metal before soldering |
| 3 | Always important when making | 31 | Must be done on metal before enamelling |
| 4 | A type of drill mainly for metal | 32 | A reddish brown metal, soft and easy to work |
| 5 | This should be part of the material used | | |

*Figure 56* Design and craft 16+ examination – criteria for assessment. Reproduced with the permission of TWYLREB and AEB

### The design folio

| Operation | Criteria for assessment |
|---|---|
| (i) Identification of need | Degree of pupil initiative |
| (ii) Analysis of problem | Identification of problem<br>Analysis of relevant factors<br>Evidence of investigation |
| Postulation of possible solutions (Feasibility of ideas to be ignored at this stage) | Variety of ideas<br>Clarity of communication |
| (iii) Selection, development and feasibility of preferred idea | Relevance to brief<br>Study of materials, constructions, components and costs<br>Evidence of experiment and the use of models or 'mock-ups' where appropriate |
| (iv) Communication and presentation of solution | Comprehensiveness<br>Clarity |

### The making process

| Operation | Criteria for assessment |
|---|---|
| (i) Personal involvement | Evidence of personal involvement as outlined in the aims of the examination |

### The making process *continued*

| Operation | Criteria for assessment |
|---|---|
| (ii) Planning the stages of production | In relation to the complexity of the job and the amount of help given by the teacher |
| (iii) Use of skills | Ability to use skills already acquired<br>Ability to acquire and use new skills appropriate to the job |

### The finished product

| Operation | Criteria for assessment |
|---|---|
| (i) Workmanship | Workmanship as demonstrated by the finished product (The design and its success as a solution to the problem to be ignored) |
| (ii) Aspects of design which can **only** be evaluated in the finished product | Quality of inter-relationships between line, form, space, colour and texture in relation to the parts of the product itself and of the product in its environment |

**Design department**   Assessment criteria

*Assessment* is related to three main categories: present attainment potential ability and individual attitudes.

*Present attainment* — this can be measured.

*Potential ability* — cannot be measured but simply inferred.

*Individual attitudes* — can be inferred from behaviour, they cannot be seen directly. The measurement here depends on the perception of the measurer.

As a department we are concerned with subjective assessment (some objective tests may be used) in relation to attainment, ability and attitudes.

The criteria for assessment must be clearly understood so that our perceptive measurements are based on like-mindedness, hence an acceptable level for the department.

Present attainment — attainment is measured in relation to:
(a)   the pupil's potential ability
(b)   the teaching group's ability range
(c)   the year group's ability range
(d)   anticipated performance at examination level

Our peception of the following will help to ensure sound, constructive comments on reports and record cards, when referring to achievement.

ability to think — convergently or divergently
concepts — does the child handle these well?
skills and techniques
workmanship
execution of ideas
contribution to discussion
initiative
use of language — written and graphic
personal research
imagination
performance in a written test
performance with homework
performance as a prediction for examination purposes

*Potential ability* — refers to potential performance. Here we must be concerned with the following:

the child's IQ
the level of work given to the child
fluctuating levels of work
individuality
performance in other curriculum areas
motivation to demand response from each child
teaching techniques

*Individual attitudes* — refers to behavioural responses. Here we must be concerned with the following:

pupil behaviour
relationship to the group
leadership qualities
conscientious work
teacher/pupil relationship
effort
personal presentation and organization
consistency
reliability
self-motivation
self discipline
initiative

**Design department** — Departmental records and school reports

The assessment criteria and record card system has the following objectives:
1   To evaluate the learning/teaching process.
2   To develop sound assessment techniques.
3   To establish and maintain an educationally sound record of pupil progress.
4   To involve all teachers in developing their personal level of assessment.
5   To make available a meaningful record for leaver reports.
6   To avoid misplacement of pupils at fourth year level re option choices.
7   To make pupils aware that their progress is being monitored within design.
8   To establish a system that will be meaningful to new staff.
9   To have a record of progress available for year tutors if required.
10   To make available a comprehensive record of progress for use at parents' evenings.

Department record cards
These cards are available for pupils in years 1, 2 and 3 and stored within each departmental section. Each card must be completed before the end of a child's course.

*Years 1 and 2*   A written comment should be compiled based on the department's assessment criteria. The emphasis here is to produce a comprehensive comment on each child.

*Year 3*   A written comment should include reference to the child's potential and suitability for a fourth year course.

*Years 4 and 5*   Individual teachers must keep a record of pupil progress. Attainment should be related to examination standards.

*Figure 57* Department assessment – determining the criteria

# CONCLUSION

It would seem inappropriate to conclude this text without reflecting briefly on its content.

Since 1958, under a theme of change, workshop activities have been subjected to considerable pressures and influences to re-define their role within a school's curriculum.

Even the changes in name have heralded a change of emphasis, or at least tried to encourage the teacher to consider a broader context for workshop activities. The tide of change has brought with it both good and ill, but the decision to accept or reject change lies with the teacher. What matters here is not the acceptance or rejection of change so much as the reasons for making the decision.

This book has emphasized the need for change from being totally product orientated to include the process of designing as well. This, to many would seem to undervalue the process of making. The assumption that making is the most important aspect of workshop activities can be questioned. Decision making is the most important feature of our lives. Hence the need for problem-solving activities, in order to allow children to develop their ability to learn through making decisions, and translating these decisions into a course of action. This approach can make designing and making activities relevant to the needs of all children as part of a general education up to the age of 16 years.

Re-defining the role of craft, design and technology will serve to develop its status as a curriculum subject. As part of a faculty structure it can attract more able pupils to its option groups at examination level.

As part of the broader concept, of design education, it offers the teacher an opportunity to make a positive contribution to a child's cognitive and affective development.

Although design education seems to suggest external pressure for internal change of a specific nature, it does offer the teacher an opportunity to work at different levels. This could be as follows:

1 Individual — a teacher working alone in a workshop.

2 Group — a teacher working as part of a department structure.

3 Inter-group — departments working together.

4 Design as a central concept — A curriculum where design and technological awareness are seen as essential components of the real world for a child, both now and in the future.

At this stage in its development at secondary level it is likely that the majority of work will occur under 1 and 2 and to a lesser extent 3.

Change must always be viewed as a challenge as long as the aims and objectives of such a change are educationally sound. In order to cope with change we need to re-model our thoughts and ideas. Preparing children for future change seems to be a worthwhile objective if we can achieve this through cognitive modelling.

The use of problem-solving activity, where problems are ill-defined leads us to the conclusion that we do not solve, but rather resolve problems. Hence the state of constant change in our lives, as new or modified needs arise.

In the workshops, within the process of designing, we are concerned with intellectual activity. Therefore we must set out to resolve in a purposeful and logical manner in order to:

define a problem
generate ideas
select and develop the preferred idea
make decisions at each stage in order to make progress
realize and resolve the problem
appraise the end product critically in terms of the initial analysis.

In 1969 the Schools Council Working Paper 26 — 'Education through the use of materials', paved the way for a new look at the role of workshop activities. Today design education offers a broader concept and room for further development.

It is hoped that this book has raised a few issues, promoted discussion, suggested possible ways for development, and helped to further the cause of design-based activities in the workshops of secondary schools today.

# REFERENCES

1. **Eggleston J** *Developments in Design Education* Open Books 1976 p 11.
2. **Willmore P R** (Ed) *Design Education in Craft and Technology* Institute of Craft Education Batsford 1976 p 56-57
3. **Jones J C** *Design Methods: Seeds of Human Futures* John Wiley and Sons Ltd 1970 p 178
4. *ibid.* p 184
5. **Bruner J S** *Towards a Theory of Education* Harvard University Press 1966

# BIBLIOGRAPHY

*Useful background reading*

**Baynes, K** *About Design* Design Council Publications 1976
**Beakley, G** and **Chilton, E G** *Design Serving the Needs of Man* Collier Macmillan 1974
**Bruner, J** *The Process of Education* Harvard University Press (Vintage Books) 1963
**De Bono, E** *Teaching Thinking* Temple Smith 1976
**De Sausmarez, M** *Basic design; the dynamics of visual form* Studio Vista 1964
**Dodd, T** *Design and Technology in the School Curriculum* Hodder and Stoughton 1978
**Eggleston, J** *Developments in Design Education* Open Books 1976
**Green, P** *Design Education, Problem Solving and Visual Experience* Batsford 1974
**Hicks, G A** et al. *The Development of Design Studies in Secondary Education* Library of Ideas Goldsmith's College 1975
**Jones, J C** *Design Methods* Wiley – Interscience 1970
**Magee, B** *Popper* Fontana Modern Masters 1973
**Ministry of Education** Crowther Report (HMSO 1958)
**Open University** *Technology for Teachers Unit 13* The Open University Press 1975
**Packard, Vance** *The Hidden Persuaders* Penguin Books 1975
**Papanek, V** *Design for the Real World* Thames and Hudson 1971
**Pirsig, R M** *Zen and the Art of Motor Cycle Maintenance* Corgi Books 1974
**Pye, D** *The Nature of Aesthetics and Design* Barrie and Jenkins 1978
**Read, H** *Education through Art* Faber and Faber 1958
**Royal College of Art** *Design in General Education* Royal College of Art 1979
**Schools Council** Working Paper 18 *Technology and Schools* 1968
**Schools Council** Working Paper 26 *Education through the use of Materials* Evans/Methuen Educational 1969
**Schools Council** Art and Craft Education 8-13 *Children's Growth through Creative Experience* Van Nostrand Reinhold 1974
**Schools Council** *Modular Course in Technology*
**Stenhouse, L** *An Introduction to Curriculum Research and Development* Heinemann 1977
**Willmore, F R** (Ed) *Design Education in Craft and Technology* Institute of Craft Education Batsford 1976
**National Association for Design Education** Working Papers and Conference Papers available

# INDEX

Analysis
 — problem 9, 12
 — product 24
Assembly 34
Assessment 68
Awareness 14, 48

Bandsaw 39, 40

Child's needs 13
Communication 14
Cutting 32
Craft worksheet
 — year 1 64
 — year 2 64
 — year 3 65
Crossword — year 1 66

Decision making 25
Department
 — structure 13
 — assessment 68
 — records 68
Design
 — brief 12
 — process 15
 — engineering method 15
Discussion 20
Drilling 41

Environment 14, 43, 44
Equipment 46
Evaluation
 — formative 50
 — summative 50
 — illuminative 50
Examinations 50

Finishing 33

Group activity 22
Group projects 56, 61

Head of department 13

Ideas 20, 24
Imagination 15
Information sheets
 — softwoods 63
 — hardwoods 63
 — plywood/multiply 63
 — blockboard/chipboard 64
 — hardboard 64

Jigsaw 40
Jigsaw exercise 22
Joining 33, 34

Learning 20
Lines
 — pencil 31
 — knife 31
 — gauge 31

Machines 39
Management 47
 — school 13
 — department 13
Marking out 30, 31
Material 41
Material — preparation to size 30
Matchett — Fundamental Design Method 18
Methodology 22

New courses 11

Organization 43

Philosophy — Department 13
Popper, K. 19
Problem solving 14, 15
Project work 61
Pupil
 — needs 13
 — ideas 24, 25
 — /teacher relationships 49

Resources 45

Safety
 — major components 26
 — pupil handout 27, 28
Sanding 40
Sawing 32
Schools Council 11
Scientific method 19
Skills and Techniques 28, 29
Softwoods

   — analysis 23
   — exercise 25
Standards 48

Teaching method 15
Terminology tree 39
Thinking — models 16, 17, 18
Tools
   — classification 37
   — cutting 38
   — measuring, marking, testing 38
   — boring 38
   — holding devices 38
   — striking tools 38
   — unclassified 38
Turning 41
Traditional courses 10

Volume production 34, 35, 36

Working drawing 10
Workshop organization 43

Printed in Great Britain
by Amazon.co.uk, Ltd.,
Marston Gate.

# 7
# Testing, Profiling, Monitoring, and Logging

> *Up till now, we were living in a perfect world, where no errors occurred. We were assuming that everything works just fine and as expected. Unfortunately, reality can be cruel and things just don't always work out as expected.*

In this chapter, we shall:

- Implement a base framework to make testing database access code easy
- Create tests to verify our data access code
- Analyze the communication of NHibernate with the database
- Configure NHibernate to log interesting information

So let's get on with it.

## Why do we need tests?

There are different reasons why we would want to write tests for our code. In test-driven development (TDD), we write tests to help us write better code. In this regard, tests are a means to improve the micro design of our application. However, more than that, tests also act as a safety net in case we start refactoring or changing our system.

# What should we test?

This is a rather philosophical question and it largely depends on the specific situation. Some development groups try to write tests for every single line of code they write. In this case, one would have 100 percent code coverage. However, this is not always possible or cost-effective.

In the latter case, we have to come up with a list of areas that are worth testing. Examples on the list can be:

- Complex mathematical or statistical algorithms
- Involved business logic or business processes
- Code that is used as the foundation or framework in an application
- The mapping of the domain model to the underlying database schema
- Complex database queries

This list is by no means complete and shall only give an indication of things that are worth testing.

# What about the database?

The database is an important part of our application and we have to include it in our tests.

Although we might create the database schema from our domain model for the first release of our application, a time will come when we have to change this schema, either manually or by using database scripts. At this point in time, we have to make sure that our mappings are still working correctly.

We might also want to test various strategies when writing (complex) database queries to minimize the number of database round trips, and/or to optimize the performance of a query.

When running tests that include the database, then each time we run a given test the database should be in the same state, otherwise our tests will not always give the same result.

There are various ways we can achieve this condition. Some solutions are more performant than the others and some, on the other hand, are easier to achieve.

- In the first approach, we wipe out the database schema each time, recreate it, and fill it with the base data we need prior to each test
- We write compensating code that removes the changes done by our tests in the clean-up method of our test class

- We wrap each test inside a transaction that is rolled back at the end of the corresponding test
- We use a snapshot of the database that is restored after each test run

Each method presented in the preceding text has its advantages and disadvantages. There is not really one ideal solution. It depends on the specific circumstances which approach makes the most sense.

## Download SQLite

Often, the first approach is selected as it offers the best repeatability of all of the approaches. Individual tests cannot have side effects on each other and the order in which the tests run do not matter.

However, trying to realize this solution with a classical RDBMS will cause the test series to run with very poor performance. If the database is installed remotely, then the situation will be even worse. Thus, we have to come up with a better solution.

SQLite is a lightweight open source database that can be used in the `in-memory` mode, which makes dropping and recreation of the database schema very fast.

SQLite can be downloaded from here: http://sourceforge.net/projects/sqlite-dotnet2/files/. On this page click on the **SQLite for ADO.NET 2.0** link. At the time of writing, the most recent version is 1.0.66.0. Navigate to the folder `1.0.66.0`. Download the file `SQLite-1.0.66.0-managedonly-binaries.zip`.

If you have a 64-bit OS installed, then copy the file `System.Data.SQlite.dll`, contained in the sub-folder `bin\x64` of the ZIP file, to the `lib` sub-folder of your `samples` folder. Otherwise, copy the same file from the `bin` sub-folder of the ZIP file to the `lib` folder.

## Pop quiz

1. What are the characteristics of tests?

    a. When used in conjunction with TDD, they help us to create better code.

    b. They introduce some maintenance overhead into the system.

    c. Tests act as a safety net when refactoring code or adding new functionality.

    d. In certain areas, writing tests can significantly reduce the time to achieve a defect free solution to a problem.

    e. All of the above.

# Preparing our environment for testing

To be able to write unit tests, we need to prepare a small framework. First of all, let's introduce a base class, which allows us to write our unit tests in a more "natural" way that resembles English text, instead of it remaining purely technical babble.

A unit test normally consists of three clearly distinguishable parts:

- Arrange – we prepare or set up the boundary conditions for our test
- Act – we execute the action whose outcome we want to test
- Assert – finally, we verify that the outcome of the action is indeed what we expect

These three steps, **arrange**, **act**, and **assert**, are sometimes also denoted with the acronym AAA. In the unit tests, we are going to write these three steps in the form of their counterparts. **Arrange** will be the **given** part, **act** will be the **when** part, and **assert** will consist of one or more tests.

We will use NUnit (http://www.nunit.org) as our unit test framework, but any other framework out there would also do the job. For example, MSTest (part of Visual Studio), MbUnit (http://www.mbunit.com/), XUnit (http://xunit.codeplex.com/), and so on.

We will call our test base class `SpecificationBase`, it looks similar to the following code snippet:

```
public class SpecificationBase
{
  [TestFixtureSetUp]
  public virtual void TestFixtureSetUp()
  {
    BeforeAllTests();
  }

  [SetUp]
  public void SetUp()
  {
    Given();
    When();
  }

  [TearDown]
  public void TearDown()
  {
    CleanUp();
  }
```

```
    [TestFixtureTearDown]
    public void TestFixtureTearDown()
    {
       AfterAllTests();
    }

    protected virtual void BeforeAllTests(){}
    protected virtual void Given(){}
    protected virtual void When(){}
    protected virtual void CleanUp(){}
    protected virtual void AfterAllTests(){}
}
```

NUnit has four important attributes with which we have to decorate `public void` methods of our class. The first attribute, `TestFixtureSetUp`, decorates a method that is only run once for all tests defined in the same class. This method can be used to execute tasks to prepare the system prior to run a test suite. Its counterpart, the `TestFixtureTearDown` attribute, decorates a method which is only called once after all tests have been executed. This method can be used to do the final cleanup after a test run.

The `SetUp` attribute decorates a method that is run prior to each test method and the `TearDown` attribute decorates the method that is called after the execution of each test method.

In our base class, all of these four methods call (empty) virtual methods, which any class that inherits from `SpecificationBase` can override. One of the advantages of this implementation is that the child classes do not have to deal with attributes anymore.

To complete the first layer of the framework, we add a `Then` attribute. This attribute is defined as a child attribute of `TestAttribute` of NUnit. We will use the `Then` attribute in our assertions block to decorate the methods that contain assertions. The code is simple, as shown in the following code snippet:

```
    public class ThenAttribute : TestAttribute {}
```

Having this `Then` attribute, we can formulate our test using a **given-when-then** syntax.

To demonstrate the usage of the preceding base class, we want to write a unit test that verifies that the properties of the `Name` value object, introduced in a previous chapter of the book, are correctly populated by the constructor. The code is as shown in the following snippet:

```
    [TestFixture]
    public class when_creating_a_name_value_object
       : SpecificationBase
    {
```

```csharp
      private string lastName;
      private string firstName;
      private string middleName;
      private Name result;

      protected override void Given()
      {
        lastName = "Schenker";
        firstName = "Gabriel";
        middleName = "N.";
      }

      protected override void When()
      {
        result = new Name(lastName, firstName, middleName);
      }

      [Then]
      public void it_should_populate_the_last_name_property()
      {
        Assert.Equals(result.LastName, lastName);
      }

      [Then]
      public void it_should_populate_the_first_name_property()
      {
        Assert.Equals(result.FirstName, firstName);
      }

      [Then]
      public void it_should_populate_the_middle_name_property()
      {
        Assert.Equals(result.MiddleName, middleName);
      }
   }
```

The name of the class reflects what we are going to verify. Sometimes, we call this the **test case**. The class name should be as close to an English phrase as possible; in fact, if we remove the underscores from `when_creating_a_name_value_object`, we obtain an intention revealing expression "when creating a name value object". Ideally, we use the title of the test case as our class name.

Next, we prepare the environment for the test, or we can say that we set up the boundary conditions for the test. This is done in the `Given` method. In this case, we define some precanned values for the last, first, and middle name that we want to use in our test.

Now, we can define the action in the `When` method. The action in our case is the instantiation of a `Name` value object. We store the result of the action in a result variable for further use. Please note that when instantiating the `Name` value object, we are using the values we (pre-) defined in the `Given` method.

Finally, in the three methods decorated with the `[Then]` attribute, we assert the outcome of the action. In our case, we make sure that all three properties of the `Name` value object have been populated correctly.

Note that the names of the three methods used for assertion of the result should again be intention revealing. The name should reflect what we expect as the result of the assertion and, again, it should be written in English prose.

Looking again at the tests, we have a **Given** [...] **When** [...] **Then** [...] schema throughout all tests. Business analysts can very easily be trained to formulate the business requirements in this way.

## Testing the mapping

To find out whether the database schema is correct and an entity is mapped correctly to the underlying database schema, we have to execute several steps. The first step is to create an entity and populate it with precanned values, as shown in the following code snippet:

```
var product = new Product
{
  Name = "Apple",
  Description = "Description for apple",
  UnitPrice = 1.50m,
  ReorderLevel = 10,
  Discontinued = true,
};
```

Then we have to try to save the product, as shown in the following code snippet:

```
session.Save(product);
session.Flush();
```

Note `session.Flush()` in the preceding code snippet. It is used to enforce the writing of all changes to the database, and in our case, to create a new `Product` record.

If the creation of a new database record is successful, then we'll want to know whether all the property values have been written to the database as defined. For this purpose, we have to load the product just written to the database, as shown in the following code snippet:

```
session.Evict(product);
var fromDb = session.Get<Product>(product.Id);
```

Note the `session.Evict(product)` statement in the preceding code snippet. We need this statement to eliminate the previously saved entity from the first level cache, and with that make sure that NHibernate does not just load the product from its first level cache, but really makes a round trip to the database to get the values.

In the test assertion part, we first make sure that the product was really stored in the database. If it hadn't been stored, then NHibernate would return null when we try to load the entity, as shown in the following code snippet:

```
Assert.That(fromDb, Is.Not.Null);
```

Now that we know the entity was stored and have successfully loaded it from the database, we have to compare the newly hydrated entity property-by-property with the original product entity, as shown in the following code snippet:

```
Assert.That(fromDb.Name, Is.EqualTo(product.Name));
Assert.That(fromDb.Description, Is.EqualTo(product.Description));
Assert.That(fromDb.UnitPrice, Is.EqualTo(product.UnitPrice));
Assert.That(fromDb.ReorderLevel, Is.EqualTo(product.ReorderLevel));
Assert.That(fromDb.Discontinued, Is.EqualTo(product.Discontinued));
```

If this test passes, we can be sure that

1. The database schema for the `Product` entity is correct.
2. The mapping for the `Product` entity has been defined correctly.

> In more advanced scenarios, we would base our persistence-related test less on the "simple" property values checking and more on the "aggregate root behavior", which includes such things as checking all cascade actions executed, either implicitly by NHibernate or explicitly by the repository operating on the aggregate root.

As we move forward in the development of our application, this test remains very valuable because it serves as a safety net when we start to extend and refactor our system. By re-running this test every time we change the application, we can be sure that we didn't break the database schema and/or the mapping of the system.

Although we have certainly recognized the great value of having tests, we still might feel a bit overwhelmed by the amount of code needed to test just a single entity.

## Testing the mapping with Fluent NHibernate

Once again, Fluent NHibernate provides us with a convenient way to test the mapping of an entity and its relations to the underlying database. Compared to the preceding example, we can reduce the amount of code to write to test a single entity by at least 50 percent.

The Fluent NHibernate assembly contains a `PersistenceSpecification<T>` class, which we can use to quickly define a test. The code needed to test the mapping for our `Product` entity would look similar to the following code snippet:

```
new PersistenceSpecification<Product>(session)
    .CheckProperty(x => x.Name, "Apple")
    .CheckProperty(x => x.Description, "Description for apple")
    .CheckProperty(x => x.UnitPrice, 1.50m)
    .CheckProperty(x => x.ReorderLevel, 10)
    .CheckProperty(x => x.Discontinued, true)
    .VerifyTheMappings();
```

Here we assume that we have an open NHibernate `session` at hand, which we provide as a parameter to the constructor of the `PersistenceSpecification` class. Note that we provide the entity we want to test as a generic parameter (in our case, `Product`).

For each property we want to test, we add a call to the `CheckProperty` method and pass a lambda expression, which describes the property as a first parameter. We then pass a precanned value as a second parameter. This precanned value will be assigned to the respective property during the test. To execute the test, we have to add a final call to the `VerifyTheMappings` method.

## Time for action – Creating the base for testing

In this exercise, we want to implement the base framework for our mapping tests.

1. Open Visual Studio and open the `OrderingSystem` solution from *Chapter 5*.

2. Add a second project to the solution. Choose **Class Library** as the project template and call the project `OrderingSystem.Tests`.

3. To the `OrderingSystem.Tests` project, add references to the assemblies `NHibernate.dll`, `NHibernate.ByteCode.Castle.dll`, and `FluentNHibernate.dll` located in the `lib` folder.

4. Make sure that the `OrderingSystem` project references the two assemblies `NHibernate.dll` and `FluentNHibernate.dll`. If not, please add these references now.

Testing, Profiling, Monitoring, and Logging

5. Download NUnit from `http://www.nunit.org/?p=download`. Only download the binaries. At the time of writing, the recommended version is `NUnit-2.5.10.11092.zip`. Open this ZIP file and extract the file `nunit.framework.dll` into the `lib` folder.

6. Add a reference to the assembly `nunit.framework.dll` of the `OrderingSystem.Tests` project.

7. Add a reference to the `OrderingSystem` project of the `OrderingSystem.Tests` project.

8. Add a class `ThenAttribute` to the project `OrderingSystem.Tests`. Make the class inherit from the `TestAttribute` class of NUnit, as shown in the following code snippet:

```
public class ThenAttribute : TestAttribute
{ }
```

9. Add a class `SpecificationBase` to the project `OrderingSystem.Tests`. Add the following code snippet to this class:

```
public abstract class SpecificationBase
{
    [TestFixtureSetUp]
    public void TestFixtureSetUp()
    {
        BeforeAllTests();
    }

    [SetUp]
    public void SetUp()
    {
        Given();
        When();
    }

    [TearDown]
    public void TearDown()
    {
        CleanUp();
    }

    [TestFixtureTearDown]
    public void TestFixtureTearDown()
    {
        AfterAllTests();
```

```
        }

            protected virtual void BeforeAllTests(){ }
            protected virtual void Given(){ }
            protected virtual void When(){ }
            protected virtual void CleanUp(){ }
            protected virtual void AfterAllTests(){ }
        }
```

**10.** Add another abstract class called `MappingSpecificationBase`, which inherits from the `SpecificationBase` class to the `OrderingSystem.Tests` project.

**11.** Add the following code snippet to the class:

```
        public abstract class MappingSpecificationBase : SpecificationBase
        {
          protected Configuration configuration;
          private ISessionFactory sessionFactory;
          protected ISession session;

          protected override void BeforeAllTests()
          {
            configuration = Fluently.Configure()
              .Database(DefineDatabase)
              .Mappings(DefineMappings)
              .BuildConfiguration();

            CreateSchema(configuration);

            sessionFactory = configuration.BuildSessionFactory();
          }

          protected ISession OpenSession()
          {
            return sessionFactory.OpenSession();
          }

          protected override void Given()
          {
            base.Given();
            session = OpenSession();
          }

          protected abstract IPersistenceConfigurer DefineDatabase();
          protected abstract void DefineMappings(MappingConfiguration m);
          protected virtual void CreateSchema(Configuration cfg){}
        }
```

12. This class configures a NHibernate `Configuration` object. The configuration object is then used to optionally create the database schema and to create the session factory, which in turn is used to create session objects. The details of the configuration must be specified by a child class, though this class only calls abstract or empty virtual methods.

13. Add a class called `entity_mapping_spec` to the `OrderingSystem.Tests` project.

14. Make this class inherit from `MappingSpecificationBase` and decorate it with a `[TestFixture]` attribute, as shown in the following code snippet:

```
[TestFixture]
public class entity_mapping_spec : MappingSpecificationBase
{
}
```

15. Override the `DefineDatabase` method and define your local SQL Server 2008 Express to be the database used for our tests, as shown in the following code snippet:

```
protected override IPersistenceConfigurer DefineDatabase()
{
   return MsSqlConfiguration.MsSql2008
    .ConnectionString("server=.\\SQLEXPRESS;"+
      "database=NH3BeginnersGuide;"+
      "integrated security=SSPI;");
}
```

16. Override the `DefineMappings` method and add the following code, which defines that we want to use fluent mappings and that all mapping classes are to be found in the assembly where the `ProductMap` class is implemented:

```
protected override void DefineMappings(MappingConfiguration m)
{
   m.FluentMappings.AddFromAssemblyOf<ProductMap>();
}
```

17. Override the method `CreateSchema` and tell the system to use the `SchemaExport` class of NHibernate to drop and recreate the schema in the database we use for testing, as shown in the following code snippet:

```
protected override void CreateSchema(Configuration cfg)
{
   new SchemaExport(cfg).Execute(false, true, false);
}
```

**18.** Add a method to the class that tests the correctness of the mapping for the `Product` entity, as shown in the following code snippet:

```
[Then]
public void it_should_correctly_map_a_product()
{
  new PersistenceSpecification<Product>(session)
    .CheckProperty(x => x.Name, "Apple")
    .CheckProperty(x => x.Description, "Some description")
    .CheckProperty(x => x.UnitPrice, 1.50m)
    .CheckProperty(x => x.ReorderLevel, 10)
    .CheckProperty(x => x.Discontinued, true)
    .VerifyTheMappings();
}
```

**19.** Run the test and verify that it executes successfully, as shown in the following screenshot:

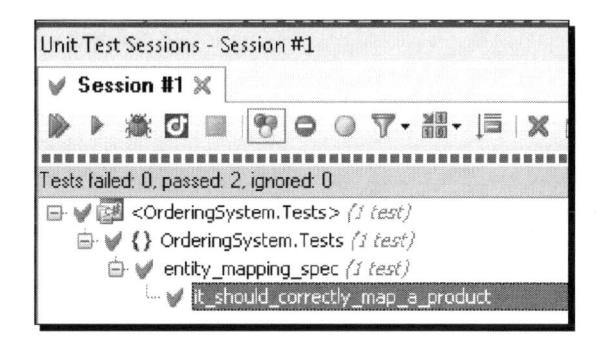

## What just happened?

We created a base (mini) framework, which allows us to write (unit) tests with little effort that verify the correctness of the mapping of the domain model to the underlying database schema. We have also implemented a test class which leverages this framework and tests the mapping of the `Product` entity.

### Have a go hero

Add code to the `entity_mapping_specs` class to test the mapping of the `Employee` class of the ordering system domain model. Use the WIKI of the Fluent NHibernate home page (http://wiki.fluentnhibernate.org/Persistence_specification_testing) to get more details about how to use the `PersistenceSpecification` class when, for example, dealing with properties of type value objects.

Testing, Profiling, Monitoring, and Logging

## Time for action – Using SQLite in our tests

In this short exercise, we will implement the necessary steps to be able to use SQLite in our database tests.

1. Open Visual Studio and load the `OrderingSystem` solution.

2. Add a folder called `UsingSqLite` to the `OrderingSystem.Tests` project.

3. Add a reference to the assembly `System.Data.SQLite.dll` of the `OrderingSystem.Tests` project. The said assembly should be located in the `lib` sub-folder of your samples folder.

4. Add a new class called `entity_mapping_spec_for_sqlite` to the preceding folder.

5. Make the class inherit from the base class `MappingSpecificationBase` and decorate it with the `TestFixture` attribute, as shown in the following code snippet:

    ```
    [TestFixture]
    public class entity_mapping_spec_for_sqlite
       : MappingSpecificationBase
    {
    }
    ```

6. Override the method `DefineDatabase` and add code to configure SQLite for **in-memory** operation. You would also require NHibernate to show the generated SQL:

    ```
    protected override IPersistenceConfigurer DefineDatabase()
    {
      return SQLiteConfiguration.Standard
        .InMemory()
        .ShowSql();
    }
    ```

7. Additionally, override the method `DefineMappings`, as shown in the following code snippet:

    ```
    protected override void DefineMappings(MappingConfiguration m)
    {
      m.FluentMappings.AddFromAssemblyOf<ProductMap>();
    }
    ```

*Chapter 7*

8.  Note that SQLite in the **in-memory** mode behaves a little bit different than any other database in that the schema is destroyed as soon as the NHibernate session is disposed, which was used to create the schema. Thus, we cannot use the same code as used in the preceding example to generate the database schema, but rather have to override the method `Given` and add the following code snippet:

    ```
    protected override void Given()
    {
      base.Given();
      new SchemaExport(configuration)
         .Execute(false, true, false, session.Connection, null);
    }
    ```

9.  Note that we use a different overload of the `Execute` method where we can pass an ADO.NET connection object, which will be used to create the schema. The NHibernate session object is already created by the base class and we can use it to get the necessary connection object.

10. Add code to test the mapping of the `Product` entity, as shown in the following code snippet. Use the same code as in the preceding example:

    ```
    [Then]
    public void it_should_correctly_map_a_product()
    {
      new PersistenceSpecification<Product>(session)
        .CheckProperty(x => x.Name, "Apple")
        .CheckProperty(x => x.Description, "Some description")
        .CheckProperty(x => x.UnitPrice, 1.50m)
        .CheckProperty(x => x.ReorderLevel, 10)
        .CheckProperty(x => x.Discontinued, true)
        .VerifyTheMappings();
    }
    ```

11. Run the test and review the output in the test runner window, as shown in the following screenshot:

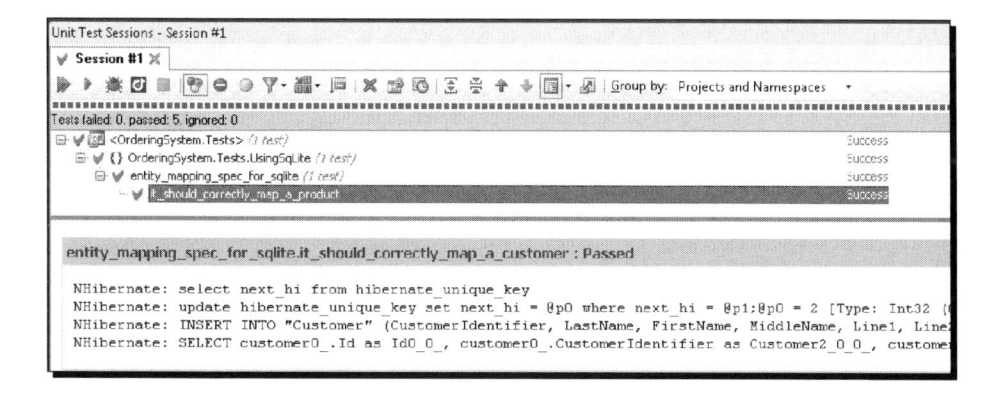

[ 197 ]

## What just happened?

We have extended our testing framework in such a way that we can use the SQLite database in the in-memory mode when executing our mapping tests. The main advantage of this approach is the speed with which the tests are executed. As the whole database resides in memory, any database-related operation is extremely fast.

## Testing queries

In Chapter 9, we will discuss various methods to learn how we can use NHibernate to query data from the database. One of the methods will be using the LINQ to NHibernate driver. NHibernate defines an extension method `Query<T>()` to the `ISession` interface. With regard to testing, there is one caveat with this approach. As the `Query` method is only an extension method to, and not part of, the interface `ISession`, this method cannot be stubbed or mocked. Any other method of the interface, such as `Get` or `Load`, can be stubbed.

> A stub is an object that is used on behalf of another object and returns precanned data when queried. A mock is similar to a stub and is also used on behalf of another object, but a mock also contains instrumentation code, which is used to monitor the behavior of the caller. Stubs and mocks are used in unit or integration tests to simulate real objects that are hard or impossible to use in a test environment. Samples of such stubs or mocks are objects accessing a database or the network, hardware drivers or objects accessing the file system, and so on.

To overcome this limitation, we can define a `Repository` class, which is a wrapper around the NHibernate `Session` object. The `Repository` class implements the interface `IRepository`, which only contains the most important members of the `ISession` interface and, most importantly, the `Query` method, as shown in the following code snippet:

```
public interface IRepository<T>
{
  IQueryable<T> Query();
  T Get(int id);
  T Load(int id);
  // possibly other members of ISession...
}
```

The implementation of the `Repository` class is trivial as every method call is directly forwarded to the contained session object, as shown in the following code snippet:

```
public class Repository<T> : IRepository<T>
{
  private readonly ISession session;
```

```
  public Repository(ISession session)
  {
    this.session = session;
  }

  public IQueryable<T> Query() { return session.Query<T>(); }
  public T Get(int id) { return session.Get<T>(id); }
  public T Load(int id) { return session.Load<T>(id); }
}
```

In our database access code, we will use the `IRepository` instead of the `ISession`.

Imagine that we have to implement a class which queries the database and returns a list of all products that are still active and need to be reordered; that is, products that have the value `UnitsOnStock` less than the value `ReorderLevel`. The list of products returned by the query shall be ordered by product `Name`. To solve this problem, we can define a class similar to the following code snippet:

```
public class GetAllProductsToOrderQueryHandler
{
  private readonly IRepository<Product> repository;

  public GetAllProductsToOrderQueryHandler(
    IRepository<Product> repository)
  {
    this.repository = repository;
  }

  public IEnumerable<Product> Execute()
  {
    // implement query here
  }
}
```

We get a repository object through constructor injection and can use it in the `Execute` method to query the database. The code in the `Execute` method will probably look similar to the following code snippet:

```
return repository.Query()
  .Where(p => !p.Discontinued && p.UnitsOnStock < p.ReorderLevel)
  .OrderBy(p => p.Name)
  .ToArray();
```

We want to write a unit test which verifies that our code produces the expected result. In the following section, we'll see how this goal can be achieved.

We have an object of the `IRepository<Product>` type that is used to get a list of `Product` entities from the database using LINQ to NHibernate, as shown in the following code snippet:

```
var products = repository.Query() …
```

We can easily stub this `repository` object in a test and make the stub object return a pre-canned list of products.

Let's create a stub for `IRepository<Product>`, which returns a well known set of products, as shown in the following code snippet:

```
public class StubbedRepository : IRepository<Product>
{
  public IQueryable<Product> Query()
  {
    return new[]
    {
      new Product {Name = "Pineapple", UnitPrice = 1.55m,
      ReorderLevel = 10, UnitsOnStock = 20,
      Discontinued = false},
      new Product {Name = "Hazelnut", UnitPrice = 0.25m,
      ReorderLevel = 100, UnitsOnStock = 20,
      Discontinued = true},
      new Product {Name = "Orange", UnitPrice = 1.15m,
      ReorderLevel = 20, UnitsOnStock = 10,
      Discontinued = false},
      new Product {Name = "Apple", UnitPrice = 1.15m,
      ReorderLevel = 20, UnitsOnStock = 50,
      Discontinued = false},
    }
    .AsQueryable();
  }

  public Product Get(int id)
  {
    throw new NotImplementedException();
  }

  public Product Load(int id)
  {
    throw new NotImplementedException();
  }
}
```

Note that in the preceding class, we only implement the method that we want to stub. We can leave all other methods unimplemented.

Additionally, note that we can convert any array of objects of type `T` to `IQueryable<T>` by using the extension method `AsQueryable` of LINQ.

We can then define a test fixture, as shown in the following code snippet:

```
public class when_querying_products_to_reorder : SpecificationBase
{
  private IRepository<Product> repository;
  private GetAllProductsToOrderQueryHandler sut;
  private IEnumerable<Product> result;

  protected override void Given()
  {
    repository = new StubbedRepository();
    sut = new GetAllProductsToOrderQueryHandler(repository);
  }

  protected override void When()
  {
    result = sut.Execute();
  }
}
```

The name of the class is once again intention revealing and tells us what scenario we are going to test. In the method `Given`, we create a stubbed repository and an object of type `GetAllProductsToOrderQueryHandler`, to which we assign a variable called `sut`, where `sut` is an acronym for **system under test**. We inject the stubbed repository into the `sut` via constructor injection.

In the `When` method, we execute the query and store the result in an instance variable `result` of type `IEnumerable<Product>`. The variable `result` can then be used in the test methods to validate the outcome of the method call.

First, we want to make sure that the code in the `Execute` method only returns active products, as shown in the following code snippet:

```
[Then]
public void it_should_only_return_active_products()
{
  Assert.That(result.Any(p => p.Discontinued), Is.False);
}
```

Next, we make sure that the property value of `ReorderLevel` is greater that the property value of `UnitsOnStock` for all returned products, as shown in the following code snippet:

```
[Then]
public void it_should_only_return_products_to_reorder()
{
   Assert.That(result.All(p => p.ReorderLevel > p.UnitsOnStock),
      Is.True);
}
```

Finally, we want to test whether the list of returned products is ordered as expected, as shown in the following code snippet:

```
[Then]
public void it_should_return_an_ordered_list()
{
   Assert.That(result.First().Name, Is.EqualTo("Apple"));
   Assert.That(result.Last().Name, Is.EqualTo("Orange"));
}
```

In the preceding code snippet, it is shown how you can create a stubbed repository, which can then be used to test the logic of the query handler class. The stub returns a list of precanned products as `IQueryable<Product>`. This is exactly the same type as the LINQ to NHibernate `Query<T>` extension method returns.

# Logging

According to the Apache project (http://www.apache.org), approximately four percent of all code written is for logging. This is a pretty significant number, especially if your application is of any real size. If we are going to write all of this code, then we might as well use a framework that will make it easier for us to configure what gets logged, where we log it, and how much of it gets logged.

## Why do we need to log?

While developing an application, we developers are used to running unit tests and using the debugger to make sure that our code runs smoothly and produces the expected results. However, once we hand over our application to the testers for quality assurance (QA), or once our product is installed in a productive environment, we do not have the possibility to use the debugger anymore to step through the code or to run unit tests to assert expected behavior and results.

However, we all know that even a very well tested application can contain bugs, and thus crash or, even worse, produce wrong results. What can we do in such situations? How can we detect a code defect or a misconfiguration of the system afterwards? What would we need to do a "post-mortem analysis"?

One of the possible answers is that we need information about which method call from the application caused the error. Additionally, we would like to have the full stack trace at the moment of the failure. It would be even better if we had a log of all the steps that happened before the error occurred. Last but not least, it would be very helpful to know the data that we operated on before and during the crash or malfunction of the system.

If our system could produce such a log of information while it is running in a test environment or in production, then, in case of a malfunction of the system, we could ask the system administrator to provide us with a copy of the logged information and use this information to detect and fix the defect.

## Logging with Log4Net

Logging is a requirement of pretty much any application. It is a standard functionality of the system and a lot of frameworks exist that provide us with this functionality. We do not and should not implement our own logging framework, but rather use one of the existing ones. One of the best known and very mature logging frameworks for .NET is Log4Net (http://logging.apache.org/log4net/index.html). This is an open source framework and is used by NHibernate. When we download NHibernate, Log4Net is included in the binaries.

## Time for action – Adding logging to our application

In this little exercise, we will create a sample application and configure it to use Log4Net as a logging framework and then create some basic logging messages.

1. Open Visual Studio and create a new project. Select **Console Application** as the project template and call the project **LoggingSample**.

2. Add a reference to the log4net.dll assembly, located in the lib folder of the project.

3. In the **Solution Explorer**, right-click on the **LoggingSample** project and select **Properties**.

4. In the project properties window, select the **Application** tab and set the **Target framework** to **.NET Framework 4**.

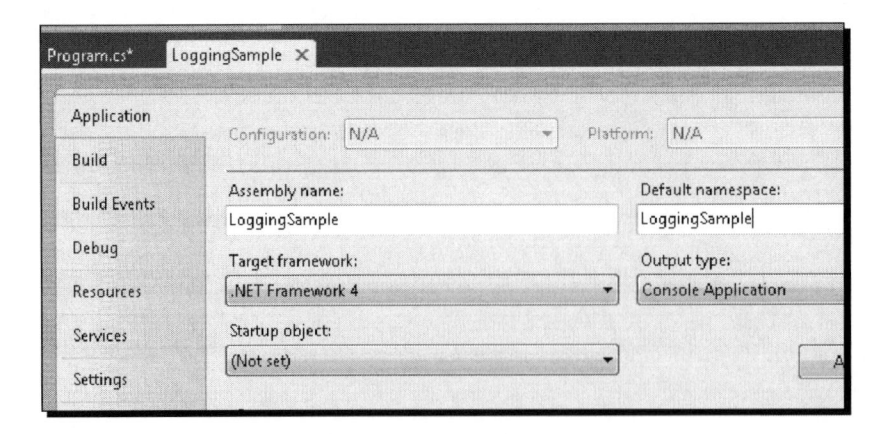

5. In the **Solution Explorer**, right-click on the **LoggingSample** project and select **Add | New Item...**. Select **Application Configuration File** as the file template and click on **OK**. A file called `App.config` is added to your project. Note that this step is only necessary if the preceding step has not already added an `App.config` file to the project.

6. In the configuration file, we add code to configure our application to use `Log4Net`. Start by adding a definition for the existence of a `log4net` section, as shown in the following code snippet:

```xml
<?xml version="1.0"?>
<configuration>
  <configSections>
    <section name="log4net"
      type="log4net.Config.Log4NetConfigurationSectionHandler,
      log4net"/>
  </configSections>
</configuration>
```

7. Next, we add the `log4net` section to the `App.config` and inside this section we define an `appender`. An `appender` is basically the target of the logging information produced by Log4Net. Various targets exist, such as files, output on the console, a database table, the registry, and so on. In our example, we want to add an `appender` that outputs the logging information to the console, as shown in the following code snippet:

```xml
<log4net>
  <appender name="ConsoleAppender"
    type="log4net.Appender.ConsoleAppender">
```

```
      <layout type="log4net.Layout.PatternLayout">
        <conversionPattern value="[%C.%M] %-5p %m%n"/>
      </layout>
    </appender>
</log4net>
```

8.  In the preceding code snippet, the tag `conversionPattern` describes how the log output should be formatted.

9.  Next, we add information to the `App.config` file to instruct Log4Net which `appender` it should use (we can define more than one `appender`!). To do this, we add the following code snippet to the `<log4net>` node:

    ```
    <root>
      <appender-ref ref="ConsoleAppender"/>
    </root>
    ```

10. Lastly, we define what `level` of debugging we want to enable. This can be done by adding the following code snippet to the `<root>` node:

    ```
    <level value="DEBUG"/>
    ```

11. In the preceding example, we define that the debug level is `DEBUG`. This means that all messages of all log levels are logged as Log4Net, starting with the configured level and including all messages with higher severity. The ranking is from lowest to highest: `DEBUG`, `INFO`, `WARN`, `ERROR`, and `FATAL`.

12. Open the `Program` class and add the `XmlConfigurator` attribute to the class file (make sure the attribute is defined outside the namespace declaration), as shown in the following code snippet:

    ```
    [assembly: log4net.Config.XmlConfigurator(Watch = true)]
    ```

13. This attribute instructs Log4Net that it should watch for configuration information in the application configuration file.

    > If you are using Log4Net to log application runtime information and you do not see any output produced, then you might have forgotten to add the `XmlConfigurator` attribute to the application.

14. Add and initialize a static class level variable of type `ILog` to the `Program` class, as shown in the following code snippet:

    ```
    private static readonly ILog log =
      LogManager.GetLogger(typeof(Program));
    ```

15. Use the logger to produce some logging messages of various log levels. You can do this by adding the following code to the `Main` method of the class:

    ```
    log.Debug("This is a Debug message.");
    log.Info("This is a Info message.");
    log.Warn("This is a Warn message.");
    log.Error("This is a Error message.");
    log.Fatal("This is a Fatal message.");
    ```

16. Add code to make the system wait for user input before exiting, as shown in the following code snippet:

    ```
    Console.Write("\r\nHit enter to exit:");
    Console.ReadLine();
    ```

17. Run the application and review its output. Your console should look similar to the following screenshot:

    ```
    [LoggingSample.Program.Main] DEBUG This is a Debug message.
    [LoggingSample.Program.Main] INFO  This is a Info message.
    [LoggingSample.Program.Main] WARN  This is a Warn message.
    [LoggingSample.Program.Main] ERROR This is a Error message.
    [LoggingSample.Program.Main] FATAL This is a Fatal message.

    Hit enter to exit:
    ```

18. In `App.config`, change the logging level to `WARN` and run the application again. What do you see this time on the console?

## What just happened?

We have created a simple program which is configured to use Log4Net to log messages of different severity levels. We have defined appenders or targets to which Log4Net outputs the logging messages via the configuration file of the application.

## Setting up logging for NHibernate

As explained earlier in this chapter, NHibernate uses Log4Net to generate logging messages. Now that we have an understanding of the most relevant parts of Log4Net and how to configure them, we can use this know-how to set up the logging for NHibernate as needed by our application requirements.

> If we only want NHibernate to log the queries it sends to the data source when running unit tests, then we don't have to configure Log4Net at all. It suffices to add the `show_sql` key to the NHibernate configuration.

# Time for action – Enable logging in NHibernate

1. Open Visual Studio and load the `OrderingSystem` solution.

2. To the project `OrderingSystem.Tests`, add a reference to the assembly `log4net.dll` located in the `lib` folder.

3. Add an `Application Configuration` (`App.config`) file to the `OrderingSystem.Tests` project and add the following code to it:

    ```xml
    <?xml version="1.0" encoding="utf-8" ?>
    <configuration>
      <configSections>
        <section name="log4net"
          type="log4net.Config.Log4NetConfigurationSectionHandler,
            log4net" />
      </configSections>
      <log4net debug="false">
        <appender name="console"
          type="log4net.Appender.ConsoleAppender, log4net">
          <layout type="log4net.Layout.PatternLayout,log4net">
            <param name="ConversionPattern"
              value="%d [%t] %-5p %c - %m%n" />
          </layout>
        </appender>
        <root>
          <level value="DEBUG" />
          <appender-ref ref="console" />
        </root>
      </log4net>
    </configuration>
    ```

4. Open the `entity_mapping_specs` class and add the following code, which initializes logging for the unit tests, as shown in the following code snippet:

    ```
    protected override void BeforeAllTests()
    {
      base.BeforeAllTests();
      log4net.Config.XmlConfigurator.Configure();
    }
    ```

## Testing, Profiling, Monitoring, and Logging

5. Run the tests and review the output in the test runner output window, as shown in the following screenshot:

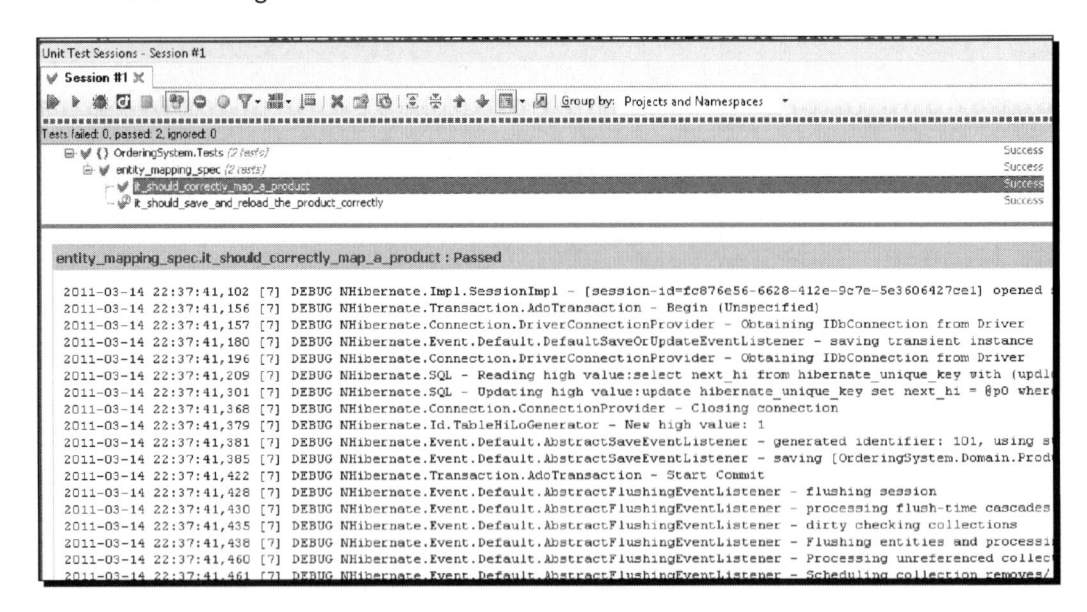

> If you don't see any output created by NHibernate via Log4Net in the test runner output window, then make sure no other listener is configured to consume the output generated by Log4Net. A sample for such a scenario could be that you have NHibernate Profiler (described later in this chapter) configured as a listener to your tests.

6. This is an overwhelming amount of information and we would like to reduce it to avoid getting lost! NHibernate defines two loggers called `NHibernate` and `NHibernate.SQL`. We can individually configure these two loggers. Add the following code snippet to the `App.config` file, just before the `<root>` tag:

```
<logger name="NHibernate">
  <level value="WARN"/>
</logger>
<logger name="NHibernate.SQL">
  <level value="ALL"/>
</logger>
```

7. In the preceding code snippet, we have set the threshold level for the chattier logger `NHibernate` to `WARN`, that is, only messages of type `WARN`, `ERROR`, or `FATAL` will be the output. The other logger `NHibernate.SQL` is configured to give an output of all logging messages of any level.

[ 208 ]

**8.** After this modification of `App.config`, run the tests again. Now the test output should look similar to the following screenshot:

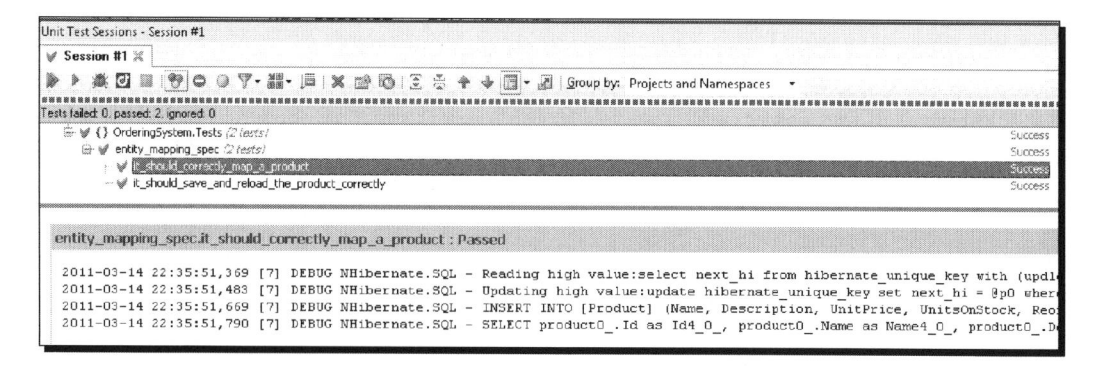

```
Unit Test Sessions - Session #1
Session #1
Tests failed: 0, passed: 2, ignored: 0
  OrderingSystem.Tests (2 tests)                                                      Success
    entity_mapping_spec (2 tests)                                                     Success
      it_should_correctly_map_a_product                                               Success
      it_should_save_and_reload_the_product_correctly                                 Success

entity_mapping_spec.it_should_correctly_map_a_product : Passed

2011-03-14 22:35:51,369 [7] DEBUG NHibernate.SQL - Reading high value:select next_hi from hibernate_unique_key with (upd
2011-03-14 22:35:51,483 [7] DEBUG NHibernate.SQL - Updating high value:update hibernate_unique_key set next_hi = @p0 wher
2011-03-14 22:35:51,669 [7] DEBUG NHibernate.SQL - INSERT INTO [Product] (Name, Description, UnitPrice, UnitsOnStock, Reo
2011-03-14 22:35:51,790 [7] DEBUG NHibernate.SQL - SELECT product0_.Id as Id4_0_, product0_.Name as Name4_0_, product0_.D
```

**9.** This is much less information! In fact, it is the same information we get when setting `ShowSql` to true in the NHibernate configuration.

## What just happened?

In our test project developed earlier in this chapter, we configured Log4Net to output all logging information to the console. Logging information, in this case, is created by NHibernate. As NHibernate produces a huge amount of logging information, we have restricted the type of logging information that is sent to the console by adding some filter information to the configuration file of the test project.

# Monitoring and profiling

Once our application is implemented and running in a test or production environment, we might want, or need, to monitor it.

Several possibilities exist for how we can monitor the database communication of our application.

## Analyzing log files

As we have seen in the *Logging* section of this chapter, NHibernate can produce a massive amount of logging data if configured accordingly. This data can be very useful to analyze what's going on under the hood. Furthermore, at least one commercial tool (NHibernate Profiler) is using the output generated by NHibernate to monitor and profile the database communication and provide a valuable insight into the usage of NHibernate.

## Using SQL Server Profiler

If you are using any commercial version of Microsoft SQL Server as your database, then you can use SQL Server Profiler to monitor the database communication produced by the application. The disadvantage of this method is that the profiler only hooks in at the database level and is not aware of NHibernate. As a consequence, we can only get a very limited insight into the usage of NHibernate through our application.

The usage of the profiler makes it possible to find errors in SQL statements and helps to detect queries or query patterns that are sub-optimal.

However, once a bad query pattern is found, it is rather hard to directly use this information to optimize the usage of NHibernate in this particular area.

## Monitoring and profiling with NHibernate Profiler

There is one commercial tool available that is strongly recommended to everyone. This tool is called NHibernate Profiler and has been written by one of the profound experts of and main contributors to NHibernate. NHibernate Profiler is a realtime visual debugger, allowing a development team to gain valuable insight and perspective into their usage of NHibernate.

This profiler offers some unique benefits that no other product can currently offer:

- Specifically built to log, monitor, and analyze the communication between the application and database through NHibernate.
- All SQL statements are nicely formatted and presented, and can be easily copied and pasted in, for example, SQL Server Management Studio for further testing.
- Analyzing access patterns and providing feedback in the form of warnings and tips on how to avoid common pitfalls when using NHibernate, and how to improve queries and commands based on best practices.
- Provides a full-stack trace of each method causing database access and allows the developer to directly jump to the relevant source code.
- Various reports with useful statistics about the database communication are available.
- The database communication is logged and can be saved for later analysis and a replay of the scenario.

NHibernate Profiler can be downloaded from `http://www.nhprof.com`. A free one month license is available to use and test the product.

Your application can easily be configured to enable profiling through NHibernate Profiler. Once the application is configured, we can then monitor and debug the database communication.

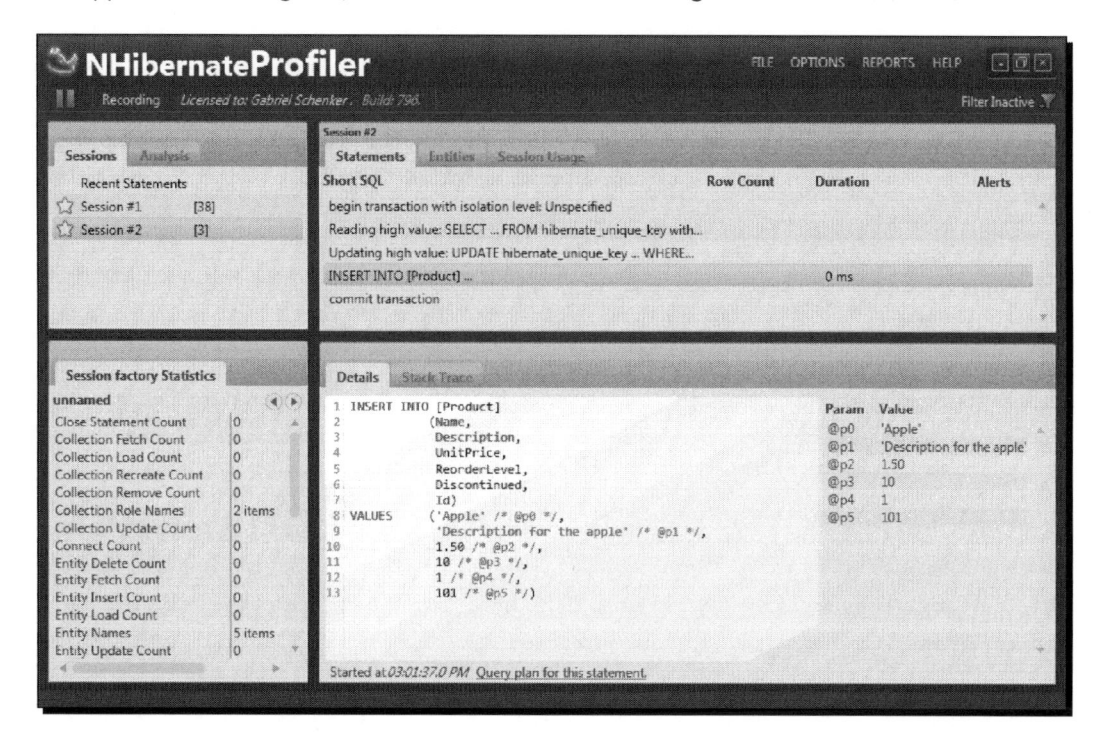

The preceding screenshot shows NHibernate Profiler in action. The profiler displays its information in four panes. The first upper left pane displays session-specific data. The second lower left pane displays statistical information regarding the session factory in use. The third upper right pane contains a list of all operations executed through the session(s), while the last lower right pane shows details of a selected statement. In this case, the nicely formatted SQL of a database insert command is shown.

## Time for action – Adding NHibernate Profiler support

In this exercise, we want to download, install, and use NHibernate Profiler to monitor the database communication caused by our unit test.

1. Download NHibernate Profiler from `http://www.nhprof.com/Download`.

2. Unpack the ZIP file (at the time of writing `NHibernate.Profiler-Build-796.zip`) into a new folder (for example, `C:\tools\NHProfiler`).

3. Navigate to the installation folder and run NHibernate Profiler by double-clicking on **NHProf.exe**. You will be presented with a dialog, as shown in the following screenshot:

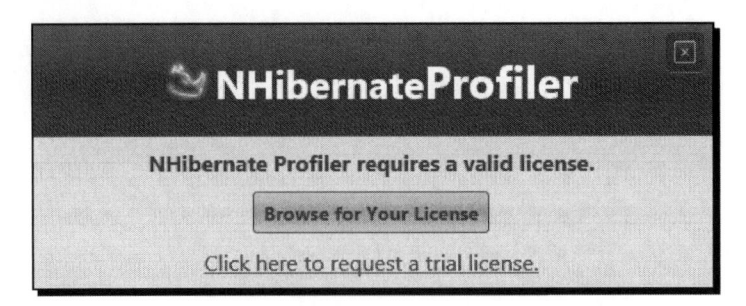

4. Request a trial license. The license will be sent to you by e-mail.

5. Create a new XML file in the application folder (for example, `MyLicense.xml`) and copy the license key from the e-mail and paste it into the XML file just created.

6. Run NHibernate Profiler again and click on **Browse for Your License**. Locate and select the `MyLicense.xml` file in the NHibernate Profiler application folder.

7. In the NHibernate Profiler application folder, locate the file `HibernatingRhinos.Profiler.Appender.dll`. Copy this file to the `lib` sub-folder of your samples folder.

8. Open Visual Studio and load the `Ordering System` solution.

9. As shown in the following screenshot, add a reference to the assembly **HibernatingRhinos.Profiler.Appender** located in the `lib` folder to the **OrderingSystem.Tests** project.

10. Furthermore, add (if you haven't already done so) a reference to the **log4net** assembly also located in the `lib` folder of the **OrderingSystem.Tests** project, as shown in the following screenshot:

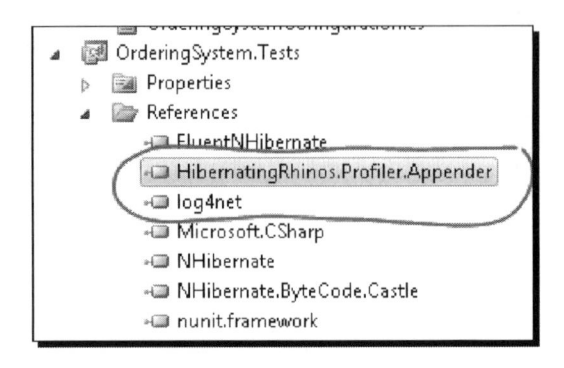

11. Open the class `MappingSpecificationBase` in the `OrderingSystem.Tests` project we implemented earlier in this chapter.

12. Add the following code snippet as the first line to the method `BeforeAllTests` to enable NHibernate Profiler to monitor the communication between our test code and the database:

    ```
    HibernatingRhinos.Profiler.Appender.NHibernate
      .NHibernateProfiler.Initialize();
    ```

    > If you configure NHibernate Profiler as a listener to your application, then all the output generated by Log4Net will be redirected to NHibernate Profiler.

13. Open the class `entity_mapping_spec` and run the tests.

14. Switch to NHibernate Profiler and review the output captured by the profiler.

15. Locate the **INSERT INTO [Product]...** statement and select it. In the lower part of the screen, review the output on the **Details** tab, as shown in the following screenshot:

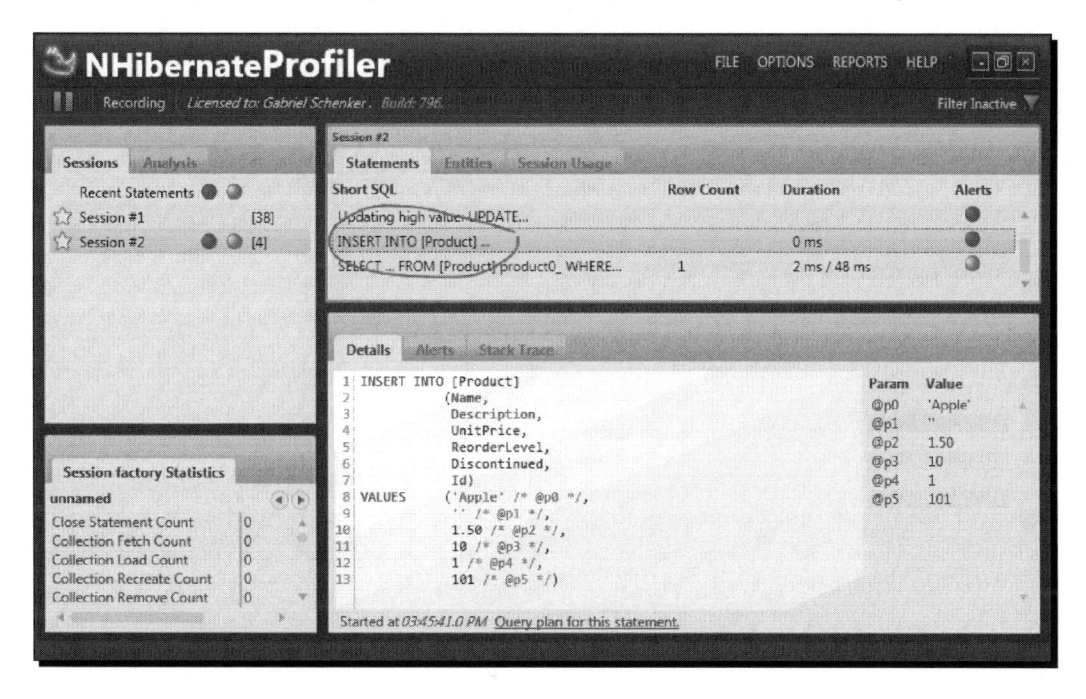

16. Note the red bullets in the **Alerts** column in the upper right side. In the lower pane, switch to the **Alerts** tab and review the error message, as shown in the following screenshot:

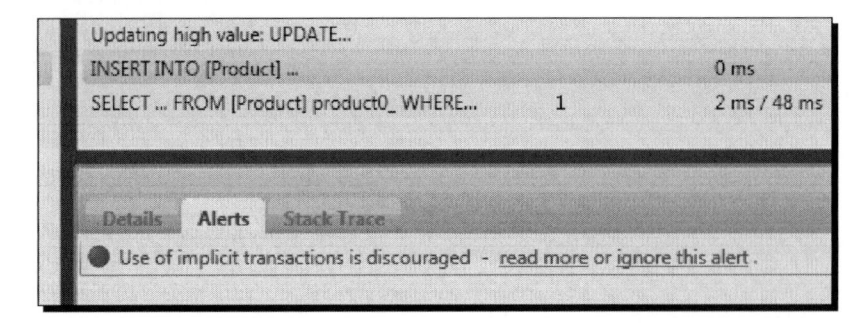

| Updating high value: UPDATE... | | |
|---|---|---|
| INSERT INTO [Product] ... | | 0 ms |
| SELECT ... FROM [Product] product0_ WHERE... | 1 | 2 ms / 48 ms |

Details | **Alerts** | Stack Trace

● Use of implicit transactions is discouraged - read more or ignore this alert.

17. The error message tells us that we have an anti-pattern in our code; we do not use explicit transactions to wrap our database access. The **read more** hyperlink provides a more thorough description of the alert, as shown in the preceding screenshot. Click on this hyperlink and review the text.

18. In the upper right pane of NHibernate Profiler, locate the **SELECT ... FROM [Product]...** entry and select it. Note the number in the **Row Count** column and the times in the **Duration** column. In our case:
    1. One record was returned as a result of the query.
    2. The query took 2 ms on the database only and 48 ms overall.

## What just happened?

We have downloaded and installed a trial license of NHibernate Profiler. Subsequently, we have configured our application to create logging information that can be used by the profiler to analyze our database communication. After this initial setup, we have run some of our tests and reviewed the output they generated in NHibernate Profiler.

NHibernate Profiler provided us with detailed information about what happened in which sequence, how long it took to execute certain queries, and how many records were returned by a given query.

## Summary

In this chapter, we learned why it is important to write tests to verify the correct mapping of the domain model to the underlying database schema. We also implemented a framework which helps us to write mapping tests with as little effort as possible.

We also discussed the value of logging and how we can configure our application to produce logging information.

Lastly, we discussed how we can monitor and profile our application during runtime. We specifically put our focus on the monitoring of the database communication of our application via NHibernate.

After this deep dive into testing and profiling, we are ready to tackle yet another important aspect of NHibernate, namely its configuration. This is the topic of the next chapter.

# 8
# Configuration

*Any complex framework that is used by many developers in very different scenarios must be configurable. With the configuration, we can influence the runtime behavior of our application that uses the framework.*

In this chapter, we will analyze in detail what a configuration is. Specifically, we will:

- Discuss why we need a configuration to begin with
- Be presented with a list of the elements of NHibernate we can configure
- Learn four different ways of how we can configure NHibernate in our applications

This chapter contains a lot of exercises that show us one-to-one how easily NHibernate can be configured.

So let's get on with it...

## Why do we need a configuration?

The runtime behavior of NHibernate depends on how we configure the system. NHibernate has been built with the idea of being very flexible and extendable. NHibernate can be used in all kinds of different scenarios. As an example, it is possible to use this framework with nearly any known and relevant relational database management system (RDBMS). Some of those supported databases are MS SQL Server, Oracle, IBM DB/2, and MySQL, to name just a few.

It is also possible to use NHibernate in brand new projects where we can choose a model-first approach, as well as in scenarios where we have to write an application on top of a legacy database.

Sometimes, we have special needs for our application. Maybe we need to add auditing capabilities to our application or maybe we want to use our own, and very specific, proxy generator.

Such a flexible and extendable system can only work if it is configurable. Therefore, what NHibernate expects from us is that we provide enough information for it at startup. Luckily, most of the settings have meaningful default values such that we only need to explicitly configure a few settings.

# Elements of the configuration

All important aspects of the runtime behavior of NHibernate are configurable by one of the methods described in detail later on in this chapter.

## Which database do we want to use?

This is probably the single most important aspect of our configuration. We have to tell NHibernate what database product we are going to use, such as SQL Server, Oracle, DB/2, MySQL, and so on. As there is no such thing as a "default database", we always have to provide these details in our configuration.

Besides the diversity of database products, each database product is also available in different versions, such as SQL Server 2000, 2005, or 2008, or Oracle 9*i*, 10*i*, or 11*g*, and so on.

Furthermore, we need to authenticate ourselves when accessing a database. Therefore, we need to provide the respective security tokens in the form of a connection string. Typically, we will find these four settings in a real-world application:

```
<property name="connection.provider">
  NHibernate.Connection.DriverConnectionProvider
</property>

<property name="connection.driver_class">
  NHibernate.Driver.SqlClientDriver
</property>

<property name="dialect">
  NHibernate.Dialect.MsSql2008Dialect
</property>

<property name="connection.connection_string">
  server=.\SQLEXPRESS;database=sample;integrated security=SSPI;
</property>
```

The preceding code snippet is part of an XML configuration file.

*Chapter 8*

The first line defines the connection provider NHibernate uses. Most of the time, we will want to use the default provider that NHibernate provides us with, but we can also define our own provider. In this case, we would have to declare this in exactly this configuration entry.

> Whenever we want to use our own implementation for a specific part of NHibernate, we have to declare this in the configuration. In this case, we have to provide the fully qualified class name combined with the assembly name in which the class is implemented. As an example, `SomeNamespace.MyDriverProvider, MyAssembly` would be the entry needed if we want to declare the usage of a class implemented in `MyAssembly` in the namespace `SomeNamespace` and with the class name `MyDriverProvider`.

The second `property` defines the database we want to use by specifying the database driver. In our case, this is the driver for MS SQL Server.

In the third entry, we define which SQL dialect we want to use. In our example, it is any of the MS SQL Server 2008 editions.

> The SQL dialect specifies things such as what types the database supports or how .NET types are mapped to the corresponding database types. Furthermore, the dialect defines which the native POID generator is or how a paginated query should look.
> NHibernate needs these dialects as SQL is not standardized enough for all databases to be compatible among each other.

Finally, in the fourth entry, we provide the connection information in the form of a connection string to NHibernate. NHibernate will use this connection string when trying to open a session with the database. In our example, we define that we want to use a locally installed SQL Server Express Edition and we want to access a database called `sample`. We further declare that we want to use `integrated security` for authentication with the database.

> Note that starting from NHibernate 3.2 (which at the time of writing had just reached general availability, or GA), the configuration has been streamlined and we need to configure less elements as NHibernate is using meaningful default values.

> **The following elements can thus be omitted:**
> - NHibernate now implements its own proxy generator. No additional external dependency is needed, and thus the configuration does not need to define the proxy factory factory element.
> - The `DriverConnectionProvider` class is the default connection provider, and thus no explicit configuration is needed.
> - Each dialect has associated a default driver, and again we can omit this declaration.

## What byte code provider and proxy factory?

When using lazy loading with NHibernate, we need to define which proxy generator NHibernate shall use. NHibernate currently natively supports three proxy generators. These three generators are part of the Castle (http://www.castleproject.org/), LinFu (http://code.google.com/p/linfu/), or Spring.NET (http://www.springframework.net/) framework. It doesn't really matter which provider you choose. You will probably want to use the proxy generator of the framework you already use. If you haven't used any of those frameworks so far, then selecting the Castle provider is a good choice.

If you are using the Castle proxy generator, then the definition in the XML configuration file will look similar to the following code snippet:

```
<property name="proxyfactory.factory_class">
   NHibernate.ByteCode.Castle.ProxyFactoryFactory,
   NHibernate.ByteCode.Castle
</property>
```

The byte code provider is responsible for creating some optimizations of the code used by NHibernate. Among others, it allows us to inject external dependencies into entities that are constructed by NHibernate. These are all advanced scenarios and usually you do not want to change the default settings there.

Note that starting from version 3.2, NHibernate has its own embedded proxy generator which is a modified version of the LinFu proxy generator. As a consequence, when using NHibernate 3.2 or higher, we don't need to reference any of the `NHibernate.ByteCode.xxx.dll`.

## Where are our mappings?

To be able to work, NHibernate has to know how we define our mappings and where the mapping information can be found.

In Chapter 5, we discussed the various ways to define a mapping between the domain model and the underlying database schema. Independent of how we define the mappings, we always have to provide these mapping definitions to NHibernate via the configuration. We can add individual mapping files or resources as well as whole assemblies which contain mappings. Using configuration in code, this declaration would look similar to the following code snippet to add a single type:

```
configuration.AddClass(typeof (Product));
```

and like the following code snippet to make NHibernate parse a whole assembly of HBM files that are stored as embedded resources:

```
configuration.AddAssembly(typeof (Product).Assembly);
```

## Do we use second level caching?

Sometimes, it makes sense to use a second layer of caching besides the first level cache (or identity map) that every NHibernate session provides. In this case, we can configure a second level cache, which is not tied to a specific session but globally available to all sessions of a given session factory.

When configuring the second level cache, we have to declare among others which cache provider we want to use.

## Do we want to extend NHibernate?

As mentioned earlier, NHibernate is a very flexible and highly extensible framework. As such, we can, for example, define custom interceptors or listeners that add functionality to NHibernate. These custom classes and their usage have to be declared to NHibernate when configuring it at startup. Note, however, that this is an advanced topic and lies outside of the focus of this book.

## XML configuration

The original way of configuring NHibernate is through XML. There are two ways we can use to define the configuration. It can either be part of the application configuration file for a classical Windows application or the `Web.config` file for a web-based application. We can alternatively define the configuration in a separate XML file.

*Configuration*

## Time for action – Configuring NHibernate using XML

In this exercise, we are going to implement a simple application which is using NHibernate to persist data to and read data from a relational database. As a database, we will use SQLite in file mode.

1. Open Visual Studio and create a new project. Select **Console Application** as the project template. Call the project `XmlConfigurationSample`.

2. Due to some incompatibility issues of SQLite, we have to adjust the target framework of our application. In the Solution Explorer, right-click on the **XmlConfigurationSample** project and select **Properties**.

3. On the Application tab, select **.NET Framework 3.5** as **Target framework**:

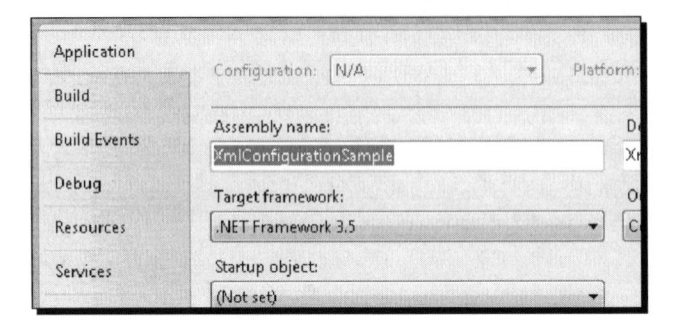

4. Switch to the **Build** tab and make sure that the **Platform Target** is set to **Any CPU**.

5. Add a reference to the three assemblies `NHibernate.dll`, `NHibernate.ByteCode.Castle.dll`, and `System.Data.SQLite.dll` to the project, as shown in the following screenshot:

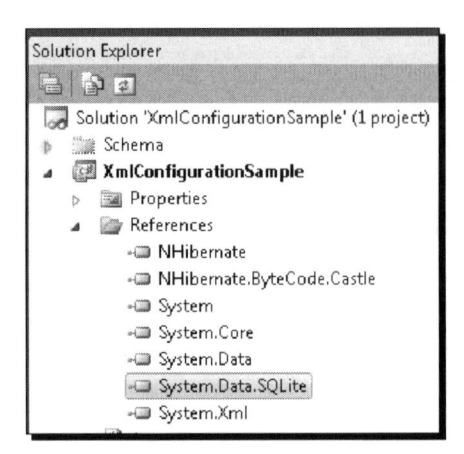

*Chapter 8*

6. In the **Solution Explorer**, right-click on the solution, select **Add | New Folder**, and name the folder `Schema`.

7. Right-click on the `Schema` solution folder and select **Add | Existing Item**. Add the two files `nhibernate-configuration.xsd` and `nhibernate-mapping.xsd` from the `lib` folder to this `Schema` folder.

8. Add a new class file called `Account.cs` to the project. Add the following code snippet to the file to define the entity `Account`:

```
public class Account
{
   public int Id { get; set; }
   public string Name { get; set; }
   public decimal Balance { get; set; }
   public string CurrencyCode { get; set; }
   public bool IsActive { get; set; }
}
```

9. Add an XML file called `Account.hbm.xls` to the project and add the following XML code to the file to define the mapping for the `Account` entity:

```xml
<?xml version="1.0" encoding="utf-8" ?>
<hibernate-mapping xmlns="urn:nhibernate-mapping-2.2"
   assembly="XmlConfigurationSample"
   namespace="XmlConfigurationSample" >
   <class name="Account" lazy="false">
     <id name="Id">
       <generator class="hilo"/>
     </id>
     <property name="Name"/>
     <property name="Balance"/>
     <property name="CurrencyCode"/>
     <property name="IsActive"/>
   </class>
</hibernate-mapping>
```

10. Set the `Build Action` property of the file to `Embedded Resource`.

11. Add a new item of type **Application Configuration File** to you project. Visual Studio adds a file named `App.config` to the project.

## Configuration

> Note that, if in step 3 you have changed the target platform of the application to .NET Framework 3.5, then Visual Studio automatically adds an App.config file to your solution. If you open this file it contains a node `<startup><supportedRuntime version="v2.0.50727"/></startup>`.
> In this case, you don't need to execute step 10 and can just delete the content of the App.config and continue with step 11.

12. To this file, add the following XML code snippet to define a section where you will define the configuration for NHibernate:

```xml
<?xml version="1.0" encoding="utf-8" ?>
<configuration>
  <configSections>
    <section name="hibernate-configuration" type=
      "NHibernate.Cfg.ConfigurationSectionHandler, NHibernate" />
  </configSections>
</configuration>
```

13. After the `configSections` definition, add the following XML code snippet to configure NHibernate:

```xml
<hibernate-configuration xmlns="urn:nhibernate-configuration-2.2">
  <session-factory>
    <property name="connection.provider">
      NHibernate.Connection.DriverConnectionProvider
    </property>
    <property name="connection.driver_class">
      NHibernate.Driver.SQLite20Driver
    </property>
    <property name="dialect">
      NHibernate.Dialect.SQLiteDialect
    </property>
    <property name="proxyfactory.factory_class">
      NHibernate.ByteCode.Castle.ProxyFactoryFactory,
      NHibernate.ByteCode.Castle
    </property>
    <property name="connection.connection_string_name">
      Sample
    </property>
    <property name="show_sql">
      true
    </property>
  </session-factory>
</hibernate-configuration>
```

Chapter 8

**14.** After the preceding code snippet, add a definition for the connection string to be used by the application (which is referenced by the `connection.connection_string_name` property above):

```
<connectionStrings>
  <add name="Sample"
    connectionString=
      "data source=xmlconfig.dbf;version=3;new=true;"/>
</connectionStrings>
```

**15.** To the `Program` class, add the following `using` statements:

```
using NHibernate.Cfg;
using NHibernate.Tool.hbm2ddl;
```

**16.** In the `Main` method of the `Program` class, add a line to create an instance of the NHibernate `Configuration` class, as shown in the following code snippet:

```
var configuration = new Configuration();
```

**17.** After the preceding statement, add code to make NHibernate scan the whole assembly where `Account` is defined for mapping files, as shown in the following code snippet:

```
configuration.AddAssembly(typeof(Account).Assembly);
```

**18.** In the `Program` class, implement a static method `BuildSchema` which uses NHibernate's `SchemaExport` class to (re)create the database schema, as shown in the following code snippet:

```
private static void BuildSchema(Configuration configuration)
{
  new SchemaExport(configuration).Execute(true, true, false);
}
```

**19.** Back in the `Main` method, add a line which calls this method and passes the configuration instance as a parameter:

```
BuildSchema(configuration);
```

**20.** Add a line of code to build a session factory from the NHibernate configuration object, as shown in the following code snippet:

```
var factory = configuration.BuildSessionFactory();
```

## Configuration

**21.** Add code to open a session. Do this in a using statement, as shown in the following code snippet:

```
using (var session = factory.OpenSession())
{
}
```

**22.** Inside the `using` statement, add code to create an `Account` entity and use the session to save it, as shown in the following code snippet:

```
var account = new Account
{
   Name = "USB-10234-R1",
   Balance = 1545.55m,
   CurrencyCode = "CHF",
   IsActive = true
};
session.Save(account);
```

**23.** Flush and clear the session, as shown in the following code snippet:

```
session.Flush();
session.Clear();
```

**24.** Add code to reload the just stored account from the database, as shown in the following code snippet:

```
var fromDb = session.Get<Account>(account.Id);
```

**25.** At the end of the `Main` method, add code which asks the user to hit *Enter* to exit the application, as shown in the following code snippet:

```
System.Console.Write("\r\n\nHit enter to exit:");
System.Console.ReadLine();
```

**26.** Run the application and review the output on the console. Your console should look similar to the following screenshot:

## What just happened?

We have created a simple application that uses a SQLite database to store the data. We have defined the configuration of NHibernate in XML as part of the application resource file.

# Configuring NHibernate in code

We do not need to provide the configuration in XML, but we can define the whole configuration in code.

## Time for action – Configuring NHibernate in code

In this exercise, we are going to implement a simple application using NHibernate which fully configures the ORM framework in code.

1. Open SQL Server Management Studio (SSMS) and create a new database called `CodeConfigurationSample`.

2. Open Visual Studio and create a new project. Select **Console Application** as the project template. Call the project **CodeConfigurationSample**.

Configuration

3. Add a reference to the two assemblies `NHibernate.dll` and `NHibernate.ByteCode.Castle.dll` to the project.

4. In the **Solution Explorer**, right-click on the solution and select **Add | New Folder** and name the folder **Schema**.

5. Right-click on the **Schema** solution folder and select **Add | Existing Item**. Add the two files, `nhibernate-configuration.xsd` and `nhibernate-mapping.xsd`, from the `lib` folder to this **Schema** folder, as shown in the following screenshot:

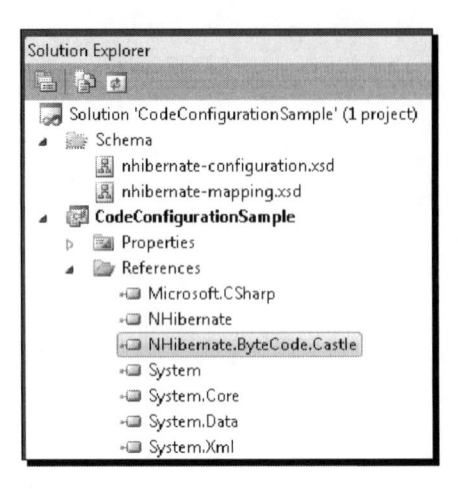

6. Add a new class file called `Product.cs` to the project and add the following code snippet to define a basic `Product` entity:

```
public class Product
{
    public int Id { get; set; }
    public string Name { get; set; }
    public decimal UnitPrice { get; set; }
    public int ReorderLevel { get; set; }
    public int UnitsOnStock { get; set; }
    public bool Discontinued { get; set; }
}
```

7. Add a new XML file to the project. Call the file `Product.hbm.xml`.

8. Set the `Build Action` property of the file to `Embedded Resource`.

9. Add the following XML code snippet to the file to define the mapping for the `Product` entity:

```
<?xml version="1.0" encoding="utf-8" ?>
<hibernate-mapping xmlns="urn:nhibernate-mapping-2.2"
  assembly="CodeConfigurationSample"
```

[ 228 ]

```
      namespace="CodeConfigurationSample" >
      <class name="Product" lazy="false">
        <id name="Id">
          <generator class="hilo"/>
        </id>
        <property name="Name"/>
        <property name="UnitPrice"/>
        <property name="ReorderLevel"/>
        <property name="UnitsOnStock"/>
        <property name="Discontinued"/>
      </class>
    </hibernate-mapping>
```

**10.** Add the following `using` statements to the `Program` class:
```
using NHibernate.Cfg;
using NHibernate.Tool.hbm2ddl;
```

**11.** Add a static method `GetConfiguration` to the `Program` class, as shown in the following code snippet:
```
private static Configuration GetConfiguration()
{
}
```

**12.** In the method body, create an instance of the type `Configuration`, as shown in the following code snippet:
```
var cfg = new Configuration();
```

**13.** With the aid of the `Add` method, add a key-value pair to the `Properties` collection of the NHibernate configuration instance that defines which driver connection provider NHibernate should use, as shown in the following code snippet:
```
cfg.Properties.Add(Environment.ConnectionProvider,
   typeof(DriverConnectionProvider).FullName);
```

> Instead of typing in a magic string `connection.provider` for the key and `NHibernate.Connection.DriverConnectionProvider` for the value, we can use a more type-safe way of defining the key-value pair. All possible configuration keys are available via the static `NHibernate.Cfg.Environment` class. For the value, we can use the `typeof(T)` function, where `T` is the class whose name we want to use as the value. The desired value can then be obtained via the `FullName` property.

14. Add more key-value pairs to the `Properties` collection to define the connection driver and the dialect, as shown in the following code snippet:

    ```
    cfg.Properties.Add(Environment.ConnectionDriver,
        typeof(SqlClientDriver).FullName);
    cfg.Properties.Add(Environment.Dialect,
        typeof(MsSql2008Dialect).FullName);
    ```

15. We also need to define the proxy factory factory class (yes, this is not a typo; it is really a factory of a factory). However, as the desired class does not live in the NHibernate assembly but in the `NHibernate.ByteCode.Castle` assembly, we cannot use the `FullName` this time, but have to use the property `AssemblyQualifiedName`, as shown in the following code snippet:

    ```
    cfg.Properties.Add(Environment.ProxyFactoryFactoryClass,
        typeof(ProxyFactoryFactory).AssemblyQualifiedName);
    ```

16. Now, we need another key-value pair to define the connection string to our database, as shown in the following code snippet:

    ```
    cfg.Properties.Add(Environment.ConnectionString,
        @"server=.\SQLEXPRESS;database= CodeConfigurationSample;" +
        "integrated security=SSPI;");
    ```

17. Finally, we want NHibernate to log the SQL sent to the database, as shown in the following code snippet:

    ```
    cfg.Properties.Add(Environment.ShowSql, "true");
    ```

18. We now need to declare which mappings we want to use. We can either do this by individually adding the entity types to the configuration, as shown in the following code snippet:

    ```
    cfg.AddClass(typeof (Product));
    ```

19. Furthermore, even better by adding the assembly which contains all XML configuration files to the NHibernate configuration object, as shown in the following code snippet:

    ```
    cfg.AddAssembly(typeof (Product).Assembly);
    ```

20. Choose one or the other from the preceding two variants.

21. Return the configuration object from this function, as shown in the following code snippet:

    ```
    return cfg;
    ```

## Chapter 8

22. Add another static method to the `Program` class that (re) creates the database schema, given the configuration, as shown in the following code snippet:

    ```
    private static void BuildSchema(Configuration configuration)
    {
      new SchemaExport(configuration).Execute(true, true, false);
    }
    ```

23. To the `Main` method of the `Program` class, add the following code snippet to create a configuration object, (re) create the database schema, and finally build a session factory:

    ```
    var configuration = GetConfiguration();
    BuildSchema(configuration);
    var factory = configuration.BuildSessionFactory();
    ```

24. Add code to open a session, as shown in the following code snippet:

    ```
    using(var session = factory.OpenSession())
    {
    }
    ```

25. Inside the `using` statement, create a product entity and use the session to save the product to the database, as shown in the following code snippet:

    ```
    var product = new Product
    {
      Name = "Apple",
      UnitPrice = 1.55m,
      ReorderLevel = 10,
      UnitsOnStock = 5
    };
    session.Save(product);
    ```

26. Additionally, inside the `using` statement, flush the session and clear the first level cache, as shown in the following code snippet:

    ```
    session.Flush();
    session.Clear();
    ```

27. Reload the product from the database using the `session` object and the ID of the previously saved product, as shown in the following code snippet:

    ```
    var fromDb = session.Get<Product>(product.Id);
    ```

28. At the end of the `Main` method, add code to wait for the user to hit *Enter* before exiting the application, as shown in the following code snippet:

    ```
    System.Console.Write("\r\n\nHit enter to exit:");
    System.Console.ReadLine();
    ```

[ 231 ]

## Configuration

**29.** Run the application and review the output in the console. It should look similar to the following screenshot:

```
    if exists (select * from dbo.sysobjects where id = object_id(N'Product') and
OBJECTPROPERTY(id, N'IsUserTable') = 1) drop table Product

    if exists (select * from dbo.sysobjects where id = object_id(N'hibernate_uni
que_key') and OBJECTPROPERTY(id, N'IsUserTable') = 1) drop table hibernate_uniqu
e_key

    create table Product (
        Id INT not null,
        Name NVARCHAR(255) null,
        UnitPrice DECIMAL(19,5) null,
        ReorderLevel INT null,
        UnitsOnStock INT null,
        Discontinued BIT null,
        primary key (Id)
    )

    create table hibernate_unique_key (
        next_hi INT
    )

    insert into hibernate_unique_key values ( 1 )
NHibernate: select next_hi from hibernate_unique_key with (updlock, rowlock)
NHibernate: update hibernate_unique_key set next_hi = @p0 where next_hi = @p1;@p
0 = 2 [Type: Int32 (0)], @p1 = 1 [Type: Int32 (0)]
NHibernate: INSERT INTO Product (Name, UnitPrice, ReorderLevel, UnitsOnStock, Di
scontinued, Id) VALUES (@p0, @p1, @p2, @p3, @p4, @p5);@p0 = 'Apple' [Type: Strin
g (4000)], @p1 = 1.55 [Type: Decimal (0)], @p2 = 10 [Type: Int32 (0)], @p3 = 5 [
Type: Int32 (0)], @p4 = False [Type: Boolean (0)], @p5 = 32768 [Type: Int32 (0)]

NHibernate: SELECT product0_.Id as Id0_0_, product0_.Name as Name0_0_, product0_
.UnitPrice as UnitPrice0_0_, product0_.ReorderLevel as ReorderL4_0_0_, product0_
.UnitsOnStock as UnitsOnS5_0_0_, product0_.Discontinued as Disconti6_0_0_ FROM P
roduct product0_ WHERE product0_.Id=@p0;@p0 = 32768 [Type: Int32 (0)]

Hit enter to exit:
```

**30.** There is one caveat in our code though. Usually, you would NOT want to define the connection string to the database in code, but rather in the configuration file of your application. To do so, add a new item of the type **Application Configuration** to you project.

**31.** Add the following XML code snippet to define the database connection:

```xml
<?xml version="1.0" encoding="utf-8" ?>
<configuration>
  <connectionStrings>
    <add name="Sample"
      connectionString="server=.\SQLEXPRESS;
      database=CodeConfigurationSample;
      integrated security=SSPI;"/>
  </connectionStrings>
</configuration>
```

**32.** In the `GetConfiguration` method, replace the statement which declares the connection string with the following code snippet:

```
cfg.Properties.Add(Environment.ConnectionStringName, "Sample");
```

**33.** Start the application again. The application should run as before, but now with the connection string defined outside the code in the configuration file.

## What just happened?

We have created an application using NHibernate to persist data to and query data from a database. We have configured NHibernate entirely in code with the exception of the connection string, which we defined in the configuration file of the application.

> In my personal career, it has been proven that the less external configuration any application needs, the easier it is to manage and support. In this regard, I personally prefer to configure as much as possible in code and only rely on external configuration where it absolutely makes sense.

## Fluent configuration

Personally, I prefer to configure NHibernate in code by using a fluent API. It makes the configuration very readable and self-expressing. Also, when defining the configuration, the individual settings are much more discoverable to the developer executing this task.

### Configuring NHibernate with Loquacious

NHibernate contains a new fluent API for configuration. This API is defined in the `Loquacious` namespace. All aspects of the configuration can be defined by using this API. The configuration in the preceding sample was already very readable, but the usage of the new fluent API will make it even more understandable.

### Time for action – Using Loquacious to configure NHibernate

As always, we do not want to talk too much about the theory, but immediately dive into an example. In this example, we use some of the concepts we discussed in earlier chapters, such as the usage of value objects and of the NHibernate Profiler tool.

**1.** Open Visual Studio and create a new project of type **Console Application**. Name the project `LoquaciousConfigurationSample`.

## Configuration

2. As we again want to use SQLite in this example, we have to overcome some of its limitations and adjust our project settings accordingly. Therefore, in the **Solution Explorer**, right-click on the project and click on **Properties**.

3. On the **Application** tab, select **.NET Framework 3.5** as **Target framework**.

4. On the **Build** tab, make sure that **Platform target** is set to **Any CPU**.

5. Add a solution folder named **Schema** to the solution.

6. In the **Solution Explorer**, right-click on the **Schema** folder and select **Add | Existing Item...**. Browse to the **lib** folder, select the `nhibernate-mapping.xsd` file, and click on **OK** to add this file to the **Schema** folder.

7. In the **Solution Explorer**, right-click on the **References** folder of the **LoquatiousConfigurationSample** project and select **Add Reference...**.

8. Navigate to the **lib** folder and select the following four files:
    1. `NHibernate.dll`
    2. `NHibernate.ByteCode.Castle.dll`
    3. `HibernatingRhinos.Profiler.Appender.dll`
    4. `System.Data.SQLite.dll`

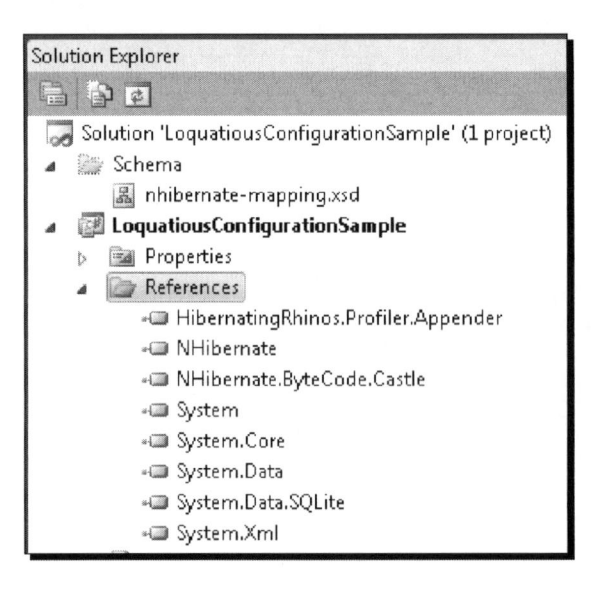

9. Again, in the **Solution Explorer**, right-click on the project and select **Add | New Item...**. Select **Application Configuration File** as the template and click on **Add**. A file called `App.config` is added to your project.

**10.** Open the `App.config` file and add a definition for the connection string we are going to use in this example. SQLite in file mode will be our database. Thus, the content of the `App.config` file should look similar to the following code snippet:

```xml
<?xml version="1.0"?>
<configuration>
  <connectionStrings>
    <add name="Sample"
      connectionString="data source=loquaciousConfig.dbf;
      version=3;new=true;"/>
  </connectionStrings>
</configuration>
```

**11.** In this example, we want to define a `Person` entity which (among others) has a `Name` property which is a **value type**. Add a new class file called `Person.cs` to the project.

**12.** Add the following code snippet to the file to define the entity:

```csharp
using System;

namespace LoquatiousConfigurationSample
{
  public class Person
  {
    public Guid Id { get; set; }
    public Name Name { get; set; }
    public string SSN { get; set; }
    public DateTime Birthdate { get; set; }
  }
}
```

**13.** Note that this time we use an `Id` of type `Guid`—which is our primary key—and not, as in preceding examples, of type `int`.

**14.** Add another new class file, `Name.cs`, to the project.

**15.** To define the `Name` value type, use the code shown in the following code snippet:

```csharp
namespace LoquatiousConfigurationSample
{
  public class Name
  {
    public string FirstName { get; set; }
    public string LastName { get; set; }
    public string MiddleName { get; set; }
  }
}
```

16. A value type always needs to implement equality based on the content of all its properties, as discussed in *Chapter 3*. Thus, add the following code snippet to the `Name` class to define this equality by overriding `Equals` and `GetHashCode`:

    ```
    public bool Equals(Name other)
    {
      if (ReferenceEquals(null, other)) return false;
      if (ReferenceEquals(this, other)) return true;
      return Equals(other.FirstName, FirstName) &&
        Equals(other.LastName, LastName) &&
        Equals(other.MiddleName, MiddleName);
    }

    public override bool Equals(object obj)
    {
      if (obj.GetType() != typeof(Name)) return false;
      return Equals((Name) obj);
    }

    public override int GetHashCode()
    {
      unchecked
      {
        int result = (FirstName != null ?
          FirstName.GetHashCode() : 0);
        result = (result*397) ^ (LastName != null ?
          LastName.GetHashCode() : 0);
        result = (result*397) ^ (MiddleName != null ?
          MiddleName.GetHashCode() : 0);
        return result;
      }
    }
    ```

17. To define the mapping, add a new file of type XML to the project. Call the file `Person.hbm.xml`.

18. In the **Solution Explorer**, select the file and make sure that in the **Properties** window, the **Build Action** is set to **Embedded Resource**.

19. Add the following XML code snippet to define the mapping of the `Person` entity:

    ```
    <?xml version="1.0" encoding="utf-8" ?>
    <hibernate-mapping xmlns="urn:nhibernate-mapping-2.2"
      assembly="LoquatiousConfigurationSample"
      namespace="LoquatiousConfigurationSample" >
      <class name="Person" lazy="false">
        <id name="Id">
          <generator class="guid.comb"/>
        </id>
        <component name="Name">
    ```

```
            <property name="FirstName"/>
            <property name="LastName"/>
            <property name="MiddleName"/>
        </component>
        <property name="SSN"/>
        <property name="Birthdate"/>
    </class>
</hibernate-mapping>
```

20. In the preceding XML definition, specifically note the usage of the ID generator class `guid.comb` which instructs NHibernate to generate `Ids` of type `Guid` that are optimized for the usage in relational databases.

21. Furthermore, note the usage of the `component` tag to define the value type `Name`.

22. We want to use the **NHibernate Profiler** application to monitor the database communication of our application through NHibernate. Thus, add code to our application to support the profiler. To the first line of the `Program` class in the `Main` method, add the following code snippet:

```
HibernatingRhinos.Profiler.Appender.NHibernate
    .NHibernateProfiler.Initialize();
```

23. Now, finally, we will use the fluent API located in the `NHibernate.Loquacious` namespace to configure NHibernate. Add a static method `GetConfiguration` to the `Program` class. The method contains the configuration code, as shown in the following code snippet:

```
private static Configuration GetConfiguration()
{
  var cfg = new Configuration();

  cfg.SessionFactory()
     .Proxy
       .Through<ProxyFactoryFactory>()
       .Mapping
       .UsingDefaultCatalog("sampleCatalog")
       .UsingDefaultSchema("dbo")
       .Integrate
       .LogSqlInConsole()
       .Using<SQLiteDialect>()
       .Connected
       .Through<DriverConnectionProvider>()
       .By<SQLite20Driver>()
       .ByAppConfing("Sample");

  cfg.AddAssembly(typeof(Person).Assembly);

  return cfg;
}
```

## Configuration

**24.** In the preceding code, we first create a new instance of type `NHibernate.Cfg.Configuration`. Then we use the extension method `SessionFactory()` to get access to the fluent configuration API. Next, we define what proxy factory factory NHibernate shall use. Then we define what the default catalog should be and the schema that NHibernate should use.

With the `Integrate` keyword, we start the declaration of the database driver and dialect we are going to use, as well as the connection string we have defined in the `App.config` file.

> Another maybe even more readable, and thus a preferable, way of configuring NHibernate is through lambda functions. The readability of the configuration through the Loquacious fluent API highly depends on the developer indenting the various statements correctly.
>
> So let's rewrite the preceding configuration by using lambdas:
>
> ```
> var cfg = new Configuration();
> cfg.Proxy(p =>
> {
>     p.ProxyFactoryFactory<ProxyFactoryFactory>();
> });
> cfg.Mappings(m =>
> {
>     m.DefaultCatalog = "NH3BeginnersGuide";
>     m.DefaultSchema = "dbo";
> });
> cfg.DataBaseIntegration(db =>
> {
>     db.ConnectionProvider<DriverConnectionProvider>();
>     db.Driver<SqlClientDriver>();
>     db.Dialect<MsSql2008Dialect>();
>     db.ConnectionStringName = "Sample2";
>     db.LogSqlInConsole = true;
> });
> ```
>
> In the preceding code snippet, we have configured NHibernate to access the `NH3BeginnersGuide` database on a SQL Server 2008.

**25.** We will now add code to use for the recreation of the database schema, as shown in the following code snippet:

```
private static void BuildSchema(Configuration configuration)
{
    new SchemaExport(configuration).Execute(true, true, false);
}
```

**26.** Having all the pieces together, we can now use them to recreate the database schema and build a session factory. Add the following code snippet to the `Main` method in the `Program` class:

```
var configuration = GetConfiguration();
BuildSchema(configuration);
var factory = configuration.BuildSessionFactory();
```

**27.** Open a new session in a `using` statement, as shown in the following code snippet:

```
using (var session = factory.OpenSession())
{
}
```

**28.** In the body of the preceding `using` statement, define a `person` object and store it in the database:

```
var person = new Person
{
    Name = new Name
    {
        LastName = "Doe",
        FirstName = "John",
        MiddleName = "A."
    },
    Birthdate = new DateTime(1977, 1, 6),
    SSN = "111-22-3333"
};
session.Save(person);
```

**29.** Moreover, inside the body of the `using` block, flush the session, clear the first level cache, and reload the just saved person from the database, as shown in the following code snippet:

```
session.Flush();
session.Clear();
var fromDb = session.Get<Person>(person.Id);
```

*Configuration*

**30.** At the end of the `Main` method, add code to ask the user to press *Enter* to terminate the application, as shown in the following code snippet:

```
Console.Write("\r\n\nHit enter to exit:");
Console.ReadLine();
```

**31.** Start the NHibernate Profiler.

**32.** Start your application and monitor its output in NHibernate Profiler. You should see something similar to the following screenshot:

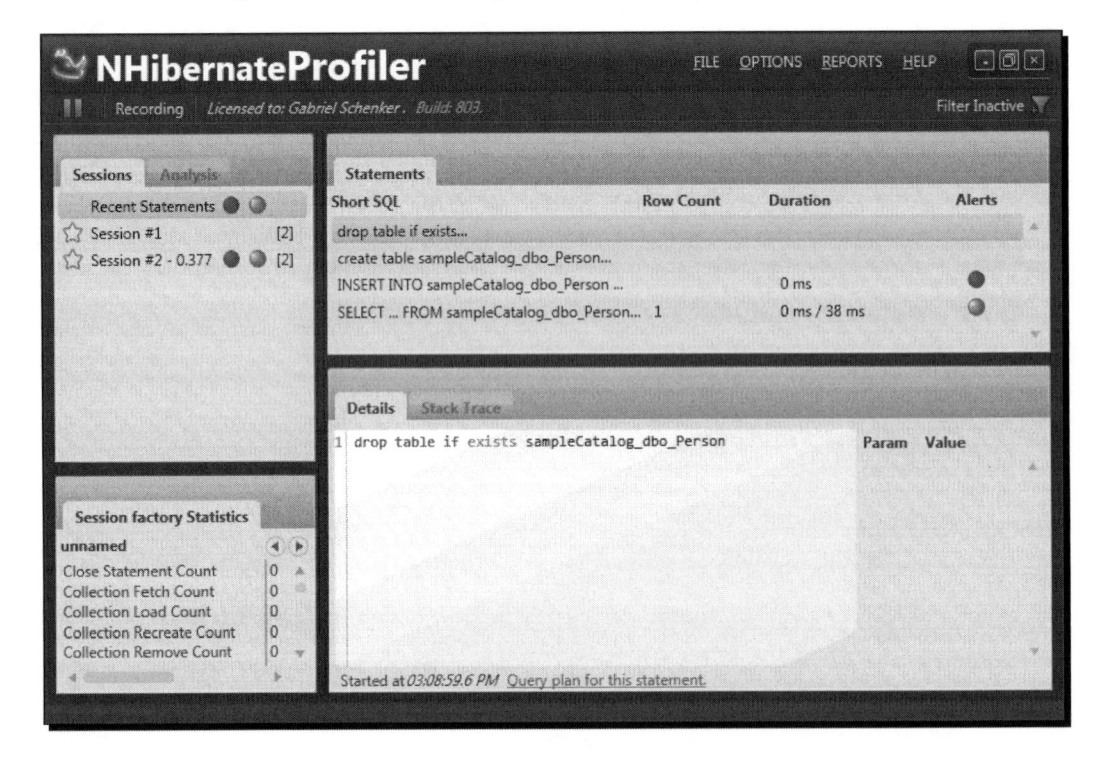

**33.** We see that two sessions were used. The first one was used to recreate the schema, while the second one was used by our code to save and reload the person object. Let's take a closer look at the table generation script, as shown in the following screenshot:

```
create table sampleCatalog_dbo_Person (
    Id          UNIQUEIDENTIFIER not null,
    FirstName   TEXT,
    LastName    TEXT,
    MiddleName  TEXT,
    SSN         TEXT,
    Birthdate   DATETIME,
    primary key ( Id ))
```

**34.** We can see that in the case of the SQLite database, the default catalog and default schema were used as prefixes in the naming of the table. In any other database product, this information would be handled differently.

**35.** Let's have a look at the **INSERT** statement, as shown in the following screenshot:

```
INSERT INTO sampleCatalog_dbo_Person
            (FirstName,
             LastName,
             MiddleName,
             SSN,
             Birthdate,
             Id)
VALUES      ('John' /* @p0 */,
             'Doe' /* @p1 */,
             'A.' /* @p2 */,
             '111-22-3333' /* @p3 */,
             '1977-01-06T00:00:00.00' /* @p4 */,
             '1e61a3d1-ae2d-4cd7-a3d4-9eab00f9aa73' /* @p5 */)
```

| Param | Value |
|---|---|
| @p0 | 'John' |
| @p1 | 'Doe' |
| @p2 | 'A.' |
| @p3 | '111-22-3333' |
| @p4 | '1977-01-06T00:00:00.00' |
| @p5 | '1e61a3d1-ae2d-4cd7-a3d4- |

**36.** And finally, the **SELECT** statement, as shown in the following screenshot:

```
SELECT person0_.Id          as Id0_0_,
       person0_.FirstName   as FirstName0_0_,
       person0_.LastName    as LastName0_0_,
       person0_.MiddleName  as MiddleName0_0_,
       person0_.SSN         as SSN0_0_,
       person0_.Birthdate   as Birthdate0_0_
FROM   sampleCatalog_dbo_Person person0_
WHERE  person0_.Id = '1e61a3d1-ae2d-4cd7-a3d4-9eab00f9aa73' /
```

*Configuration*

## What just happened?

In the preceding exercise, we used the fluent API provided in the Loquacious namespace to configure NHibernate. This API allows us to configure the system in a type-safe and discoverable manner. We have used two slightly different approaches to define the configuration, one that uses a fully-fluent style and the other that uses a mixture of fluent API and lambda expressions for an even improved readability.

We have used XML documents to map our (simple) domain, we have also used NHibernate Profiler to monitor the output of the application. The application writes and reads entities of type product to and from the database.

### Pop quiz

1. Prior to using NHibernate in our applications, we have to configure this framework. Which of the following are elements that are mandatory in our configuration?

    a. Second level cache.

    b. Connection string.

    c. SQL dialect.

    d. ADO.NET batch size.

    e. Default schema.

## Configuring NHibernate with Fluent NHibernate

Throughout the examples in this book, we have used the fluent API of Fluent NHibernate to configure NHibernate. Thus, let's keep this section rather short and there will also be no example included. Suffice to say that any aspect of NHibernate can be configured in a very user-friendly and discoverable way when using this interface.

There is a sample solution in the code that accompanies this book. The sample solution is called `FNHConfigurationSample.sln`. Let's take a look at this sample and experiment with it.

### Have a go hero

Take a copy of the preceding exercise and convert it to use Fluent NHibernate to configure NHibernate and map the domain to the underlying database.

## Convention over configuration

As we have seen, nearly every aspect of NHibernate can be configured, and thus influences the corresponding runtime behavior. With a lot of configuration possibilities and flexibility comes a lot of responsibility. We have to be aware of the fact that with the wrong configuration settings in place, we can severely impact the performance and general behavior of the system.

Having to explicitly define each and every possible configuration setting of a complex framework such as NHibernate can be a tedious and error-prone task. Even if we are very careful and do not create any wrong settings, then it is at least a boring task to do.

Using conventions instead gives us more freedom to concentrate on the important elements of the configuration. As for (nearly) each possible setting, there are meaningful defaults defined. Thus, we only need to explicitly define the exceptions or deviations from the defaults.

It has been proven in real life that complex exception-based systems are much more manageable than systems where everything has to be configured explicitly.

## Summary

In this chapter, we have been diving deep into the details of why and how to configure NHibernate.

Specifically, we covered:

- How to configure NHibernate when using XML configuration files
- Configuring every aspect of NHibernate in code
- Using the new fluent API of NHibernate to configure the system

We also briefly discussed the configuration via Fluent NHibernate and the difference between configuration and convention, and why we should prefer the usage of conventions when configuring our system.

Now that we've learned about configuration, we're ready to send queries to the database – which is the topic of the next chapter.

# 9
# Writing Queries

*Nearly every application collects data, loads of data, and stores it in some database. In the end, users want to get some valuable information out of the data. That's why reports are always the most important part an application provides to the end user. To get those reports on-screen or on paper, we first query the data from the database. Consequently, querying the database can be considered the backbone of our solution.*

In this chapter, we shall:

- Learn how to use LINQ (Language Integrated Queries) to NHibernate to retrieve data from the database
- Query the database using the criteria query API
- Use the original object-oriented SQL dialect called Hibernate Query Language (HQL)
- Discuss entities with properties that can be lazy loaded
- Confront eager loading with lazy loading, as well as looking at how to batch queries

So, let's not lose any time and dive into the topic.

Writing Queries

# How can we get to our data?

When using NHibernate to persist and retrieve data to and from the database, we have various means available to query the data we previously stored in the database. Originally, there was only one kid on the block called HQL. HQL is similar to SQL used by most of the relational databases to query data. However, HQL is more object-oriented and, when writing HQL queries, we do not reference database tables or views. Rather, we reference the entities defined in our domain model. HQL is still a valuable way to query data and is probably the most complete of all APIs. It's reasonable to state that if you can't solve a query problem using HQL, you probably can't solve it using any of the other APIs.

Later on, NHibernate introduced a second API to query data from the database. This API was called the criteria query API. Queries are created in a modular way by defining criteria and combining them. Originally, the definition of such criteria elements needed the use of strings to, for example, reference properties of an entity. With the introduction of NHibernate 3, we have a new and more type-safe variant of the criteria query API. This API is also called **QueryOver**.

NHibernate has offered a third API for some time now. This third API was a LINQ provider for NHibernate. In NHibernate 2.x, LINQ to NHibernate was not part of the core NHibernate and was only available as a contribution project. This LINQ provider was created on top of the Criteria API. Furthermore, the LINQ provider was very incomplete; complex queries were not supported. For the release of NHibernate 3, the LINQ provider has been completely rewritten and is now part of the core NHibernate framework. This new provider is built on top of HQL.

The LINQ to NHibernate provider nowadays is the preferred way to query data and can be used to write nearly all queries. Only in very specific and possibly convoluted scenarios may we want to use HQL.

Finally, let's not forget, there is a fourth way to define queries in NHibernate. We can write queries by using native SQL, though this is a double-edged sword. On the positive side, you can leverage all features of your database product; on the negative side you tightly bind yourself to a specific database product and cannot easily switch to another database, say from Oracle to MS SQL Server or MySQL, and vice versa.

Note that even if you write your queries in native SQL, the result of the query is an entity or a list of entities and not an ADO.NET recordset.

Please also note that most of the code examples discussed in this chapter can be found in the `QuerySamples` solution accompanying this book.

# The LINQ to NHibernate provider

The introduction of LINQ in .NET 3.5 has changed the way developers deal with sets of data. Where in the times prior to LINQ, the `foreach` loop has ruled the game when dealing with sets or lists of data, it is now LINQ that is the king of the game.

LINQ to objects is centered on the interface `IEnumerable<T>` and manipulates sets of objects that live in-memory. LINQ to NHibernate, on the other hand, is a LINQ provider used to access the database and retrieve data in the same way one would access and manipulate in-memory objects. The LINQ to NHibernate driver is centered on the `IQueryable<T>` interface.

## Defining the root of our query

It all starts with a simple extension method for the NHibernate session object or, more specifically, with an extension method to the `ISession` interface. The extension method is generic in T, as shown in the following code snippet:

```
var list = session.Query<Product>();
```

The method `Query<Product>` returns a "collection object" implementing the interface `IQueryable<Product>`.

Note that the preceding query is not executed immediately, but only if we start to access and use the data, probably by enumerating the list, as shown in the following code snippet:

```
var list = session.Query<Product>();
foreach(var product in list)
{
   // do something with product
}
```

This behavior is called **lazy evaluation** and is something we have to get used to.

The preceding LINQ query would generate a SQL statement on the database, equivalent to this:

```
SELECT [list of all mapped fields] FROM PRODUCT
```

The preceding query loads all mapped fields for all records of the database table PRODUCT.

## Limiting the number of records returned

It is an anti-pattern to define queries that can possibly return an unlimited set of records from the database. Just imagine having a query like the following code snippet:

```
var orders = session.Query<Order>();
```

This query returns all orders stored in the `Order` table. What might not be a problem during the first time your application goes into production, can become a real bottleneck over time when more and more orders are defined and added to the system. Modern e-commerce sites, such as Amazon, store millions of orders in their databases over time.

Thus, we should always limit the number of records to a reasonable maximum. This can easily be done by using the `Take` function, as shown in the following code snippet:

```
var orders = session.Query<Order>().Take(200);
```

The preceding query would return a maximum of 200 orders from the database.

## Filtering a set of records

Of course this, in most of the cases, is not what we want. Normally we not only want to load the first 200 or so records from a given table, but rather a well-defined subset of the records. When extracting a subset of records, we call it filtering. The keyword used for filtering is `Where`. LINQ defines a method `Where`, which takes as a parameter, a predicate of `T`. A predicate is a function with one parameter that returns a Boolean, as shown in the following code snippet:

```
Func<T, bool> predicate
```

Let's say we want a list of all discontinued products. The query would then look similar to the following code snippet:

```
var discontinuedProducts = session
    .Query<Product>
    .Where(p => p.Discontinued);
```

In the preceding query, we used a lambda expression `p => p.Discontinued` to define the predicate. This expression means: Given a product `p`, take the content of its property `Discontinued`, and return it. If the return value is `true`, then the corresponding product is included in the resulting filtered set.

Sometimes, people also refer to the act of filtering a set of data as reducing a set of data, and the filter function is called a **reduce function** or operation.

## Mapping a set of records

Returning a set of records including all fields of the source database table is not always what we want. Thus, we need a way to select the subset of fields that we really want. For this purpose, we can use the `Select` function, which again is an extension method for the `IQueryable<T>` interface. The select method takes a mapping function as parameter. The definition of the mapping function is as shown in the following code snippet:

```
Func<TSource, TResult> mapper
```

Let's say, we want to load a list of discontinued products, but with only the `Id` and `Name` of the product mentioned. For this purpose, we first define a class `NameID`, as shown in the following code snippet:

```
public class NameID
{
   public int Id {get; set;}
   public string Name {get; set;}
}
```

Our query will then look as shown in the following code snippet:

```
var discontinuedProducts = session
  .Query<Product>
  .Where(p => p.Discontinued)
  .Select(p => new NameID{Id = p.Id, Name = p.Name});
```

Again, we have defined the mapper function as a lambda expression, as shown in the following code snippet:

```
p => new NameID{Id = p.Id, Name = p.Name}
```

This, put in words, means: take a `Product` object p and return an object of type `NameID`, whose properties, `Id` and `Name`, correspond to the `Id` and `Name` of the product p. So, we have mapped a `Product` entity into a `NameID` object.

## Sorting the resulting set

Filtering and mapping is not always enough. Sometimes, we also want to sort the resulting set of data. The NHibernate LINQ provider can do this for us too. Let's assume that we want to get a list of `Person` objects sorted by their last name, as shown in the following code snippet:

```
var people = session.Query<Person>()
   .OrderBy(p => p.LastName);
```

# Writing Queries

If we also want it to be sorted by their first name, then the query will look similar to the following code snippet:

```
var people = session.Query<Person>()
  .OrderBy(p => p.LastName)
  .ThenBy(p => p.FirstName);
```

Note that we can sort by as many columns as we want by simply appending the `ThenBy` method calls. Also, note that the `OrderBy` and `ThenBy` methods have their counterparts `OrderByDescending` and `ThenByDescending`, which, of course, sort in the reverse order.

```
var people = session.Query<Person>()
  .OrderByDescending(p => p.LastName)
  .ThenByDescending(p => p.FirstName);
```

Thus, the preceding code snippet returns a reversely sorted list of people.

## Grouping records

If we want to count how many people have their last name starting with the same letter, and this also for each letter of the alphabet, then we can do so with the help of a "clever" group function, as shown in the following code snippet:

```
var personsPerLetter = session.Query<Person>()
  .GroupBy(p => p.LastName.SubString(0,1))
  .Select(g => new { Letter = g.Key, Count = g.Count() });
```

This returns a list of anonymous types, which contain the desired result.

The `GroupBy` method returns `IEnumerable<IGrouping<T,V>>`, where `T` represents the type of the value by which we group and `V` represents the type which is grouped. In the preceding sample, `T` would be of type `string` and `V` of type `Person`. The `IGrouping` interface offers us a list of very useful aggregate functions that allow us to count, summarize or average values, as well as get the minimum or maximum of a value, where the value is one of the properties of `V`.

## Forcing a LINQ query to execute immediately

As mentioned earlier, a LINQ query is always lazy executed, that is only when we start to iterate over the result set is the query effectively executed. Sometimes, we do not want this behavior. Instead, we want to force the LINQ driver to immediately execute the query and return the result. We have different ways of doing so. First, we can end a query with a call to the extension methods `ToArray` or `ToList`. These two methods immediately start to enumerate the result set and put the resulting objects into an array or a list of `T`, respectively:

```
var products = session.Query<Product>()
  .Where(p => p.ReorderLevel > p.UnitsOnStock)
  .ToArray()
```

The preceding query loads a list of all products that need to be reordered and puts them into an array.

There is another very useful method that forces a LINQ query to execute immediately. It is the `ToDictionary` function. This function is handy when we want to retrieve a list of entities from the database and store them in a collection using a unique key per instance. Let's give an example, as shown in the following code snippet:

```
var personsPerLetter = session.Query<Person>()
    .GroupBy(p => p.LastName.SubString(0,1))
    .Select(g => new { Letter = g.Key, Count = g.Count() })
    .ToDictionary(x => x.Letter, x => x.Count);
```

The preceding query creates a dictionary with the number of people whose last name starts with a given letter. The key is the starting letter of the last name and the value is the number of persons. As you can imagine, the first lambda expression defines the value we use as the key and the second lambda expression defines the corresponding value in the collection.

## Changing from querying the database to querying in-memory objects

Sometimes, we want to query some data from the database, and then further manipulate this data in creative ways using functionality that is not supported by the underlying database. For these scenarios, we need a way to instruct the LINQ to NHibernate provider that from this point on all manipulations will be done in-memory and NOT on the database. The method we can use for this purpose is the `AsEnumerable` method.

Let's have a look at an example. Let's assume that there is an `Email` entity which contains a lot of records. We now want to generate a filtered list of e-mails, where the filter is actually a regular expression. However, regular expressions are not supported by most database products. Thus, the filtering has to be done in-memory, as shown in the following code snippet:

```
var statusList = session.Query<Email>()
    .Select(e => e.EmailAddress)
    .AsEnumerable()
    .Where(e => SomeFilterFunctionUsingRegExp(e));
```

In the preceding example, the projection happens in the database, but the filtering is done in-memory.

Writing Queries

# Creating a report using LINQ to NHibernate

To get familiar with the usage of the LINQ to NHibernate provider, we want to create a couple of different reports that we'll print on-screen.

In the following example, which is divided into two parts, our domain model is part of astronomy, and more precisely, of star classification. We will use an XML configuration file and XML mapping files to map our domain model.

## Time for action – Preparing the system

To be able to create reports, we first define the domain model, create the mappings and the database schema, and finally, create some data. Let's do this now:

1. Open SQL Server Management Studio and create a new empty database called `LinqToNHibernateSample`.

2. Open Visual Studio and create a new **Console Application** type project. Name the project `LinqToNHibernateSample`.

3. Set **Target Framework** of the project to **.NET Framework 4**.

4. Add references to the `NHibernate` and `NHibernate.ByteCode.Castle` assembly projects located in the `lib` folder.

5. Add a new solution folder called `Schema` to the solution.

6. Add the two files `nhibernate-configuration.xsd` and `nhibernate-mapping.xsd`, located in the `lib` folder to this `Schema` solution folder.

7. Add a class file, `Star.cs`, to the project and add the following code snippet to the file to define the `Star` entity:

    ```
    public class Star
    {
      public virtual Guid Id { get; set; }
      public virtual string Name { get; set; }
      public virtual IList<Planet> Planets { get; set; }
      public virtual StarTypes Class { get; set; }
      public virtual SurfaceColor Color { get; set; }
      public virtual double Mass { get; set; }
    }
    ```

8. Add a class file, `Planet.cs`, to the project and add the following code snippet to the file to define the `Planet` entity:

```
public class Planet
{
  public virtual Guid Id { get; set; }
  public virtual string Name { get; set; }
  public virtual bool IsHabitable { get; set; }
  public virtual Star Sun { get; set; }
}
```

9. Add a class file, `SurfaceColor.cs`, to the solution. Define `enum SurfaceColor` in this file, as shown in the following code snippet:

```
public enum SurfaceColor
{
  Blue, BueToWhite, WhiteToYellow, OrangeToRed, Red
}
```

10. Furthermore, add a class file, `StarTypes.cs`, to the project. Inside this class define `enum StarTypes`, as shown in the following code snippet:

```
public enum StarTypes
{
  O, B, A, F, G, K, M
}
```

11. Add an XML file to the project and name it `Star.hbm.xml`. Make sure that you set `Build Action` of the file to `Embedded Resource`.

12. In this new XML file, define the mapping for the `Star` entity, as shown in the following code snippet:

```
<?xml version="1.0" encoding="utf-8" ?>
<hibernate-mapping xmlns="urn:nhibernate-mapping-2.2"
  assembly="LinqToNHibernateSample"
  namespace="LinqToNHibernateSample">
  <class name="Star">
    <id name="Id">
      <generator class="guid.comb"/>
    </id>
    <property name="Name"/>
    <property name="Mass"/>
    <property name="Class" type="StarTypes"/>
    <property name="Color" type="SurfaceColor"/>
    <bag name="Planets" inverse="true"
      cascade="all-delete-orphan">
```

```xml
            <key column="StarId" />
            <one-to-many class="Planet"/>
        </bag>
    </class>
</hibernate-mapping>
```

13. Note how the two `enum` type properties, `Color` and `Class`, of the `Star` entity are mapped. We use the `type` attribute to specify that NHibernate shall map these properties as database columns of type `int` (the base type of an `enum` is `int`). Also, note how the list of planets of a star is mapped. Specifically, review the `inverse` and `cascade` attributes, as well as the type of collection we use. Furthermore, note that we are using the `Guid` generator, which is optimized for usage in the database.

14. Add another XML file `Planet.hbm.xml` to the project and also set its `Build Action` to `Embedded Resource`.

15. Add the following code snippet to the file to map the `Planet` entity:
    ```xml
    <?xml version="1.0" encoding="utf-8" ?>
    <hibernate-mapping xmlns="urn:nhibernate-mapping-2.2"
      assembly="LinqToNHibernateSample"
      namespace="LinqToNHibernateSample">

      <class name="Planet">
        <id name="Id">
          <generator class="guid.comb"/>
        </id>
        <property name="Name"/>
        <property name="IsHabitable"/>
        <many-to-one name="Sun" class="Star" column="StarId"/>
      </class>
    </hibernate-mapping>
    ```

16. Note how we use the `column` attribute in the `many-to-one` tag to match the `key` definition of `bag` in the `Star.hbm.xml` mapping file.

17. Add a new XML file to the project. Name the file `hibernate.cfg.xml`. This file will contain the configuration information, as shown in the following code snippet:
    ```xml
    <?xml version="1.0" encoding="utf-8" ?>
    <hibernate-configuration xmlns="urn:nhibernate-configuration-2.2">
      <session-factory name="Sample">
        <property name="connection.provider">
          NHibernate.Connection.DriverConnectionProvider
        </property>
        <property name="connection.driver_class">
    ```

```
      NHibernate.Driver.SqlClientDriver
    </property>
    <property name="dialect">
      NHibernate.Dialect.MsSql2008Dialect
    </property>
    <property name="connection.connection_string">
      server=.\SQLEXPRESS;database=LinqToNHibernateSample;
        integrated security=true
    </property>
    <property name="proxyfactory.factory_class">
      NHibernate.ByteCode.Castle.ProxyFactoryFactory,
      NHibernate.ByteCode.Castle
    </property>
  </session-factory>
</hibernate-configuration>
```

**18.** Set the `Copy to Output Directory` property of the preceding file to `Copy always`.

**19.** To the `Main` method of the `Program` class, add code to instantiate a NHibernate `Configuration` object, as shown in the following code snippet:

```
var configuration = new Configuration();
```

**20.** Call the method `Configure` of the configuration object. This will search for a file called `hibernate.cfg.xml` in the current directory and, if found, take all configuration values out of it, as shown in the following code snippet:

```
configuration.Configure();
```

**21.** Add code to tell the configuration object to parse the assembly, where the entity `Star` is defined for occurrences of HBM files, and use them to map the domain, as shown in the following code snippet:

```
configuration.AddAssembly(typeof(Star).Assembly);
```

**22.** Add code to (re) create the database schema, as shown in the following code snippet:

```
new SchemaExport(configuration).Execute(true, true, false);
```

**23.** Use the configuration object to create a session factory, as shown in the following code snippet:

```
var factory = configuration.BuildSessionFactory();
```

*Writing Queries*

**24.** Add a call to the method `CreateData`, which will contain the code to create some precanned data and store it in the database. Pass the session factory as the parameter, as shown in the following code snippet:

```
CreateData(factory);
```

**25.** Once we have data available in the database, we want to use some LINQ queries to create on-screen reports. Thus, add a call to a reporting method, as shown in the following code snippet:

```
QueryData(factory);
```

**26.** As the last two lines of the `Main` method, add the following code snippet:

```
Console.Write("\r\n\nHit enter to exit:");
Console.ReadLine();
```

**27.** Now, implement the `CreateData` method. This method creates two stars with planets, our Sun, and a star called `61 Virginis`, which has three planets. Some more stars, having no known planets, are created as well. For each star, we define its name, relative mass (our sun has mass equal to 1), the surface color, and the classification. All stars, including their planets, are then stored in the database, as shown in the following code snippet:

```
private static void CreateData(ISessionFactory factory)
{
  var sun = new Star {Name = "Sun", Mass = 1, Class = StarTypes.G,
    Color = SurfaceColor.WhiteToYellow};
  var planets = new List<Planet>
  {
    new Planet{Name = "Merkur", IsHabitable = false, Sun = sun},
    new Planet{Name = "Venus", IsHabitable = false, Sun = sun},
    // please consult the sample code for full list of planets
  };
  sun.Planets = planets;

  var virginis61 = new Star { Name = "61 Virginis", Mass = 0.95,
    Class = StarTypes.G,
    Color = SurfaceColor.WhiteToYellow };
  var planets2 = new List<Planet>
  {
    new Planet{Name = "Planet 1", IsHabitable = false,
    Sun = virginis61},
    new Planet{Name = "Planet 2", IsHabitable = true,
    Sun = virginis61},
    new Planet{Name = "Planet 3", IsHabitable = false,
```

```
      Sun = virginis61},
};
virginis61.Planets = planets2;

var stars = new List<Star>
{
  sun, virginis61,
  new Star{Name = "10 Lacertra", Mass = 60,
  Class = StarTypes.O, Color = SurfaceColor.Blue},
  new Star{Name = "Spica", Mass = 18,
  Class = StarTypes.B, Color = SurfaceColor.Blue},
  // please consult the sample code for full list of stars
};

using (var session = factory.OpenSession())
using (var tx = session.BeginTransaction())
{
  foreach (var star in stars)
  {
    session.Save(star);
  }
  tx.Commit();
}
}
```

## What just happened?

In the preceding exercise, we prepared our system such that we will be able to create some reports using LINQ to NHibernate. We first defined a domain, and then we added XML mapping files to the project to map the domain to the underlying database. Then we configured NHibernate, created some data, and used NHibernate to persist the data to the database.

## Time for action – Creating the reports

Now that we have prepared the system, we are ready to generate some reports based on the data just persisted in the database using the LINQ to NHibernate provider.

1.  First, implement the method `QueryData` in the `Program` class, as shown in the following code snippet:

    ```
    private static void QueryData(ISessionFactory factory)
    {
      using (var session = factory.OpenSession())
    ```

## Writing Queries

```
        using (var tx = session.BeginTransaction())
        {
          PrintListOfStars(session);
          PrintListOfBigBlueStars(session);
          PrintSumOfStarMassPerClass(session);
          PrintListOfHabitablePlanets(session);
          tx.Commit();
        }
      }
```

2. Note how this method creates a session, a transaction, and, inside the transaction, calls four reporting methods, passing the session object to each of them.

3. Let's implement the first of these methods, which shall print a list of all stars ordered by their respective names on-screen, as shown in the following code snippet:

```
    private static void PrintListOfStars(ISession session)
    {
      Console.WriteLine("\r\n\nList of stars ----------------\r\n");

      var stars = session.Query<Star>()
        .OrderBy(s => s.Name);

      foreach (var star in stars)
      {
        Console.WriteLine("{0} ({1}, {2})",
          star.Name, star.Class, star.Color);
      }
    }
```

4. Note how, in the preceding code snippet, we use the `Query` extension method to get `IQueryable<Star>`, which we can then sort by using the `OrderBy` method. Furthermore, note that the query is only executed the moment we start iterating over it (in the `foreach` loop).

5. Next, we want to try filtering and ordering by multiple properties, even in the reverse order. The goal is to print on-screen a list of all stars with a blue surface color and a relative mass greater than 15:

```
    private static void PrintListOfBigBlueStars(ISession session)
    {
      Console.WriteLine("\r\n\nList of big blue stars -------\r\n");

      var stars = session.Query<Star>()
        .Where(s => s.Color == SurfaceColor.Blue && s.Mass > 15)
        .OrderByDescending(s => s.Mass)
        .ThenBy(s => s.Name);
```

```
   foreach (var star in stars)
   {
     Console.WriteLine("{0} ({1}, {2}, Mass={3})",
       star.Name, star.Class, star.Color, star.Mass);
   }
}
```

6.  In the next reporting method, we want to group our list of stars and use an aggregate function (Sum) to calculate the total relative mass of the stars stored in the database, grouped by their class. We then want to print the class and the total relative mass on-screen, as shown in the following code snippet:

    ```
    private static void PrintSumOfStarMassPerClass(ISession session)
    {
       Console.WriteLine("\r\n\nSum of masses per class -------\r\n");

       var starMasses = session.Query<Star>()
         .GroupBy(s => s.Class)
         .Select(g => new {Class = g.Key,
           TotalMass = g.Sum(s => s.Mass)});

       foreach (var mass in starMasses)
       {
         Console.WriteLine("Class={0}, Total Mass={1}",
           mass.Class, mass.TotalMass);
       }
    }
    ```

7.  Lastly, we implement a method that prints a list of habitable planets sorted by the Sun and by the planet name, as shown in the following code snippet:

    ```
    private static void PrintListOfHabitablePlanets(ISession session)
    {
       Console.WriteLine("\r\n\nList of habitable planets------\r\n");

        var planets = session.Query<Planet>()
         .Where(p => p.IsHabitable)
         .OrderBy(p => p.Sun.Name)
         .ThenBy(p => p.Name);

       foreach (var planet in planets)
       {
         Console.WriteLine("Star='{0}', Planet='{1}'",
           planet.Sun.Name, planet.Name);
       }
    }
    ```

8.  Note how we query a list of planets (and not suns) in the preceding code snippet.

## What just happened?

We used the LINQ to NHibernate provider to define various queries, which include filtering, sorting, grouping, and aggregating. We used the resulting datasets to print an on-screen report.

# Criteria queries

NHibernate defines an alternative API that we can use to query our data from the database. These kinds of queries are called criteria queries. The queries are created by composing a set of criteria. Different types of criteria exist for filtering, sorting, projecting (or mapping), as well as grouping sets of records. In the past, it was only possible to define queries using magic strings. With the introduction of NHibernate 3, it is also possible to define strongly-typed criteria queries.

## Untyped criteria queries

In this section, we shall see how we can create criteria queries that result in the same set of records as in the examples used when we discussed the LINQ to NHibernate provider.

All of it starts by defining the root of our criteria query, as shown in the following code snippet:

```
var query = session.CreateCriteria<Product>();
```

The method `CreateCriteria` returns an object that implements the interface `ICriteria`. If we want to get a list of all products, then we need to use the method `List<T>` of the interface `ICriteria`, as shown in the following code snippet:

```
var products = session.CreateCriteria<Product>().List<Product>();
```

The method `List<Product>()` returns `IList<Product>`. Contrary to LINQ to NHibernate, the query is executed immediately when the `List` method is called.

There is also a non-generic `List` method defined on the `ICriteria` interface. This method returns an object of type `IList`. The individual elements of this list are arrays of objects, that is, `object[]`. The number of objects and their order depends on the number of fields and their respective orders in the query.

If we want to limit the number of records to be returned by the query, then we can use the `SetMaxResults` function. To get the first ten products from the database, use this query, as shown in the following code snippet:

```
var first10Products = session.CreateCriteria<Product>()
    .SetMaxResults(10)
    .List<Product>();
```

Now, let's get a filtered list of products, say only all discontinued products, as shown in the following code snippet:

```
var discontinuedProducts = session.CreateCriteria<Product>()
  .Add(Restrictions.Eq("Discontinued", true))
  .List<Product>();
```

Please note the usage of a magic string to define the property name, which we want to use for filtering in the preceding query.

Filtering is done by adding one to many restriction criteria to the query. Thus, if we want to get a list of all active products that need to be reordered, we would use the following code snippet:

```
var discontinuedProducts = session.CreateCriteria<Product>()
  .Add(Restrictions.Eq("Discontinued", false))
  .Add(Restrictions.GeProperty("ReorderLevel", "UnitsOnStock"))
  .List<Product>();
```

Although this is certainly very flexible, it is also very error prone when compared to the usage of LINQ to NHibernate. Imagine you make a typo when defining the restrictions in the preceding query and name the property `UnitSonStock` instead of `UnitsOnStock`. You would only realize this error during runtime.

The static class `Restrictions` has many more handy functions for defining filter criteria of all kinds.

Now, let's discuss how we can map a set of records. This is also called a projection. We are projecting one type and receive another type as a result of the operation. Unfortunately, projections using the Criteria API are not as easy as when using LINQ. We have to first define what fields we want to project. Then we additionally define a transformer, which takes those values and puts them into the desired target type, as shown in the following code snippet:

```
var productsLookup = session.CreateCriteria<Product>()
  .SetProjection(Projections.ProjectionList()
    .Add(Projections.Property("Id"))
    .Add(Projections.Property("Name"))
  )
  .SetResultTransformer(
    new AliasToBeanResultTransformer(typeof (NameID)))
  .List<NameID>();
```

## Writing Queries

In the preceding example, we used the `SetProjection` method to define the mapping. We selected the properties `Id` and `Name` of the product and we want to put them into an object of type `NameID`. The class `NameID` is defined as shown in the following code snippet:

```
public class NameID
{
   public int Id { get; set; }
   public string Name { get; set; }
}
```

We are using `AliasToBeanResultTransformer` defined by NHibernate to transform the results of the query into a list of `NameID` objects. Note that the names of the properties in the target object must match the names of the projected properties. If this is not the case, then the `Add` method of the `ProjectionList` has an overload where we can define an alias. The alias has to correspond with the name in the target object.

> NHibernate 3 brings some slight improvements to the Criteria API. In most cases, the usage of magic strings can now be avoided and lambda expressions can be used to define the properties of interest in a type-safe way. Instead of defining a projection like this `Projections.Property("Name")`, we can now use `Projections.Property<Product>(p => p.Name)`.

Sorting a result set is straightforward. We just add another criterion to our query, as shown in the following code snippet:

```
var sortedProducts = session.CreateCriteria<Product>()
   .AddOrder(Order.Asc("Name"))
   .List<Product>();
```

To define a list of products that is sorted in reverse order, we just use the `Desc` method of the static `Order` class. We can sort by as many properties as we want. Just add another sort criterion for each additional field to the query.

Grouping, which was a separate function in the LINQ provider, is part of the projection in the criteria query API. Assuming we want to group our products by the property `Category` and count the number of rows per category, we would use the following query:

```
var productsGrouped = session.CreateCriteria<Product>()
   .SetProjection(Projections.ProjectionList()
     .Add(Projections.GroupProperty("Category"))
     .Add(Projections.RowCount(), "Num")
   )
   .List();
```

The criteria API is best suited if we have to dynamically generate queries based on, say, user selections. As an example, consider an application which allows a user to flexibly select filter criterions.

Other than that, a LINQ or a HQL query are more readable, and thus more maintainable on the long run.

## Strongly-typed criteria queries

A new feature of NHibernate 3 is the ability to define criteria queries that do not use "magic" strings but are strongly-typed. For this purpose, the method `QueryOver<T>` has been added to the `ISession` interface. Here, the generic parameter `T` represents the entity type we want to query.

When using the `QueryOver` API, we specify the root of our queries, as shown in the following code snippet:

```
var query = session.QueryOver<Product>();
```

To simply get a list of all products in the database, use this query, as shown in the following code snippet:

```
var products = session.QueryOver<Product>().List();
```

Here, in contradiction to the Criteria API, we do not have to specify the return type in the list as it is already declared at the `QueryOver` level.

If we want to limit the number of records returned by a query, then we can use the `Take` method. Our query then looks very similar to the one we used when discussing LINQ to NHibernate, as shown in the following code snippet:

```
var first10Products = session.QueryOver<Product>()
  .Take(10)
  .List();
```

The API allows us also to filter the result set by using the familiar `Where` method. To get a list of all discontinued products use the following code snippet:

```
var discontinuedProducts = session.QueryOver<Product>()
  .Where(p => p.Discontinued)
  .List();
```

We can, of course, combine multiple filters to, for example, get a list of all active products that need to be reordered, as shown in the following code snippet:

```
var productsToReorder = session.QueryOver<Product>()
  .Where(p => p.Discontinued == false)
  .Where(p => p.ReorderLevel >= p.UnitsOnStock)
  .List();
```

# Writing Queries

Instead of using multiple `Where` statements, we can also use a single one and combine the individual predicates into one, using Boolean operators:

```
var productsToReorder = session.QueryOver<Product>()
    .Where(p => p.Discontinued == false &&
      p.ReorderLevel >= p.UnitsOnStock)
    .List();
```

So far, so good! If you are familiar with LINQ, then the preceding expressions should not be of any surprise to you.

Sorting the results is again very similar to LINQ when using the `QueryOver` API. The only difference is that LINQ defines `OrderBy` and `OrderByDescending` to define ascending and descending ordering, while the `QueryOver` API only defines an `OrderBy` method. However, this method has to be combined with a call to either `Asc` or `Desc`. When sorting by multiple fields, both the API have a `ThenBy` (and `ThenByDescending` for LINQ) method.

To get a list of products sorted by `Name` ascending and by `UnitPrice` descending, we use the following code snippet:

```
var sortedProducts = session.QueryOver<Product>()
    .OrderBy(p => p.Name).Asc
    .ThenBy(p => p.UnitPrice).Desc
    .List();
```

As it was in the Criteria API, it is also the hardest part to define a mapping using the QueryOver API. If I only want to retrieve `Id` and `Name` of all products and fill them into an array of `NameID` objects, then it can be done using the following code snippet:

```
var productsLookup = session.QueryOver<Product>()
    .Select(p => p.Id, p => p.Name)
    .TransformUsing(Transformers.AliasToBean<NameID>())
    .List<NameID>();
```

Note how we use the `Select` method to define the list of properties we want to select (or project). Each property is defined by a lambda expression, for example, `p => p.Name` to select the `Name` property. Then, we use the `TransformUsing` method to declare how NHibernate should transform the result of the projection. In the preceding case, we selected the `AliasToBean` transformer declaring `NameID` as the target type of the transformation. There are other transformers defined by NHibernate and you can even implement your own ones. The static class `Transformers` gives us a list of available transformers.

Finally, we end the query with a call to the `List<NameID>` method. We declare the target type here; otherwise, NHibernate would assume that the target type is still `Product`, as declared when calling the `QueryOver` method.

> A transformer used by a criteria query or a `QueryOver` query must implement the interface `IResultTransformer`. This interface has two methods that allow transformations on the row level, as well as transformations of the result set as a whole.
>
> When looking at the transformation at the row level, the transformer has a simple task to do; namely, to transform a tuple of objects (`object[] tuple`) to whatever target type we want. The tuple contains the value of the fields we declared in the projection.
>
> In the case where we select the properties `Id` and `Name` of the `Product` entity, we would have to convert a tuple with two elements (`object[2] tuple`) to a target type `NameID` by mapping `tuple[0]` to the property `Id` of the `NameID` object and `tuple[1]` to the `Name` property of the `NameID` object.

When transforming data by using projections, we can also group the result sets and apply aggregate functions to the fields. To group all products by `Category` and then count the number of rows for each category, as well as evaluate the average unit price per category, and the sum of units on stock per category, we would have the following query:

```
var productsGrouped = session.QueryOver<Product>()
   .Select(Projections.Group<Product>(p => p.Category),
      Projections.Avg<Product>(p => p.UnitPrice),
      Projections.Sum<Product>(p => p.UnitsOnStock),
      Projections.RowCount())
   .List<object[]>();
```

To keep things simple, we didn't define a transformation in the preceding example and just let NHibernate return the rows of the result set as tuples of objects.

## Time for action – Using QueryOver to retrieve data

In this example, we want to add some products to the database and use the `QueryOver` method to retrieve a special selection of these products.

We want to use the Loquacious configuration and `ConfOrm` mapping in this example to refresh our memory a bit.

1. Open SQL Server Management Studio and log in to your local SQL Server Express edition.
2. Create a new database called `QueryOverSample`.
3. Open Visual Studio and create a new project. Use the **Console Application** template and name the project `QueryOverSample`.

## Writing Queries

4. Add references to the `NHibernate.dll`, `NHibernate.ByteCode.Castle.dll`, and `ConfOrm.dll` assemblies, located in the `lib` folder of the project.

5. Add a new class to the project. Name it `Category.cs`.

6. Add the following code snippet to define a `Category` entity for this new class file:

   ```
   using System;

   namespace QueryOverSample
   {
     public class Category
     {
       public virtual Guid Id { get; set; }
       public virtual string Name { get; set; }
       public virtual string Description { get; set; }
     }
   }
   ```

7. Add a new class file to the project. Name it `Product.cs`.

8. Add the following code snippet to the file to define a `Product` entity:

   ```
   using System;

   namespace QueryOverSample
   {
     public class Product
     {
       public virtual Guid Id { get; set; }
       public virtual string Name { get; set; }
       public virtual Category Category { get; set; }
       public virtual decimal UnitPrice { get; set; }
       public virtual bool Discontinued { get; set; }
       public virtual int ReorderLevel { get; set; }
       public virtual int UnitsOnStock { get; set; }
     }
   }
   ```

9. To the `Program` class, add a static method to create an NHibernate `Configuration` object using Loquacious configuration and pointing to the local SQL Server Express edition database named `QueryOverSample`:

   ```
   private static Configuration GetConfiguration()
   {
     var cfg = new Configuration();
   ```

```
cfg.SessionFactory()
  .Proxy
  .Through<ProxyFactoryFactory>()
  .Integrate
  .LogSqlInConsole()
  .Using<MsSql2008Dialect>()
  .Connected
  .Through<DriverConnectionProvider>()
  .By<SqlClientDriver>()
  .Using(new SqlConnectionStringBuilder
  {
    DataSource = @".\SQLEXPRESS",
    InitialCatalog = "QueryOverSample",
    IntegratedSecurity = true
  });
  return cfg;
}
```

> If the preceding code snippet looks strange to you, then please have a look at *Chapter 8, Configuration*, and re-read the section which introduces configuration via the Fluent API defined in NHibernate's Loquacious namespace.

10. Now we want to add a method to the `Program` class to define the mappings for our domain. To do this, we use mapping by the convention provided by `ConfOrm`, as shown in the following code snippet:

```
private static void AddMappings(Configuration configuration)
{
  var types = new[] {typeof (Category), typeof (Product)};

  var orm = new ObjectRelationalMapper();
  orm.TablePerClass(types);

  var mapper = new Mapper(orm);
  var hbmMappings = mapper.CompileMappingFor(types);
  configuration.AddDeserializedMapping(hbmMappings, "MyDomain");
}
```

> You can find more details about how to use convention-based mappings using `ConfOrm` in *Chapter 5, Mapping the Model to the Database*, of this book.

## Writing Queries

11. Add a static method to the `Program` class to (re) create the database schema given an NHibernate configuration object, as shown in the following code snippet:

    ```
    private static void BuildSchema(Configuration configuration)
    {
      new SchemaExport(configuration).Execute(true, true, false);
    }
    ```

12. Now add another static method to the `Program` class, which will create our data, as shown in the following code snippet:

    ```
    private static void AddProductsAndCategories(
      ISessionFactory sessionFactory)
    {
    }
    ```

13. Add code to this method, which creates five categories with names `Category 1`, `Category2`, and so on. Each category will have a random number of 0 to 9 associated products. Each product has a random value for the properties `UnitPrice`, `UnitsOnStock`, and `ReorderLevel`. The product is set as discontinued if a random number between 0 and 10 is greater than 8 (that is rather rare), as shown in the following code snippet:

    ```
    var categories = new List<Category>();
    var products = new List<Product>();
    var random = new Random((int) DateTime.Now.Ticks);
    for (var i = 1; i <= 5; i++)
    {
      var category = new Category
      {
        Name = string.Format("Category {0}", i)
      };
      categories.Add(category);
      var count = random.Next(10);
      for (var j = 1; j <= count; j++)
      {
        var product = new Product
        {
          Name = string.Format("Product {0}", i*10+j),
          Category = category,
          UnitPrice = (decimal)random.NextDouble() * 10m,
          Discontinued = random.Next(10) > 8,
          UnitsOnStock = random.Next(100),
          ReorderLevel = random.Next(20)
        };
        products.Add(product);
      }
    }
    ```

*Chapter 9*

14. After adding the code snippet which defines the categories and products, add code to save the entities to the database using a session object and a transaction, as shown in the following code snippet:

    ```
    using (var session = sessionFactory.OpenSession())
    using (var tx = session.BeginTransaction())
    {
      foreach (var category in categories)
      {
        session.Save(category);
        foreach (var product in products)
        {
          session.Save(product);
        }
      }
      tx.Commit();
    }
    ```

15. Now, the interesting part, we want to use the `QueryOver` method of the `ISession` interface to create some reports of the data just generated and saved in the database.

16. Create a method that creates a session and a transaction, and will be used to call all report creation methods, as shown in the following code snippet:

    ```
    private static void PrintReports(ISessionFactory sessionFactory)
    {
      Console.WriteLine();
      Console.WriteLine("--------------------");
      Console.WriteLine("|  Prining Reports  |");
      Console.WriteLine("--------------------");
      using (var session = sessionFactory.OpenSession())
      using (var tx = session.BeginTransaction())
      {
        // here we will call the reporting methods…
        tx.Commit();
      }
    }
    ```

# Writing Queries

17. Add a static field for the session factory to the `Program` class, as shown in the following code snippet:

    ```
    private static ISessionFactory sessionFactory;
    ```

18. Add the following code to the `Main` method of the `Program` class to create the configuration, add the mappings, recreate the database schema, create a session factory, create and store category and product entities in the database, and finally, call the `PrintReports` method, as shown in the following code snippet:

    ```
    var configuration = GetConfiguration();
    AddMappings(configuration);
    BuildSchema(configuration);
    sessionFactory = configuration.BuildSessionFactory();
    AddProductsAndCategories(sessionFactory);

    PrintReports(sessionFactory);

    Console.Write("\r\n\nHit enter to exit:");
    Console.ReadLine();
    ```

19. As a first report, we want to retrieve a list of all categories sorted by their name in an ascending order. Having this list, we want to print the name of those reports on the screen, as shown in the following code snippet:

    ```
    private static void PrintListOfCategories(ISession session)
    {
      Console.WriteLine("\r\nList of categories:\r\n");
      var categories = session.QueryOver<Category>()
        .OrderBy(c => c.Name).Asc
        .List();
      foreach(var category in categories)
      {
        Console.WriteLine("Category: {0}", category.Name);
      }
    }
    ```

20. Add the following code snippet just before the `tx.Commit();` statement in the `PrintReports` method to call the preceding reporting method:

    ```
    PrintListOfCategories(session);
    ```

*Chapter 9*

**21.** Run the application. You should see something similar to the following screenshot:

```
| Prining Reports |

List of categories:

NHibernate: SELECT this_.Id as Id0_0_, this_.Name as Name0_0_, this_.Description
 as Descript3_0_0_ FROM Category this_ ORDER BY this_.Name asc
Category: Category 1
Category: Category 2
Category: Category 3
Category: Category 4
Category: Category 5

Hit enter to exit:
```

**22.** Review the query that NHibernate sent to the database server to retrieve the list of categories.

**23.** Add another reporting method that retrieves the list of all products that are not discontinued and that need to be reordered as the respective reorder level is equal or higher than the number of units on stock. The list of products shall be ordered by category name, and then by product name, as shown in the following code snippet:

```
private static void PrintProductsToReorder(ISession session)
{
  Console.WriteLine("\r\nList of products to reorder:\r\n");
  Product productAlias = null;
  Category categoryAlias = null;

  var products = session.QueryOver<Product>(() => productAlias)
    .JoinAlias(() => productAlias.Category, () => categoryAlias)
    .Where(() => productAlias.Discontinued == false)
    .Where(() => productAlias.ReorderLevel >=
      productAlias.UnitsOnStock)
    .OrderBy(() => categoryAlias.Name).Asc
    .ThenBy(() => productAlias.Name).Asc
    .List();

  Console.WriteLine();
  foreach (var product in products)
  {
    Console.WriteLine(
    "Category: {0}, Product: {1} (Units on stock: {2})",
    product.Category.Name, product.Name,
    product.UnitsOnStock);
  }
}
```

Writing Queries

24. Add code to the `PrintReports` method to call the preceding method.

25. Run the application and you should see something similar to the following screenshot (note that due to the usage of random numbers, the number of products listed can vary with each run):

```
List of products to reorder:

NHibernate: SELECT this_.Id as Id1_1_, this_.Name as Name1_1_, this_.Category as
  Category1_1_, this_.UnitPrice as UnitPrice1_1_, this_.Discontinued as Disconti5
  _1_1_, this_.ReorderLevel as ReorderL6_1_1_, this_.UnitsOnStock as UnitsOnS7_1_1
  _, categoryal1_.Id as Id0_0_, categoryal1_.Name as Name0_0_, categoryal1_.Descri
  ption as Descript3_0_0_ FROM Product this_ inner join Category categoryal1_ on t
  his_.Category=categoryal1_.Id WHERE this_.Discontinued = @p0 and this_.ReorderLe
  vel >= this_.UnitsOnStock ORDER BY categoryal1_.Name asc, this_.Name asc;@p0 = F
  alse [Type: Boolean (0)]

Category: Category 3, Product: Product 33 (Units on stock: 10)
Category: Category 3, Product: Product 35 (Units on stock: 7)
Category: Category 4, Product: Product 46 (Units on stock: 16)
Category: Category 5, Product: Product 54 (Units on stock: 7)

Hit enter to exit:
```

26. Again, review the SQL statement created by NHibernate to retrieve the list of products to reorder.

## What just happened?

We created a simple domain and mapped it, with the aid of ConfORM, to the underlying database. We then added some data to the database and, finally, we used the QueryOver API to create some basic reports whose results we have output to the console.

## Have a go hero

Define yet another reporting method, which returns the top ten (active) products with the highest number of units in stock. The list must be sorted by the number of units in stock. For each product, print the category name, product name, and units in stock on the screen.

## Hibernate Query Language

This is the original query language of NHibernate. It strongly resembles SQL, but is more object-oriented than its counterpart. HQL queries are defined as strings, and thus are not type-safe. On the other hand, and on a positive note, HQL gives support to dynamic entities for which a class does not exist at all.

Parameters in HQL queries are defined by prefixing a name with a colon, for example : name.

In this section, we will see how to write HQL queries that are equivalent to the queries introduced in the section *The LINQ to NHibernate provider*. Each HQL query is created by calling the `CreateQuery` method of the `ISession` interface and passing the HQL string as a parameter. To query a list of all products, one would write the following code snippet:

```
var products = session.CreateQuery("from Product p").List<Product>();
```

Note the familiar `List<T>` method we already encountered when discussing the criteria query API.

To limit the number of records returned from a query, we can use the method `SetMaxResults`. To skip a number of records, we can use the `SetFirstResult` method:

```
var first10Products = session.CreateQuery("from Product p")
   .SetFirstResult(10)
   .SetMaxResults(10)
   .List<Product>();
```

> Starting with NHibernate 3.2, we can write the preceding query as `"from Product skip 10 take 10"`, which is a more concise way than when using the `SetFirstResult` and `SetMaxResult` methods.

We can filter the list of products and, say, retrieve all discontinued products only, as shown in the following code snippet:

```
var discontinuedProducts = session
  .CreateQuery("from Product p where p.Discontinued")
  .List<Product>();
```

We can define filters using the parameters, as shown in the following code snippet:

```
var hql = "from Product p" +
  " where p.Category = :category" +
  " and p.UnitPrice <= :unitPrice";
var cheapFruits = session
   .CreateQuery(hql)
   .SetString("category", "Fruits")
   .SetDecimal("unitPrice", 1.0m)
   .List<Product>();
```

Note in the preceding code snippet how we use the `SetString` and `SetDecimal` methods to define the values of the corresponding parameters. The first parameter of the `SetString` and `SetDecimal` method is the name of the parameter without the leading colon.

## Writing Queries

If we want to project (or map) a list of entities, then we can use result transformers as explained in detail in the section about the criteria query API, as shown in the following code snippet:

```
var productsLookup = session
    .CreateQuery("select Id as Id, Name as Name from Product")
    .SetResultTransformer(Transformers.AliasToBean<NameID>())
    .List<NameID>();
```

Note that in order to work, you absolutely have to define an alias for each column, even if the alias is the same as the column in the select statement.

Sorting is achieved by using the `order by` keyword, and we can sort by multiple columns as well in the ascending and descending order, as shown in the following code snippet:

```
var sortedProducts = session
    .CreateQuery("from Product p order by p.Name, p.UnitPrice desc")
    .List<Product>();
```

If we want to group a set of records by one or more fields, then we can do so by using the `group by` keywords. All fields that are occurring in the select list and are not part of the grouping must have an aggregate function applied, as shown in the following code snippet:

```
var productsGrouped = session
    .CreateQuery("select p.Category as Category," +
    "          count(*) as Count," +
    "          avg(p.UnitPrice) as AveragePrice" +
    " from    Product p" +
    " group by p.Category")
    .List();
```

In the preceding example, we group by `Category` and we return `Category`, the count of records per category, as well as the average unit price per category.

Due to the lack of a transformation, the result set that is returned is `IList`. Each list item is an array of objects (`object[]`).

We can define a transformation and use some LINQ to objects "magic" to make the returned data set more "developer-friendly":

```
var productsGrouped = session
    .CreateQuery("select p.Category as Category," +
    "          count(*) as Count," +
    "          avg(p.UnitPrice) as AveragePrice" +
    " from    Product p" +
    " group by p.Category")
    .SetResultTransformer(Transformers.AliasToEntityMap)
    .List<IDictionary>()
    .Select(r => new
```

```
{
  Category = r["Category"],
  Count = r["Count"],
  AveragePrice = r["AveragePrice"],
});
```

The `AliasToEntityMap` transformer converts the type of each row of the result set from `object[]` to `IDictionary`, where the keys correspond to the column alias of the query. With the final (LINQ) `Select` statement, we map `IDictionary` to an anonymous type with the fields `Category`, `Count`, and `AveragePrice`.

# Lazy loading properties

A new feature of NHibernate 3 is the ability to lazy load specific properties of an entity. This feature comes in handy whenever your entity has a property with potentially large content, such as a photo. Most probably, you won't need to always access the content of such a property if you work with the entity. It makes sense to not load the property by default and only load it whenever it is explicitly accessed by your code.

When using XML to define the mapping of an entity, we have the new `lazy` attribute on a property, as shown in the following code snippet:

```
<property name="SomeProperty" lazy="true" ... />
```

However, we can also define lazy properties using Fluent NHibernate's fluent mapping API, as shown in the following code snippet:

```
Map(x => x.SomeProperty).LazyLoad();
```

Let's analyze what SQL NHibernate generates if we query an entity `Book` that has a lazy property `Review`, as the content of the `Review` property can be quite large. Here is the definition of the (simplified) entity, as shown in the following code snippet:

```
public class Book
{
  public virtual int Id { get; set; }
  public virtual string BookTitle { get; set; }
  public virtual int YearOfPublication { get; set; }
  public virtual string Review { get; set; }
}
```

*Writing Queries*

Using Fluent NHibernate to map the entity, we have the following code snippet:

```
public class BookMap : ClassMap<Book>
{
  public BookMap()
  {
    Id(x => x.Id);
    Map(x => x.BookTitle);
    Map(x => x.YearOfPublication);

    Map(x => x.Review)
       .CustomType("StringClob")
       .LazyLoad();
  }
}
```

Note how the `Review` property is mapped. We use a custom type `StringClob`, which when used in conjunction with MS SQL Server, will be converted into a `VARCHAR(MAX)` column type. We also use the `LazyLoad` method call to define that `Review` is a lazy property.

Now, let's load the entity by ID. The query generated by NHibernate is shown in the following screenshot:

```
1  SELECT book0_.Id                as Id1_0_,
2         book0_.BookTitle         as BookTitle1_0_,
3         book0_.YearOfPublication as YearOfPu3_1_0_
4  FROM   [Book] book0_
5  WHERE  book0_.Id = 1 /* @p0 */
```

Note that the column `Review` is missing in the preceding `SELECT` statement, which is good. If we now try to access the `Review` property of the book entity, then NHibernate lazy loads this property by generating this SQL statement, as shown in the following screenshot:

```
1  SELECT book_.Review as Review1_
2  FROM   [Book] book_
3  WHERE  book_.Id = 1 /* @p0 */
```

Note that if you have more than one lazy property defined on an entity, NHibernate loads them all at once the first time you access one of the properties.

## Have a go hero

Implement a simple solution where you have a `Category` entity defined, as shown in the following code snippet:

```
public class Category
{
  public virtual Guid Id { get; set; }
  public virtual string Name { get; set; }
  public virtual string Description { get; set; }
  public virtual byte[] Photo { get; set; }
}
```

When mapping the category, define the two properties `Description` and `Photo` as lazy loaded.

Write code to create and store a category entity in the database. Load the category from the database and analyze the query that is generated by NHibernate. Then access the `Description` property and again review what NHibernate does.

## Executing multiple queries in a batch

Up to now, each query we executed caused a round trip to the database server. Sometimes, we know that we need to execute multiple queries to, for example, populate a complex screen of our application with data. In this scenario, we can improve the performance of our application significantly if we send all queries as a batch to the database. The database, in turn, will send us a list of query result sets instead of a single result set.

The LINQ to NHibernate provider defines a `ToFuture` extension method just for this purpose. All queries that are terminated with `ToFuture` are sent to the database as a batch at the moment when the data of the first query is accessed. Let's assume that our application is an ordering system and we want to load the list of categories, the list of active products of a given category, as well as the count of the returned products in one go. Our code snippet would look similar to the following:

```
using (var session = factory.OpenSession())
using (var tx = session.BeginTransaction())
{
  var categories = session.Query<Category>().ToFuture();
  var query = session.Query<Product>()
    .Where(p => !p.Discontinued)
    .Where(p => p.Category.Name == "Fruits");
  var products = query
    .ToFuture();
  var count = query
```

## Writing Queries

```
        .GroupBy(p => p.Discontinued)
        .Select(x => x.Count())
        .ToFutureValue();

    // get the results
    var result = new Result
    {
        Categories = categories.ToArray(),
        Products = products.ToArray(),
        ProductCount = count.Value
    };
}
```

The query batch generated by NHibernate and sent to the database looks similar to the following screenshot:

```
 1  select  category0_.Id              as Id0_,
 2          category0_.Name            as Name0_,
 3          category0_.Description     as Descript3_0_
 4  from    [Category] category0_
 5
 6
 7  select  product0_.Id               as Id1_,
 8          product0_.Name             as Name1_,
 9          product0_.UnitPrice        as UnitPrice1_,
10          product0_.Discontinued     as Disconti4_1_,
11          product0_.ReorderLevel     as ReorderL5_1_,
12          product0_.UnitsOnStock     as UnitsOnS6_1_,
13          product0_.Category_id      as Category7_1_
14  from    [Product] product0_,
15          [Category] category1_
16  where   product0_.Category_id = category1_.Id
17          and not (product0_.Discontinued = 1)
18          and category1_.Name = 'Fruits' /* @p0 */
19
20
21  select  cast(count(*) as INT) as col_0_0_
22  from    [Product] product0_,
23          [Category] category1_
24  where   product0_.Category_id = category1_.Id
25          and not (product0_.Discontinued = 1)
26          and category1_.Name = 'Fruits' /* @p1 */
27  group by product0_.Discontinued
28
```

Please review the preceding code snippet. Certainly, you might wonder about how the query for the count of products has been defined. Intuitively, one would expect that the query should look rather similar to the following code snippet:

```
var count = query.Count().ToFuture();
```

However, the preceding query would not work as expected as the `Count()` method causes LINQ to immediately execute the query even before `ToFuture` is applied. Thus, we have to resort to a trick and use a grouping by an invariant field. As we have already filtered by the `Discontinued` method, this field is indeed invariant and we can use it for grouping. The result is as shown in the following code snippet:

```
var count = query
  .GroupBy(p => p.Discontinued)
  .Select(x => x.Count())
  .ToFutureValue();
```

Note that all other query APIs support the batching of multiple queries as well.

# Eager loading versus lazy loading

Let's assume we have the following simple domain with a **Person** entity that has a set of **Hobby** entities, as shown in the following screenshot:

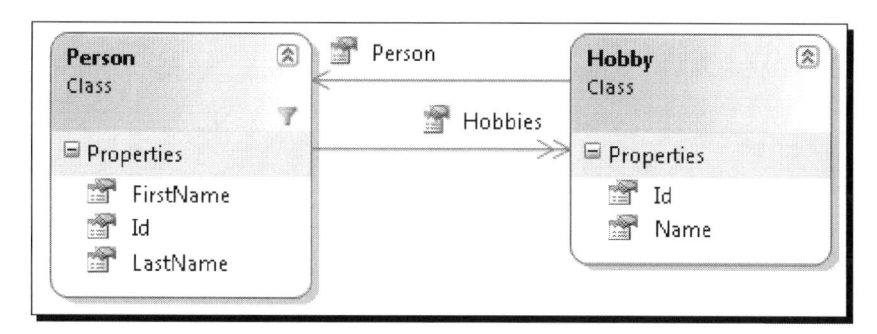

If we have stored, for example, three person entities in the database and we execute the following code snippet:

```
var listOfPersons = session.Query<Person>();
foreach (var person in listOfPersons)
{
  Console.WriteLine("{0} {1}", person.LastName, person.FirstName);
  foreach (var hobby in person.Hobbies)
  {
    Console.WriteLine("   {0}", hobby.Name);
  }
}
```

Then the result in the NHibernate profiler will look similar to the following screenshot:

| Short SQL | Row Count |
|---|---|
| begin transaction with isolation level: Unspecified | |
| SELECT ... FROM "Person" person0_ | 3 |
| SELECT ... FROM "Hobby" hobbies0_ WHERE hobbies0_.Person_id =... | 2 |
| SELECT ... FROM "Hobby" hobbies0_ WHERE hobbies0_.Person_id =... | 3 |
| SELECT ... FROM "Hobby" hobbies0_ WHERE hobbies0_.Person_id =... | 2 |
| commit transaction | |

```
1  SELECT hobbies0_.Person_id as Person3_1_,
2         hobbies0_.Id        as Id1_,
3         hobbies0_.Id        as Id0_0_,
4         hobbies0_.Name      as Name0_0_,
5         hobbies0_.Person_id as Person3_0_0_
6  FROM   "Hobby" hobbies0_
7  WHERE  hobbies0_.Person_id = '5ff9f9ed-fbb9-4811-a7a0-9eb8007ff110'
```

This is a typical select (n+1) problem. NHibernate first loads the list of all person and then when we access the hobbies of each person, it lazy loads its respective list of hobbies. In many circumstances, this might be the desired behavior, specifically if we know that we only want to access properties of the person entity but not its hobbies, or if we only want to access the hobbies of a few people of potentially many person.

If, on the other hand, we know in advance that we need to access the hobbies of all person that we load from the database, then there is a better way to load the data. We can instruct NHibernate to eagerly load all hobbies together with the person entities.

In LINQ to NHibernate, we have the `Fetch` method for this purpose. The following query causes NHibernate to only send one statement to the database:

```
var persons = session.Query<Person>()
    .Fetch(p => p.Hobbies);
```

The SQL generated by NHibernate looks similar to the following screenshot:

```
 1  select person0_.Id              as Id1_0_,
 2         hobbies1_.Id             as Id0_1_,
 3         person0_.FirstName       as FirstName1_0_,
 4         person0_.LastName        as LastName1_0_,
 5         hobbies1_.Name           as Name0_1_,
 6         hobbies1_.Person_id      as Person3_0_1_,
 7         hobbies1_.Person_id      as Person3_0__,
 8         hobbies1_.Id             as Id0__
 9  from   "Person" person0_
10         left outer join "Hobby" hobbies1_
11            on person0_.Id = hobbies1_.Person_id
```

NHibernate uses an outer join to load the person and hobbies data in one go. This, of course, is a clear improvement over the first version, which caused (n+1) queries to be sent to the database, where n is the number of person we retrieve from the database.

The same result can also be achieved when using criteria queries, as shown in the following code snippet:

```
var persons = session.CreateCriteria<Person>("p")
    .CreateCriteria("p.Hobbies", JoinType.LeftOuterJoin)
    .List<Person>();
```

Here, we use the `CreateCriteria` method to define how the dependent Hobbies collection should be treated and we have declared that we want NHibernate to use a left outer join. The resulting database query is the same as the one generated by the LINQ provider.

Note that we use `left outer join` and not `inner join`, as the person can have no hobbies and in this case, `inner join` would not retrieve this person.

Lastly, we can also use HQL to achieve the same result by using a `left join fetch` operation between the person and hobbies, as shown in the following code snippet:

```
var hql = "select p from Person as p left join fetch p.Hobbies as h";
var listOfPersons = session.CreateQuery(hql)
    .List<Person>();
```

Once again, the database query generated by NHibernate looks the same as the one generated by the LINQ provider.

*Writing Queries*

# Bulk data changes

In previous chapters we learned how we can—with the aid of NHibernate—add new records to the database, change, and delete existing ones. These operations have been executed on a single record base. This is the expected behavior and fulfills our requirements in most cases. However, sometimes we would like to execute changes on a set of data as a whole in one go. NHibernate allows us to execute some bulk data changes by using HQL. For this purpose, we can use the `ExecuteUpdate` method, which is defined on the `IQuery` interface. Let's try to update the unit price of all products in the system with one single query, as shown in the following code snippet:

```
var hql = "update Product p set p.UnitPrice = 1.1 * p.UnitPrice";
session.CreateQuery(hql).ExecuteUpdate();
```

NHibernate sends the following command to the database, as shown in the following screenshot:

```
1  update "Product"
2  set     UnitPrice = 1.1
3                   * UnitPrice
```

Bulk deletes are also possible. Let's try to remove all discontinued products from the system, as shown in the following code snippet:

```
var hql = "delete Product p where p.Discontinued=true";
session.CreateQuery(hql).ExecuteUpdate();
```

Finally, we can execute bulk inserts by using HQL, as shown in the following code snippet :

```
var hql = "insert into Product(Id, Name, Category, UnitPrice) " +
   "select t.Id, t.Name, t.Category, t.UnitPrice " +
   "from ProductTemp t";
session.CreateQuery(hql).ExecuteUpdate();
```

A couple of notes to the bulk insert:

- The source of data has to be a (mapped) table of the database
- All of the column types between the source and target tables must match
- We cannot use `Id` columns whose values are auto-generated by the database, such as identity columns in MS SQL Server

## Pop quiz – Some remarkable points

1. The following are four questions. Take some time and try to respond to them on your own prior to reading the given answers.

    a. Explain in your own words: why querying a database is such a crucial task for most business applications?

    b. What can you do to group multiple LINQ to NHibernate queries and send them in one batch to the database server?

    c. Explain what the select (n+1) anti-pattern is and how you can avoid it.

    d. You want to update the value of a column in the product table for thousands of records stored in your database in an efficient way. How would you do that?

# Summary

We learned a lot in this chapter about how to retrieve data stored in the database. Querying data from a database is one of the most important aspects of an application. Users, in general, want to use the collected data to generate some meaningful reports displayed on-screen or printed on paper. Furthermore, in a typical application, read operations are much more frequent than write operations. In this regard, we would consider this chapter as one of the most important ones of the whole book.

In this chapter, we specifically covered:

- How to query data by using the LINQ to NHibernate provider, which is new in NHibernate 3
- Alternative methods provided by NHibernate to retrieve data such as the criteria query API, the `QueryOver` API, which is new in NHibernate 3 and the Hibernate Query Language (HQL)
- Lazy loading properties of an entity, which is a new addition to NHibernate 3
- How to send multiple queries to the server in one go
- The possibility to execute bulk data operations when using HQL

We learned a lot about data retrieval. As users expect the data they retrieve from the system to be in a valid and consistent state, we need to make sure that no invalid data can be persisted in our system. That's why in the next chapter, we will discuss how we can validate the data prior to saving it to the database.

# 10
# Validating the Data to Persist

*Most applications we write today allow users to enter new data into the system or modify existing data. Often, the user can manipulate many different types of entities with complex interactions. Sometimes, the interactions of different entities are so complex that the user cannot completely oversee them. The expectation now is that the application should guide the users in such situations and not allow the entry of wrong or incomplete data.*

This is the background to this chapter. So, let's get on with it.

## What is validation and why is it so important?

When we are talking about validation, then we mean to make sure that the data collected by the users of our application is complete, valid, and consistent. As an example, take the delivery address of an order managed by an ordering system. If the address is incomplete or wrong, then the order cannot be delivered, which would result in frustration on the side of the person who ordered something, as well as an added cost for the supplier of the goods. This is an inacceptable situation and we better make sure that our application prevents the users from entering, or generating wrong or incomplete data.

## Who owns the database?

When writing an application, one of the first things to do is to make sure that our application owns the database. Having this boundary condition enforced significantly decreases the complexity of our solution and saves us from writing a lot of unnecessary error-handling code.

Once our solution is in production, we don't let any other application integrate with our application on the database level; that is, we don't give any other application direct access to our tables and views, or more generally speaking, to our raw data.

These are bold statements, but experience with real projects more than justifies them. They are based on personal experiences throughout many small, mid-size to enterprise level projects. A lot of problems that we faced had to do with the fact that our application did not exclusively own the database. On the other hand, projects having their own exclusive database have always been very successful.

Nevertheless, how can we achieve this goal?

1. We have some pre-existing database whose data we need to use in our application.
2. We have some legacy application that is still in use and produces data that our new application has to use.
3. Our Customer wants to integrate our application with other applications and exchange data between them.
4. Our Customer wants to create ad-hoc reports from the data stored in our database.
5. The data in the database belongs to the Customer and we cannot forbid them to access this data, and so on.

These are all valid concerns and they tend to come up over and over again. On the other hand, we also have to face the requirements of producing a solution that has a short time to market, is robust and reliable, is flexible regarding new business requirements, and has the highest possible data quality.

Having these requirements in mind, there are some suggestions about how to solve the challenges listed above:

1. Import the legacy data into your database using some ETL (Extract, Transform, and Load) tool. This can be either a one-time task or a recursive task, scheduled to happen every couple of hours or so.
2. You can either use the solution proposed above using an ETL tool or, if that doesn't work, try to access the new or changed data of the legacy application by using, for example, web services or file transfer (export/import).
3. Provide other integration points like a web service interface, through which the other applications can query or push data from and to our application.
4. Either provide a reporting client to the customer that allows ad-hoc queries, or implement a web service interface through which a third-party reporting tool, such as MS Excel, can access (part of) the data produced by our application.

5.  We cannot forbid our Customers to get access to their data. However, that doesn't mean that we give them access to the raw data. This raw data has no meaning without our application. Only the combination of data and business logic implemented in our application gives the data a meaning. The data alone does not reflect the whole picture. It can even be misleading as the data might be, say, denormalized for performance reasons, or might be incomplete as certain values are calculated values and depend on each other.
    We can give the Customer access to this data by providing other interfaces to the data, such as web services.

All in all, we can say that if our goal is to deliver an application which is robust and reliable, then we need to trade in something. We cannot give our Customers a sharp knife to play with and expect them to not hurt themselves. Ultimately, our Customers will blame our application if it produces wrong or misleading results even though the cause of these wrong results is the fact that the Customer changed the raw data either manually or through another application.

# Why, what, and where do we validate?

Adding validation logic to our software increases its size and complexity considerably. As adding validation to the solution is not free, we must have very good reasons to add this additional logic. Let's face them.

## Why validate?

Users that use our application can enter invalid or incomplete data, either by mistake or on purpose. The latter case is better known as "trying to hack a system", whereas the former can happen even to well-disposed users. In either case, we have to prevent this. If our system uses wrong data, then this can result in undesired outcomes. As an example, consider the case that a malicious user tries to order some goods with our e-commerce software and wants to use a falsified credit card to pay. We have to make sure that the credit card number provided by the user is valid and only then accept the order.

## What data?

Here we could simply state that we need to validate all data that is entered. And often, that is also a requirement when we implement the application. If we do not validate all the data that a user enters, then we have to at least concentrate on the part of the data that is mission critical. By mission critical we mean data that, if incomplete or wrong, could negatively impact our business in a direct or indirect way.

## Where to validate?

If we want to write an application that performs well, is robust, and pleasant to use, then we have to validate data at various points. We should validate the data:

- At the presentation layer
- On the server, inside our domain model
- At the database level

On the presentation layer, we do the "easy" validations; such as whether the user:

- provides a value for a mandatory field
- enters data of the right type (a number in a numeric field, a valid date in a date field, and so on)
- does not enter strings longer than permitted
- enters numbers or dates in the expected range

In the domain model, we repeat the same validations as we did in the presentation layer and, additionally, we execute complex validations to validate interactions between entities. An example would be to only accept an order of a customer over a certain threshold value, if the customer has no unpaid invoices.

In the domain model, we also have to do the basic validation similar to the one executed in the presentation layer, otherwise hackers might try to bypass the UI validation logic. However, they will fail if we re-validate all input again.

In the database, we add constraints which serve as a last resort, if all the other validations did not catch invalid data. Typical constraints are foreign key constraints, unique constraints, or even check constraints.

## Validating single properties

For simple validations happening at, for example, the presentation layer, we can use validation based on the content of individual properties of an object. There is a project available in the **NHibernate Contributions** that does just this. This project defines attributes that can be used to decorate the properties of our entities, and it also defines the validation engine, which we can use to validate our entities against the rules we defined by placing those validation attributes on top of the properties. This project is called NHibernate. Validator. You can find and download the source of the NHibernate Contribution projects via SVN from the following URL: https://nhcontrib.svn.sourceforge.net or, more conveniently, you can just use the NHibernate.Validator.dll assembly in the code library accompanying this book.

## Configuring the validator

Once we have referenced the `NHibernate.Validator` assembly in our solution, we need to configure the validation engine. For this purpose, the project defines a fluent API. First, we have to define an instance of the validator configuration, as shown in the following code snippet:

```
var nhvConfig =
   new NHibernate.Validator.Cfg.Loquacious.FluentConfiguration();
```

Note that this is not the same as the NHibernate configuration.

Using the fluent API, we can now configure the preceding configuration object and define:

- Which validation mode we want to use
- Where the validation definitions can be found (in our example, we instruct the validator engine to parse the assembly where our domain is defined)
- How we want to integrate validation with NHibernate

```
nhvConfig
    .SetDefaultValidatorMode(ValidatorMode.UseAttribute)
    .Register(typeof (Product).Assembly.ValidationDefinitions())
    .IntegrateWithNHibernate
    .ApplyingDDLConstraints()
    .And
    .RegisteringListeners();
```

In the preceding code snippet, we have defined that we want to (only) use attributes to define the validation rules. We also instruct the validator engine to parse the assembly where our domain is defined for validation definitions; these are the attributes we will use to decorate our entities. Finally, we ask the validator engine to use the metainformation available in the validation attributes applied to the domain to enrich the schema definition (the `ApplyDDLConstraints` call), and we also ask it to register two interceptors with NHibernate, which validate the properties transparently whenever we want to insert or update an entity (the `RegisteringListeners` call).

Having this validator configuration, we can now create a validator engine object and configure it using the preceding configuration object, as shown in the following code snippet:

```
var validatorEngine = new ValidatorEngine();
validatorEngine.Configure(nhvConfig);
```

## Validating the Data to Persist

Finally, we can use the `Initialize` extension method for the NHibernate configuration object, which is defined by the `NHibernate.Validator` project. We pass the validator engine object as a parameter to the `Initialize` method, as shown in the following code snippet:

```
nhibernateConfig.Initialize(validatorEngine);
```

After all this setup, we are ready to (re)create the database schema. We do this in the usual way, by using the `SchemaExport` class of NHibernate, as shown in the following code snippet:

```
new SchemaExport(c).Execute(false, true, false);
```

## Defining validation rules

Once we have our system configured and the database schema created, we can start decorating our entities with attributes.

Each attribute defines, among others, a `Message` parameter, which we can set to define the validation message the system shall display in case the validation of an entity fails.

One of probably the most common scenarios is to validate that the user has entered a value for a mandatory field. For this purpose, the validator project defines the `NotNull` attribute. A typical target of such an attribute would be the `Name` property of a `Product` class. A product must have a valid name:

```
[NotNull(Message = "Product must have a valid name")]
public string Name { get; set; }
```

Usually, the `Name` of a Product entity must be at least one or two characters long and not exceed 50 characters. We can enforce this with the `Length` attribute:

```
[NotNull(Message = "Product must have a valid name")]
[Length(Min = 2, Max = 50,
   Message = "Name of product must be between 1 and 50 char"]
public string Name { get; set; }
```

As you can see in the preceding example, we can have multiple attributes on a single property of an entity. Of course, they should not contradict each other.

## Fluently configure validation rules

If we don't want to pollute the entities of our domain model with attributes and keep concerns separated, then we can also define the validation rules externally in a separate class. To make things simple and transparent, NHibernate validator offers a fluent API to configure the validation of our entities.

For each entity we want to validate, we define a class that inherits from the generic class `ValidationDef<T>`, where `T` is the entity we want to validate. In the case where we want to validate the Product entity, we have:

```
public class ProductValidator : ValidationDef<Product>
{ }
```

In the constructor of the preceding class, we can then use the fluent API provided by `NHibernate.Validator` to declaratively define the validation logic to be applied to the entity. To achieve the same result as in the preceding example, where we were using attributes to decorate the `Name` property of the product, we can write:

```
Define(x => x.Name)
  .NotNullable()
  .WithMessage("The product name cannot be undefined")
  .And
  .LengthBetween(2, 50)
  .WithMessage("Product name must be between 2 and 50 char")
```

## Enforcing validation

When configuring the validator, we have registered two NHibernate listeners that are triggered whenever an entity is either inserted or updated. These listeners validate the entity and throw an exception if the entity is in an invalid state.

Usually, we might want to avoid such a situation where the system throws an exception due to failed validation. A better solution is to validate our entities prior to trying to save or update them. Nothing is easier than that. We can use the validator engine to validate our modified entities and react accordingly, as shown in the following code snippet:

```
var product = new Product {...};
var validator = new ValidatorEngine();
var invalidValues = validator.Validate(product);
if (invalidValues.Length > 0)
   ShowInvalidValues(product, invalidValues);
else
   session.Save(product);
```

## Validating the Data to Persist

In the preceding code snippet, we create a new product entity. We then use the validator engine to validate the product. The validate method returns an array of `InvalidValue` objects. If the product is in a valid state, then this array has zero length, otherwise each element of the array contains information about a failed validation. We only save the product if the validation succeeds, otherwise we might want to display the messages of the failed validations, as shown in the following code snippet:

```
private static void ShowInvalidValues
   (object entity, IEnumerable<InvalidValue> invalidValues)
{
   Console.WriteLine(entity.GetType().Name);
   foreach (var invalidValue in invalidValues)
     Console.WriteLine("   Property {0}: {1}",
        invalidValue.PropertyName,
        invalidValue.Message);
}
```

## Time for action – Using property validation

In this example, we want to implement a simple domain that is validated using attributes to decorate the properties of our entities. We will use NuGet to set up our project and have a quick start.

1. Open Microsoft SQL Server Management Studio (SSMS) and log in to your local SQL Server Express. Create a new empty database called `BasicValidationSample`.

2. Open Visual Studio and add a new **Console Application** type project. Call the project `BasicValidationSample`.

3. Set **Target framework** of the project as **.NET Framework 4.0**.

4. Make sure you have the latest **NuGet Package Manager** extension installed. At the time of writing, this is version 1.2.x.

> **Installing NuGet Package Manager Extension**
>
> To be able to use NuGet from within Visual Studio, you first need to install the NuGet Package Manager extension. This is very simple, but only works for VS 2010 Professional or higher. In VS 2010, navigate to **Tools | Extension Manager...**. In the **Extension Manager** dialog window, click on **Online Gallery** on the left side. Enter `NuGet Package Manager` into the search textbox in the right-hand upper corner of the dialog and hit *Enter*. In the list of available downloads, the NuGet package manager should be the first one. Click on **Download** and follow the instructions on the screen.

5. In **Solution Explorer**, right-click on the **References** folder and, from the context menu, select **Add Library Package Reference…**:

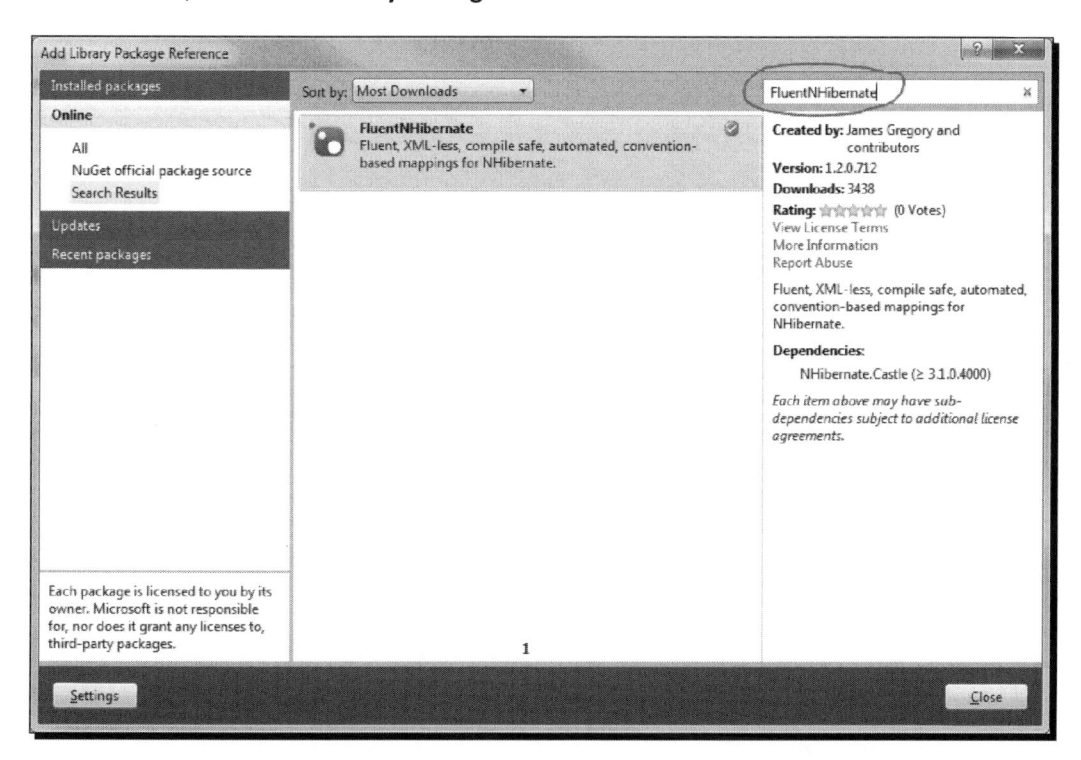

6. In the **Add Library Package Reference** dialog window, select **Online** on the left side. Then, add **FluentNHibernate** into the search box on the top right of the window. From the list of packages that appear, select **FluentNHibernate**. This will install and reference Fluent NHibernate together with NHibernate.

7. Add references to the assemblies `Castle.Core.dll`, `FluentNHibernate.dll`, `Iesi.Collections.dll`, `NHibernate.dll`, `NHibernate.ByteCode.Castle.dll`, and `NHibernate.Validator.dll`, found in the `lib` folder of the code accompanying this book.

8. Add a `Category` class to the project containing the following code:

```
public class Category
{
    public virtual Guid Id { get; set; }
    public virtual string Name { get; set; }
}
```

*Validating the Data to Persist*

9. Add a mapping class for the `Category` class and name it `CategoryMap`, as shown in the following code snippet:

    ```
    public class CategoryMap : ClassMap<Category>
    {
        public CategoryMap()
        {
            Id(x => x.Id).GeneratedBy.GuidComb();
            Map(x => x.Name);
        }
    }
    ```

10. Furthermore, add a `Product` class to the project, as shown in the following code snippet:

    ```
    public class Product
    {
        public virtual Guid Id { get; set; }
        public virtual string Name { get; set; }
        public virtual Category Category { get; set; }
        public virtual decimal UnitPrice { get; set; }
        public virtual int UnitsOnStock { get; set; }
        public virtual int ReorderLevel { get; set; }
        public virtual bool Discontinued { get; set; }
    }
    ```

11. And finally, add the mapping class for the `Product` class and name it `ProductMap`, as shown in the following code snippet:

    ```
    public class ProductMap : ClassMap<Product>
    {
        public ProductMap()
        {
            Id(x => x.Id).GeneratedBy.GuidComb();
            Map(x => x.Name);
            References(x => x.Category);
            Map(x => x.UnitPrice);
            Map(x => x.UnitsOnStock);
            Map(x => x.ReorderLevel);
            Map(x => x.Discontinued);
        }
    }
    ```

12. Add a `NotNullNotEmpty` attribute to the `Name` property of the `Category` class, as shown in the following code snippet:

    ```
    [NotNullNotEmpty(Message = "The category name cannot
      be undefined.")]
    public virtual string Name { get; set; }
    ```

13. Furthermore, add a `Length` attribute to the `Name` property of the `Category` class. The length of the name has to be between 2 and 50 characters, as shown in the following code snippet:

    ```
    [NotNullNotEmpty(Message = "The category name cannot
      be undefined.")]
    [Length(Min = 2, Max = 50, Message =
      "The category name must be between 2 and 50 characters long")]
    public virtual string Name { get; set; }
    ```

14. Add a `NotNull` attribute to each of the following properties of the `Product` class: `Category`, `UnitPrice`, `UnitsOnStock`, `ReorderLevel`, and `Discontinued`. An example of which is shown in the following code snippet:

    ```
    [NotNull]
    public virtual bool Discontinued { get; set; }
    ```

15. Add a `Min` attribute to the `ReorderLevel` and `UnitsOnStock` properties, which asserts that the corresponding value cannot be negative, for example:

    ```
    [NotNull]
    [Min(1, Message = "Reorder level must be a positive number.")]
    public virtual int ReorderLevel { get; set; }
    ```

16. To the `Program` class, add a constant defining the connection string, as shown in the following code snippet:

    ```
    const string connString =
      "server=.\\SQLEXPRESS;database=BasicValidationSample;" +
      "integrated security=true";
    ```

## Validating the Data to Persist

17. To the `Main` method of the `Program` class, add code to fluently create a session factory using Fluent NHibernate's API, as shown in the following code snippet:

```
var factory = Fluently.Configure()
   .Database(   MsSqlConfiguration
        .MsSql2008
        .ConnectionString(connString)
        .ShowSql()
    )
    .Mappings(m => m.FluentMappings
        .AddFromAssemblyOf<Product>()
    )
    .ExposeConfiguration(ExportSchema)
    .BuildSessionFactory();
```

18. Define the `ExportSchema` method that is called in the preceding code snippet by the `ExposeConfiguration` method. In this method, we have to configure the validation engine and then initialize the NHibernate configuration with this validator configuration, as shown in the following code snippet:

```
private static void ExportSchema(Configuration c)
{
   var nhvConfig = new FluentConfiguration();
   nhvConfig.SetDefaultValidatorMode(ValidatorMode.UseAttribute)
        .Register(typeof (Product).Assembly.ValidationDefinitions())
        .IntegrateWithNHibernate
        .ApplyingDDLConstraints().And.RegisteringListeners();

   var validatorEngine = new ValidatorEngine();
   validatorEngine.Configure(nhvConfig);

   c.Initialize(validatorEngine);

   new SchemaExport(c).Execute(true, true, false);
}
```

19. At the end of the `Main` method, add code to prevent the application from exiting without the user saying so, as shown in the following code snippet:

```
Console.Write("Hit enter to exit:");
Console.ReadLine();
```

*Chapter 10*

> **How to localize the validation messages**
>
> If you are writing an application for the international market, then you might want to localize the validation messages. In this case, instead of adding a hard coded message to the respective validation attributes, you can add a key. That is, instead of having a string such as `Message="Category name cannot be undefined."`, you use a key `Message="CategoryNameCannotBeUndefined"`. Instead of displaying the validation message, you can use this key value to look up the string in the correct language from your resource files. For more in-depth information about how to localize validation messages, you might want to read the following two blog posts that provide a very complete description of the topic:
>
> `http://fabiomaulo.blogspot.com/2009/10/nhibernatevalidator-customizing.html`
>
> `http://fabiomaulo.blogspot.com/2009/10/nhibernatevalidator-customizing_28.html`

## What just happened?

In the preceding exercise, we used NuGet to quickly add Fluent NHibernate and NHibernate to our solution. We also added the `NHibernate.Validator.dll` assembly found in the NHibernate Contribution projects to the solution. We then used the attributes defined in the latter assembly to decorate our entities with validation attributes. Finally, we configured NHibernate to use the validator engine of the validator assembly to validate the entities prior to persisting them to the database.

## Have a go hero

Add a `ProductCode` (string) property to the `Product` class. Do not forget to map this new property. Add a `PatternAttribute` validation attribute to this property and make sure the `ProductCode` matches a given pattern (for example, "P-00-000-0", where "0" is a placeholder for any number).

## Validating complex business rules

To validate complex business rules, attributes are not enough. In this case, we need some alternatives.

*Validating the Data to Persist*

## Enforcing always valid entities

One way to validate the data entered by the user is to require the entities and value objects in our domain model to always be in a valid state and reject any data changes if this rule is violated. If we postulate that in our domain, entities and value objects can always only be in a valid state, then we have to write much less error-handling code. Any code dealing with entities can always assume that the respective entity is in a valid state.

How can we achieve an entity or a value object that is always in a valid state? Let's look at a simple example: our application has a person entity. The first and last name of a person object must always be defined. Earlier in this book, we introduced a Name value object, which consists of the three properties: FirstName, MiddleName, and LastName. We can now add some validation logic to this class to guarantee that a person always has a complete and valid name. As a value object is immutable, it is always constructed through a parameterized constructor, which contains a parameter for each value. In our case, these are the said three parameters: last, middle, and first name. In the constructor, we validate that the first and last name are indeed defined and valid, as shown in the following code snippet:

```
public class Name
{
  public Name(string lastName, string middleName, string firstName)
  {
    if(string.IsNullOrWhiteSpace(lastName) ||
       lastName.Length < 2 || lastName.Length > 50)
      throw new ArgumentException("Invalid last name. " +
        "Must be between 2 and 50 charaters long.");

    if(string.IsNullOrWhiteSpace(firstName) ||
       firstName.Length < 2 || firstName.Length > 50)
      throw new ArgumentException("Invalid first name." +
        "Must be between 2 and 50 charaters long.");

    LastName = lastName;
    MiddleName = middleName;
    FirstName = firstName;
  }

  public string LastName { get; private set; }
  public string MiddleName { get; private set; }
  public string FirstName { get; private set; }
}
```

Note that we have implied that the mandatory first and last name must each be at least 2 characters long, but not more than 50 characters long.

Note also that all properties are read-only to enforce the immutability of the value object.

Another example of enforcing the validity of an entity is the case of a bank account. The application can only credit an account entity if there are sufficient funds in the account, an example is shown in the following code snippet:

```
public class Account
{
  public decimal Balance { get; private set; }

  public void Credit(decimal amount)
  {
    if(Balance - amount < 0.0m)
      throw new ArgumentException("Not enough funds.");
    Balance -= amount;
  }
}
```

Another advantage of always having valid entities and value objects is that we can pass those entities around and the code we call can assume they are valid. And thus, we do not need special error-handling code that deals with the fact that an entity could be invalid.

## Using validation classes

To handle complex validation requirements, we might want to put our validation logic into special validation classes. In doing so, we honor the single responsibility principle (SRP), which states that a class should have one and only one responsibility. In this case, the responsibility is that of validating the entity. Following this principle can lead to a code base, which is more robust and maintainable.

For our ordering system, let's assume that each order has to be approved by an employee. Now consider the case where we want to make sure that orders above a certain amount, say 1000 US$, can only be approved by an employee who has the status of a manager, and that the approval can only succeed if the customer has no pending invoices. This kind of validation is a multi-step operation, and thus it makes sense to implement a class specifically with the purpose of this validation. Furthermore, by doing so, we can focus better on the task at hand and are not distracted by other details.

In the preceding scenario, we could, for example, call the validator class `OrderApprovalValidator` and the logic inside this validator would:

1. Verify that the logged in employee is indeed a manager.
2. Verify that the customer who placed the order has no pending invoices.

*Validating the Data to Persist*

The code of this validator might look similar to the following code snippet:

```
public class OrderApprovalValidator
{
  public IEnumerable<string> GetBrokenRules(Order entity)
  {
    if(user_is_not_manager)
      yield return "you are not a manager.";
    if (customer_has_pending_invoices)
      yield return "customer has pending invoices";
  }

  // more code, omitted for clarity...
}
```

Note that the preceding code snippet contains pseudocode and is not complete. It shall only help to clarify the concept.

`GetBrokenRules` returns `IEnumerable` of error messages. If the returned collection of error messages is empty, then the operation causing a state transition of the order entity is valid and will put the order into a valid state.

## Time for action – Validating user input

In this exercise, we want to create a simple product inventory application. As part of this application, we want to validate the user input when adding, say, new product categories or deleting existing categories. We will implement this solution as a WPF application.

1. Open Microsoft SQL Server Management Studio (SSMS) and log in to your local SQL Server Express. Create a new empty database called `AdvancedValidationSample`.

2. Open Visual Studio and add a new **WPF Application** project. Call the project `AdvancedValidationSample`.

3. Add references to `NHibernate.dll`, `NHibernate.ByteCode.Castle.dll`, and `FluentNHibernate.dll` to the project.

4. Set **Target framework** of the project as **.NET Framework 4.0**.

5. Add a `Category` class to the project, as shown in the following code snippet:
   ```
   public class Category
   {
     public Guid Id { get; set; }
     public string Name { get; set; }
   }
   ```

*Chapter 10*

**6.** Add a `Product` class to the project, as shown in the following code snippet:
```
public class Product
{
  public Guid Id { get; set; }
  public string Name { get; set; }
  public Category Category { get; set; }
  public decimal UnitPrice { get; set; }
  public int ReorderLevel { get; set; }
  public bool Discontinued { get; set; }
}
```

**7.** Add a `CategoryMap` class to the project to map the `Category` entity using Fluent NHibernate, as shown in the following code snippet:
```
public class CategoryMap : ClassMap<Category>
{
  public CategoryMap()
  {
    Not.LazyLoad();
    Id(x => x.Id).GeneratedBy.GuidComb();
    Map(x => x.Name).Not.Nullable().Length(50);
  }
}
```

**8.** For once, we don't want to use lazy load, and thus need to declare this in the mapping with the `Not.LazyLoad()` statement. As a consequence, we do not need to declare the properties of our `Category` entity as virtual.

**9.** Add a `ProductMap` class to the project to map the `Product` entity, as shown in the following code snippet:
```
public class ProductMap : ClassMap<Product>
{
  public ProductMap()
  {
    Not.LazyLoad();
    Id(x => x.Id).GeneratedBy.GuidComb();
    Map(x => x.Name).Not.Nullable().Length(50);
    References(x => x.Category).Not.Nullable();
    Map(x => x.UnitPrice).Not.Nullable();
    Map(x => x.ReorderLevel).Not.Nullable();
    Map(x => x.Discontinued).Not.Nullable();
  }
}
```

## Validating the Data to Persist

10. Add an interface `IValidator<T>` to the project. This interface will be implemented by all validator classes we define in this project, as shown in the following code snippet:

    ```
    public interface IValidator<in T> where T : class
    {
        IEnumerable<string> BrokenRules(ISession session, T entity);
    }
    ```

11. Add a `SaveCategoryValidator` class to the project. This class implements the preceding interface and verifies that the category entity to save is in a valid state, as shown in the following code snippet:

    ```
    public class SaveCategoryValidator : IValidator<Category>
    {
        public IEnumerable<string> BrokenRules(ISession session,
            Category entity)
        {
        }
    }
    ```

12. To the `BrokenRules` method, add code to validate that the `Name` property of the category entity is defined, as shown in the following code snippet:

    ```
    if (string.IsNullOrWhiteSpace(entity.Name))
        yield return "Name of category must be defined.";
    ```

13. Add code to verify that the length of the `Name` entity is between 2 and 50 characters long, as shown in the following code snippet:

    ```
    if (entity.Name.Length < 2 || entity.Name.Length > 50)
        yield return "Name of category must be between 2 and 50" +
            " characters long";
    ```

14. Finally, add code that verifies that the chosen name is unique. For this purpose, we have to query the database and find out whether there already exists another category with the same name, as shown in the following code snippet:

    ```
    if (session.Query<Category>()
        .Where(c => c.Id != entity.Id)
        .Any(c => c.Name == entity.Name))
        yield return "Duplicate category name.";
    ```

15. Please note how we use the `yield return` keyword to return all the possible error messages as `IEnumerable<string>`.

**16.** Add a class `DeleteCategoryValidator` to the project. The class also implements the `IValidator<T>` interface and contains code to verify that the category to delete is not referenced by any product stored in the system:

```
public class DeleteCategoryValidator : IValidator<Category>
{
  public IEnumerable<string> BrokenRules(ISession session,
    Category entity)
  {
    if (session.Query<Product>()
      .Any(p => p.Category.Id == entity.Id))
      yield return "Cannot delete category that" +
        " is referenced.";
  }
}
```

**17.** Now we want to add a validator that is called when saving a new or changed product. Add a class `SaveProductValidator` to the project. Add code to validate that the name of the product is defined, unique, and in the given length limits, as well as that the unit price is at least one cent and the reorder level is a positive number (including zero), as shown in the following code snippet:

```
public class SaveProductValidator : IValidator<Product>
{
  public IEnumerable<string> BrokenRules(ISession session,
    Product entity)
  {
    if (!string.IsNullOrWhiteSpace(entity.Name))
      yield return "Name of product must be defined.";
    if (entity.Name.Length < 2 || entity.Name.Length > 50)
      yield return "Name of product must be between" +
        " 2 and 50 characters long";
    if (session.Query<Product>()
      .Where(p => p.Id != entity.Id)
      .Any(p => p.Name == entity.Name))
      yield return "Duplicate product name.";
    if (entity.UnitPrice < 0.01m)
      yield return "Unit price must be at least 1 cent";
    if (entity.ReorderLevel < 0)
      yield return "Reorder level must be a positive number";
  }
}
```

Validating the Data to Persist

18. Open the `App.xaml.cs` file. Override the `OnStartup` method and add a call to a method that will create the session factory, as shown in the following code snippet:

```
public partial class App : Application
{
  private const string connString = "server=.\\SQLEXPRESS;"+
    "database=AdvancedValidationSample;"+
    "integrated security=true";

  public static ISessionFactory SessionFactory { get; private set; }
}

  protected override void OnStartup(StartupEventArgs e)
  {
    base.OnStartup(e);
    CreateSessionFactory();
  }
}
```

19. Add the `CreateSessionFactory` method to the `App` class, which uses the fluent configuration API of Fluent NHibernate, as shown in the following code snippet:

```
private static void CreateSessionFactory()
{
  SessionFactory = Fluently.Configure()
    .Database(MsSqlConfiguration.MsSql2008
      .ConnectionString(connString)
      .ShowSql()
      )
    .Mappings(m => m.FluentMappings
      .AddFromAssemblyOf<Category>())
    .ExposeConfiguration(c => new SchemaExport(c)
      .Execute(false, true, false))
    .BuildSessionFactory();
}
```

20. Now we define a view model, which will contain the presentation logic of our simple application. Add a class `MainViewModel` to the project.

21. Add a public read-only property `Categories` of type `ObservableCollection<Category>` to the view model class, as shown in the following code snippet:

```
public ObservableCollection<Category> Categories
    { get; private set; }
```

[ 304 ]

**22.** Add a public property `SelectedCategory` of type `Category` to the view model, as shown in the following code snippet:

```
public Category SelectedCategory { get; set; }
```

**23.** Add a field of type `SaveCategoryValidator` and a field of type `DeleteCategoryValidator` to the class, as shown in the following code snippet:

```
private readonly DeleteCategoryValidator deleteCategoryValidator;
private readonly SaveCategoryValidator saveCategoryValidator;
```

**24.** Add a constructor to the class to initialize the two validator fields and the categories collection, as shown in the following code snippet:

```
public MainViewModel()
{
  deleteCategoryValidator = new DeleteCategoryValidator();
  saveCategoryValidator = new SaveCategoryValidator();

  Categories = new ObservableCollection<Category>();
}
```

**25.** Add a method `SaveCategory`, which contains the code to validate and, if successful, save `SelectedCategory` to the database, as shown in the following code snippet:

```
public void SaveCategory()
{
  if (SelectedCategory == null) return;

  using (var session = App.SessionFactory.OpenSession())
  using (var tx = session.BeginTransaction())
  {
    var category = session.Get<Category>(SelectedCategory.Id) ??
      new Category();
    category.Name = SelectedCategory.Name;
    var brokenRules = saveCategoryValidator
      .BrokenRules(session, category)
      .ToArray();
    if (brokenRules.Any())
    {
      MessageBox.Show(
        string.Join(Environment.NewLine, brokenRules),
        "Validation errors");
      return;
    }
```

## Validating the Data to Persist

```
        session.SaveOrUpdate(category);
        tx.Commit();

        SelectedCategory.Id = category.Id;
      }
    }
```

26. In the preceding code snippet, we use the session factory defined in the `App` class to get a session. We start a transaction and then first validate the category entity. If the validation fails, then we show the result in a message box and cancel the transaction. If, on the other hand, the validation succeeds, then we save the entity to the database. We are using the `SaveOrUpdate` method of the session as, at that point, we do not know whether the current category is new, or it is an existing one we want to update. However, NHibernate knows it and can handle it for us.

27. Now we add code to be able to delete a category if it is not used. Add a method `DeleteCategory` to `MainViewModel`, as shown in the following code snippet:

```
public void DeleteCategory()
{
  if (SelectedCategory == null) return;

  using (var session = App.SessionFactory.OpenSession())
  using (var tx = session.BeginTransaction())
  {
    var brokenRules = deleteCategoryValidator
      .BrokenRules(session, SelectedCategory)
      .ToArray();
    if (brokenRules.Any())
    {
      MessageBox.Show(
        string.Join(Environment.NewLine, brokenRules),
        "Validation errors");
      return;
    }
    session.Delete(SelectedCategory);
    tx.Commit();

    Categories.Remove(SelectedCategory);
    SelectedCategory = null;
  }
}
```

28. In the preceding code snippet, we first check whether there is actually a selected category. If not, then we do nothing. Otherwise, we open a session and start a transaction. Then we validate that we can indeed delete the category. If not, we display the validation error in a message box and abandon the transaction. If the validation succeeds, on the other hand, then we use the delete method of the session to remove the category from the database. We then also have to remove it from our categories collection. Finally, we set the `SelectedCategory` property to null.

29. Now, we need a method that adds a new category to the categories collection and makes it the selected category, as shown in the following code snippet:

```
public void AddNewCategory()
{
  var category = new Category { Name = "(New Category)" };
  Categories.Add(category);
  SelectedCategory = category;
}
```

30. With this, our view model is complete; or is it? Not so fast my friend! Once we define the view, we will want to bind certain controls on it by putting controls on the properties of the model. To make this binding two-way, we need to implement the interface `INotifyPropertyChanged` by the view model and trigger the `PropertyChanged` event whenever `SelectedCategory` changes.

31. Make `MainViewModel` implement the interface `INotifyPropertyChanged`, as shown in the following code snippet:

```
public class MainViewModel : INotifyPropertyChanged
{
  public event PropertyChangedEventHandler PropertyChanged;

  // other code...
}
```

32. Add a method `OnPropertyChanged`, which triggers the `PropertyChanged` event, as shown in the following code snippet:

```
private void OnPropertyChanged(string propertyName)
{
  if (PropertyChanged != null)
    PropertyChanged(this,
      new PropertyChangedEventArgs(propertyName));
}
```

## Validating the Data to Persist

33. Modify the property `SelectedCategory` such that it triggers the `OnPropertyChanged` event when its value changes, as shown in the following code snippet:

    ```
    private Category selectedCategory;
    public Category SelectedCategory
    {
      get { return selectedCategory; }
      set
      {
        selectedCategory = value;
        OnPropertyChanged("SelectedCategory");
      }
    }
    ```

34. Now we are done with the view model and can start to implement the view.

35. Open the `MainWindow.xaml` file and add `TabControl` with two tabs. Set the title of the first tab to `Categories` and the title of the second tab to `Products`. Design the first tab as the following screenshot:

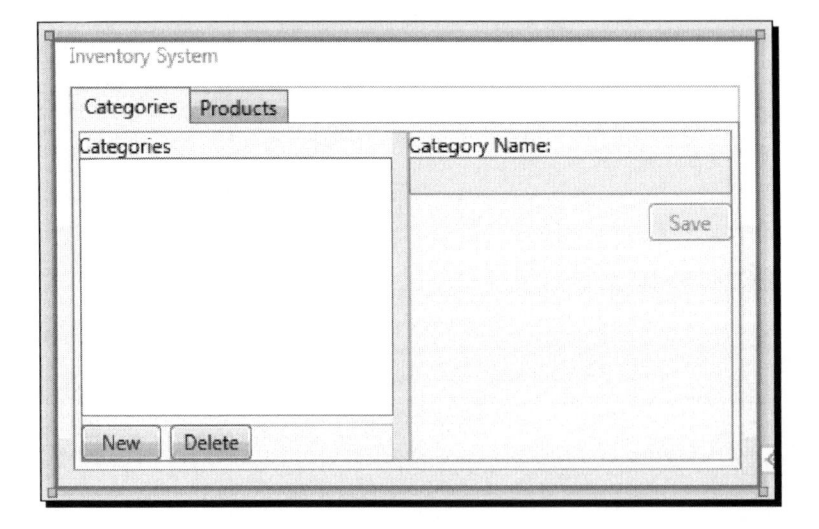

36. Please open the solution in the accompanying code bundle to see the full XAML needed to do this.

37. Open the code behind the window for `MainWindow` and add a field for the main view model, as shown in the following code snippet:

    ```
    private readonly MainViewModel viewModel;
    ```

## Chapter 10

**38.** Add code to constructor to instantiate the view model and assign it as `DataContext`, as shown in the following code snippet:

```
public MainWindow()
{
   InitializeComponent();

   viewModel = new MainViewModel();
   DataContext = viewModel;
}
```

**39.** Implement the event handler called `OnSelectedCategoryChanged` for the `SelectedItemChanged` event of the categories list box. In this method, we want to set the accessibility of the **Save** button and the category name textbox, depending on whether an item is selected or not, as shown in the following code snippet:

```
private void OnSelectedCategoryChanged(object sender,
   SelectionChangedEventArgs e)
{
   var canEdit = lstCategories.SelectedItem != null;
   saveCategory.IsEnabled = canEdit;
   txtCategoryName.IsEnabled = canEdit;
}
```

**40.** Implement the event handler for the click event of the **Save** button. The code in the view shall remain as simple as possible. Thus, we just want to delegate to the main view model, as shown in the following code snippet:

```
private void OnSaveCategory(object sender, RoutedEventArgs e)
{
   // needed when user uses accelerator key
   // to trigger notify property changed event
   saveCategory.Focus();

   viewModel.SaveCategory();
}
```

**41.** Do the same thing for the event handler for the **Delete** button, as shown in the following code snippet:

```
private void OnDeleteCategory(object sender, RoutedEventArgs e)
{
   viewModel.DeleteCategory();
}
```

*Validating the Data to Persist*

**42.** Finally, implement the event handler for the **New** button. In this method, we want to set the focus to the category name textbox and select the content to make editing a pleasure, as shown in the following code snippet:

```
private void OnNewCategory(object sender, RoutedEventArgs e)
{
  viewModel.AddNewCategory();
  txtCategoryName.Focus();
  txtCategoryName.SelectionLength = txtCategoryName.Text.Length;
}
```

**43.** Run the application and add some new categories, edit existing ones, and delete existing ones, as shown in the following screenshot:

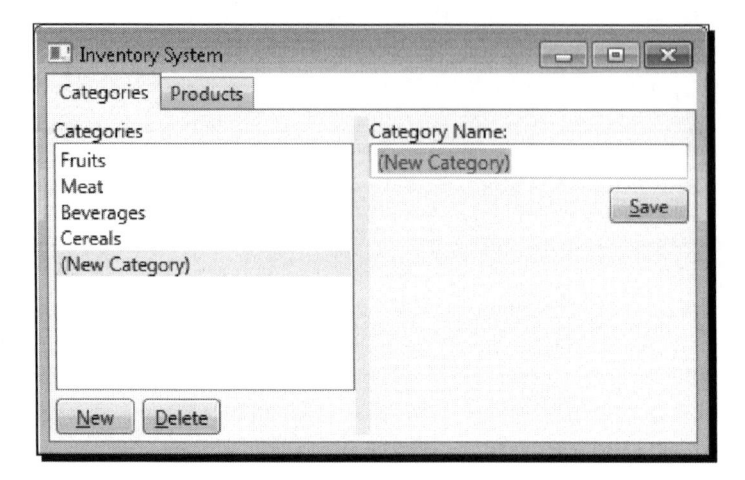

## What just happened?

We implemented (part of) a simple product inventory application. Referring to this chapter, the important part of the application is that when saving or deleting a category, the category is first validated. As the validation is relatively complex and we, for example, need to access the database, we chose to implement validator classes for this purpose. If the validation results in errors, then those errors are presented to the user and the operation is aborted.

### Have a go hero

Try to complete the preceding exercise and implement the part where the user can add new products and update or delete existing products. Implement the user interface of the second tab of the above project.

# What to do if we don't own the database?

Here, we face a serious problem! We have no guarantees that the data in the database conforms to the rules we defined in our application. If our application, for example, expects and postulates that there can be no order in the system without an associated Customer, and another application that we do not control has written orders to the database that do not have this association, then a subsequent load operation for this order might fail and our application throws an exception.

Is this behavior acceptable? If not, what should we do? Basically, we have two possible strategies:

1. Do not load wrong or incomplete data. Inform the user about the fact that the data is not in the expected format. The user can then decide how to continue and, say, try to manually fix the data.
2. We are relaxing our own rules in our solution and making, for example, the domain model more tolerant to incomplete or wrong data. However, this leads to a lot of other problems. All of a sudden, our own application can produce and store incomplete or wrong data.

It is strongly recommended to go with the first approach and write a data cleaning tool to give the user the possibility to fix wrong data. In complex applications, the second approach is just too dangerous and leads to brittle code.

## Pop quiz

1. Why do we add validation logic to our application?
    a. To prevent malicious users from compromising our system by using wrong or incomplete data.
    b. To avoid situations where users enter wrong or incomplete data by mistake.
    c. To make our application more robust and reliable.
    d. To prevent our application from calculating and displaying wrong results on-screen and in reports on paper.
    e. All of the above.

# Summary

We learned a lot in this chapter about how important it is to always validate the data our application produces and works with.

Specifically, we covered:

- How to use attributes to decorate the properties of the entities in the domain model and use the added metadata to validate those entities.
- The usage of always valid entities and value objects. We learned that this convention cannot only be used to validate data that the users enter into the system, but also to significantly reduce the complexity and size of our code base.
- How to address more complex validation requirements by using special validator classes. By implementing classes that have only the responsibility of validating the data entered by the users, we follow the single responsibility principle (SRP) and make our code more maintainable.
- Last but not least, what we can do if our solution does not own the database and we have to deal with the fact that the database contains incomplete or invalid data.

Now that we've learned about validation, it is time to come to an end and look at some of the most common pitfalls when using an object relational mapper framework, such as NHibernate, which is the topic of the next chapter.

# 11
# Common Pitfalls—Things to Avoid

*After having learned so much about NHibernate, it is time to think about some scenarios which can lead us to use NHibernate in the wrong way if we do not pay attention and can lead to a system which is unsatisfactory. One of the most obvious side effects of wrong usage or configuration of NHibernate is bad performance. Our application starts to crawl and in some situations even times out.*

In this chapter we shall discuss some of the most frequent mistakes developers make when using NHibernate. We will also show how to do it right. The topics discussed are:

- Avoid mappings that are too verbose or inefficient
- Wrong mapping for read-only access
- Never blindly rely on NHibernate but rather make informed decisions
- The anti-pattern of using implicit transactions
- Why not to use database generated IDs
- Using LINQ to NHibernate the wrong way
- How to avoid troubles with lazy loading
- Considering using a read and a write model in complex domains
- Phantom updates and what causes them
- Is NHibernate the one and only solution to persist data

So let's get on with it...

## Requesting the obvious

NHibernate, Fluent NHibernate or ConFORM define a lot of sensible conventions regarding the mapping of the domain model with its entities to the underlying database schema. Still, I see a lot of users defining very verbose mappings; but defining too much, especially unnecessary things, can obfuscate the important elements of the mapping. It is harder to read and harder to quickly understand such a mapping file and even harder to spot a defect.

Let's look at the following perfectly legal snippet of an XML mapping:

```
<property name="OrderDate" lazy="false" access="Property"
          type="DateTime" insert="true" update="true"
          unique="false">
   <column name="OrderDate" not-null="true" sql-type="DateTime" />
</property>
```

Although the snippet is quite long it only defines the mapping for one single property of an entity. In this case, the `OrderDate` property of the `Order` entity is mapped.

The very same result can be achieved by using this snippet:

```
<property name="OrderDate" not-null ="true"/>
```

Isn't the latter snippet way more readable? It is also more maintainable and less error prone.

Let's look at the unnecessary attributes in detail and give some reasons why they are superfluous in most cases:

- `lazy`: By default, all properties mapped with the `<property>` tag are not lazy loaded. Thus, `false` is the default value.
- `access`: NHibernate by default uses property setters and getters to access the data of the entities. Thus, no need to declare this explicitly in this example.
- `type`: NHibernate uses reflection to determine the type of a mapped property. In most cases this is the expected behavior, only in rare cases we need to "help" NHibernate to find the right property type. Samples are when using, for example, `CLOB` or `BLOB` type fields in conjunction with an Oracle database.
- `insert`: By default, the value of the mapped property is used when inserting a new record into the database. In other words the default value for `insert` is `true`.
- `update`: Similar to `insert` discussed above, the value of the mapped property is used when updating an existing record in the database. Consequently the default value of `update` is `true`.
- `unique`: By default, NHibernate assumes that the values of a given database column must not be unique. Thus, the default value of `unique` is `false`.

- `column name`: By default, NHibernate uses the same name as the property when mapping to the underlying database table field. Thus, this definition is only needed when the database field name differs from the property name of the mapped entity.
- `column sql-type`: In most cases NHibernate is able to correctly map the .NET data types to the matching types used by the underlying database. The mappings are defined in the dialect strategies that NHibernate uses. We select the correct strategy when configuring NHibernate.

Consequently, my advice is: do only declare the absolute minimum of what is required. Rely as much as possible on the default conventions of the framework. It is highly unlikely that these conventions are ever going to change, too many existing applications would break.

## Wrong mapping for read-only access

Often we might need to access some data in read-only mode. This data can be denormalized and aggregated to, for example, produce a report on screen or on paper. In this case, we might want to use database views to retrieve the data and map data transfer objects (DTOs) to those views.

A typical sample would be retrieving a list of the top 10 customers of the month including the customer name, the number of orders, and the total value of the orders placed during the month of interest. Let's assume we have created a database view to collect all this data. The view is called `Top10CustomersOfMonth` and has the fields `CustomerId`, `CustomerName`, `NbrOfOrders`, `Total`, `Month`, and `Year`.

Let's also assume we have the DTO `Top10Customers` and want to map this DTO to the view. This time we are using Fluent NHibernate for the mapping. What is often observed in such mappings is similar to the following code snippet:

```
public class Top10CustomersMap : ClassMap<Top10Customers>
{
  public Top10CustomersMap()
  {
    Table("Top10CustomersOfMonth");
    Id(x => x.CustomerId).GeneratedBy.GuidComb();
    Map(x => x.CustomerName).Length(50).Not.Nullable();
    Map(x => x.NbrOfOrders).Not.Nullable();
    Map(x => x.Total).Not.Nullable();
    Map(x => x.Month).Not.Nullable();
    Map(x => x.Year).Not.Nullable();
  }
}
```

# Common Pitfalls—Things to Avoid

Although this works, it is inefficient in one part and too verbose in other parts. The correct mapping would look similar to the following code snippet:

```
public class Top10CustomersMap2 : ClassMap<Top10Customers>
{
  public Top10CustomersMap2()
  {
    Table("Top10CustomersOfMonth");
    ReadOnly();
    Not.LazyLoad();
    SchemaAction.None();

    Id(x => x.CustomerId);
    Map(x => x.CustomerName);
    Map(x => x.NbrOfOrders);
    Map(x => x.Total);
    Map(x => x.Month);
    Map(x => x.Year);
  }
}
```

First of all, we have said that this view is for read-only access. Let's tell NHibernate about this fact by calling the `ReadOnly()` method.

As this database view is providing us with a denormalized and aggregated view of the data is crafted specifically for the purpose to retrieve the data as quickly as possible, we do not want NHibernate to use lazy loading in this case. By calling `Not.LazyLoad()` we turn lazy load off. By avoiding lazy load, NHibernate does not have to create proxies to wrap the DTOs and is thus slightly more efficient.

If we are generating the database schema from the domain model with the aid of NHibernate's `SchemaExport` class, then we must instruct NHibernate not to generate a table for the above mapping. Note that NHibernate is not able and will never be able to correctly create a view. The meta information we provide through the mapping file is just not enough information to know how the view should be constructed. That is why we add the `SchemaAction.None()` statement.

When defining a mapping between a DTO and a database view or table, and the mapping is used for read-only access, then we do not need to define other elements than the `name` and, in rare cases, the `type` of the mapping. There is no need to define the strategy used to generate IDs since we are not creating IDs but just reading data. We also do not need to define whether a field is nullable or not, nor define the `length` of a string type field.

# Blindly relying on NHibernate

NHibernate is a very helpful tool and makes the lives of us developers much easier when we have to deal with data that is persisted in relational databases. However, NHibernate is and remains only a tool. NHibernate is designed in such a way that it uses one of the best strategies to access data in most common scenarios. However, if we blindly rely on NHibernate to always use the best possible strategy, then we will be surprised.

A lot of scenarios exist where NHibernate just cannot make the right decision for us. In such situations, we have to "help" the tool and give it some context-specific hints.

A possible scenario is where we want to retrieve a list of parent entities, each having a collection of child entities. If, during our operation, we are executing that we want to access properties of all child entities, then we better tell NHibernate that we are planning to traverse all child entities and thus inform the tool that it should load everything in one go and not rely on the default lazy load behavior. We will specifically discuss this topic in a later section of this chapter when we are talking about the select (n+1) problem.

Another scenario is where we have a parent entity with two different collections of child entities. An example would be a blog entity with a collection of posts and a collection of authors.

If we try to force NHibernate to load the blog entity and its two child collections in a single request, then we might cause NHibernate to execute a cross join between the involved tables. A cross join basically combines each record of one table with each record of the other table. As a result, way too much data is loaded from the database. If both tables contain a lot of records, then this can put a lot of pressure on a system.

# Using implicit transactions

It is highly recommended practice to always wrap database operations into explicit transactions when using NHibernate. If we do not explicitly define the boundaries of our transactions, then the database uses implicit transactions to wrap each single statement. In most scenarios, this is inefficient as we usually execute multiple statements inside a business transaction of our system. As the boundaries of a business transaction are defined by the feature we implement, we should always make this explicit by opening and closing a transaction at the appropriate location. The simplest form in doing so is to begin a transaction immediately after opening a session, and to end and commit the transaction immediately before we close the session.

Throughout many of the examples accompanying this book I use this very simple approach:

```
using(var session = sessionFactory.OpenSession)
using(var tx = session.BeginTransaction())
{
  // do some database operations
  tx.Commit();
}
```

In a web application, you would probably want to start the transaction in the `BeginRequest` handler and to commit and end the transaction in the `EndRequest` handler of, for example, the `Global.asax` file.

## Using database-generated IDs

Using database-generated IDs for our entities at first glance seems very appealing and straightforward. However, a closer look at the problem at hand reveals that using database-generated IDs is effectively an anti-pattern and should be strictly avoided.

Database-generated IDs only make sense in scenarios where our application is sharing the database with other applications that can also update the data therein. In this case, we might want to rely on the database to generate the necessary primary keys and guarantee their uniqueness. However, I have already discussed in earlier chapters of this book why we should prevent this scenario from happening and insist that our application owns its own database.

NHibernate provides us with many ways to create or define primary key values for new entities. Two ID generators that I personally recommend are either the `HiLo` generator or the `GuidComb` generator.

While the `HiLo` generator generates integral numbers as primary key values, the `GuidComb` algorithm generates **GUIDs** that are created in a way which is optimized for indexing in the database. The standard algorithm used by the .NET framework to generate GUIDs is not very well suited for this purpose and thus NHibernate provides its own implementation in the form of the `GuidComb` generator.

If we are, for example, using an architectural pattern called **Command Query Responsibility Segregation (CQRS)** where query operations are strictly separated from data manipulation operations (commands), then we might even consider using client side generated IDs. To guarantee uniqueness of those IDs, the only reasonable type of IDs are GUIDs in this case. It is relatively easy to implement an algorithm that can be used by the client and that generates GUIDs that are optimized for indexing in the database. One way is to copy the code used by NHibernate which should not be a problem since the source code for NHibernate is freely available.

# Using LINQ to NHibernate the wrong way

LINQ to NHibernate is a really nice addition to the framework and makes querying the database much easier and more enjoyable. The queries are also much more readable than the same queries written in HQL, Criteria Query, or QueryOver syntax. Also, LINQ queries are composable in the same way we used from LINQ to objects.

However, there also lies the danger of this API if not used carefully. To fully leverage LINQ we have to understand the system boundaries.

As long as we stay in the context of LINQ to NHibernate, we are dealing with sets of results of type `IQueryable<T>` where `T` is the placeholder for the entity we are querying, for example, `Product` or `Order`.

LINQ queries are always executed by lazy loading. That is, we can define a LINQ query without that the system tries to execute it. For example, the following statement does not cause the system to execute the query:

```
var products = session.Query<Product>().Where(p => p.Discontinued);
```

The moment we start to iterate over the query (result), the query is effectively executed on the source:

```
foreach(var product in products)
{
  // do something with product
}
```

In the case of LINQ to NHibernate the source is the database. The moment we try to iterate over such a query, the NHibernate LINQ provider parses the query expression tree and generates a SQL statement which is then executed on the database.

As mentioned earlier, LINQ queries are composable. If we do want to take the above query and group the result by category names and then print a list of category names followed by the names and unit price of all its products, we could do this as follows:

```
using (var session = factory.OpenSession())
using(var tx = session.BeginTransaction())
{
  var products = session.Query<Product>()
    .Where(p => p.Discontinued);

  foreach (var productGroup in products.GroupBy(
    p => p.Category.Name))
  {
    Console.WriteLine("Category: {0}", productGroup.Key);
```

```
            foreach (var product in productGroup)
            {
               Console.WriteLine("   {0} - {1}",
                  product.Name, product.UnitPrice);
            }
      }
   }
```

In the above code snippet we have taken the products query from the previous definition and applied a `GroupBy` operation to it. We then iterate over the product groups and print the category name (which happens to be the key of the grouping) and then a list of all products belonging to that group.

If we run this code the following query will be sent to the database:

```
 1  select    product0_.Id            as Id1_,
 2            product0_.Name          as Name1_,
 3            product0_.UnitPrice     as UnitPrice1_,
 4            product0_.Discontinued  as Disconti4_1_,
 5            product0_.Category_id   as Category5_1_
 6  from      [Product] product0_,
 7            [Category] category1_
 8  where     product0_.Category_id = category1_.Id
 9            and product0_.Discontinued = 1
10  group by category1_.Name
```

This causes an exception to be triggered as the query is invalid. Only fields that occur in the group by statement can also occur in the select list. However, we need the data of all those fields, and thus we have to find another solution.

We know that we need all products, and thus can force NHibernate to load them before the `GroupBy` operation is applied. To achieve this we simply add an `AsEnumerable()` statement into the mix. The combined query would then look similar to the following code snippet:

```
var productGroups = session.Query<Product>()
   .Where(p => p.Discontinued)
   .AsEnumerable()
   .GroupBy(p => p.Category.Name);
```

Now the query works and the expected result is printed on the screen.

The `AsEnumerable` statement is used to switch the context from LINQ to NHibernate to LINQ to objects without triggering the execution of the query. Now, whenever we iterate over the result of the query, the LINQ provider knows which part of the expression tree to take and to convert into a SQL statement, which can then be executed from the database.

# The trouble with lazy loading

Lazy loading is a very handy feature that NHibernate offers to us, but if we are not careful enough this little feature can turn against us and cause our system to crawl. We might be surprised by the fact that to retrieve the data for a seemingly simple view can take a very long time, or in extreme cases time out.

Lazy loading is useful if we define a domain model where the different entities are related to each other via references or one to many associations. It was introduced to prevent NHibernate from always loading all associated entities when we only deal with one specific entity. Let's have a look at a simple blog engine. We have a **Blog** entity which has a collection of **Post** entities, as shown in the following screenshot. By default, the Post entities of each Blog entity are only loaded on demand, that is, they are lazy loaded.

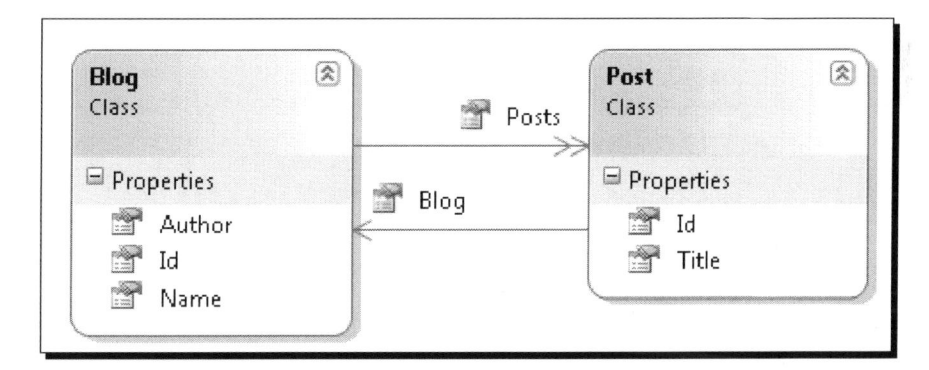

## The select (n+1) problem

When we load a blog entity from the database by using the following code snippet:

```
using (var session = factory.OpenSession())
using (var tx = session.BeginTransaction())
{
  blog = session.Load<Blog>(1001);
  tx.Commit();
}
```

NHibernate generates this query on the database:

```
1  SELECT  blog0_.Id       as Id0_0_,
2          blog0_.Name     as Name0_0_,
3          blog0_.Author   as Author0_0_
4  FROM    [Blog] blog0_
5  WHERE   blog0_.Id = 1001 /* @p0 */
```

Note that only the Blog table is queried and the Post table is not accessed so far. As long as, in our code, we only access properties of the blog entity (such as the blog name or author), the posts will not be loaded.

The moment we try to access the Posts collection of the blog, with code like:

```
var nbrOfPosts = blog.Posts.Count;
```

something interesting happens. NHibernate creates an additional query on the database to retrieve all posts associated with the blog we are currently working with:

```
1  SELECT  posts0_.Blog_id  as Blog3_1_,
2          posts0_.Id       as Id1_,
3          posts0_.Id       as Id1_0_,
4          posts0_.Title    as Title1_0_,
5          posts0_.Blog_id  as Blog3_1_0_
6  FROM    [Post] posts0_
7  WHERE   posts0_.Blog_id = 1001 /* @p0 */
```

Let's assume now that we want to generate a report which prints the name and author of all blogs in our system, followed by the list of the titles of the posts of each blog. We could do this using the following code snippet:

```
using (var session = factory.OpenSession())
using (var tx = session.BeginTransaction())
{
  var blogs = session.Query<Blog>();
  foreach (var blog in blogs)
  {
    Console.WriteLine("Blog {0} by {1}", blog.Name, blog.Author);
    foreach (var post in blog.Posts)
    {
```

```
            Console.WriteLine("  {0}", post.Title);
        }
    }
    tx.Commit();
}
```

The result is as shown in the following screenshot:

```
begin transaction with isolation level: Unspecified
SELECT ... FROM [Blog] blog0_
SELECT ... FROM [Post] posts0_ WHERE posts0_.Blog_id = 1001
SELECT ... FROM [Post] posts0_ WHERE posts0_.Blog_id = 1002
SELECT ... FROM [Post] posts0_ WHERE posts0_.Blog_id = 1003
commit transaction
```

In the preceding example we have three different blogs. Each blog has a couple of posts. With the preceding code snippet, NHibernate creates one query to retrieve all blogs and then an additional query for each blog to retrieve its posts. Mathematically, if we have n blogs then NHibernate creates (n+1) queries in total. This is the infamous select (n+1) query problem.

Having only a few blogs, this seems to be a minor issue. However, if we have hundreds or even thousands of blogs, then this is a real bummer. Nevertheless, do not worry, we can easily fix this by giving NHibernate a hint to eagerly load the posts when loading the blogs, as shown in the following code snippet:

```
using (var session = factory.OpenSession())
using (var tx = session.BeginTransaction())
{
    var blogs = session.Query<Blog>()
        .Fetch(b => b.Posts);
    foreach (var blog in blogs)
    {
        Console.WriteLine("Blog {0} by {1}", blog.Name, blog.Author);
        foreach (var post in blog.Posts)
        {
            Console.WriteLine("  {0}", post.Title);
        }
    }
    tx.Commit();
}
```

In the preceding LINQ to NHibernate query, we have used the Fetch method to indicate that we want to eagerly load the posts together with the blog. This is the only change needed. Everything else stays the same.

After this little change in the query, NHibernate creates a query for us, as shown in the following screenshot:

```
Statements  Entities  Session Usage
Short SQL                                            Row Count
begin transaction with isolation level: Unspecified
SELECT ... FROM [Blog] blog0_ left outer join [Post]...   11
commit transaction
```

```
Details  Alerts  Stack Trace
 1  select blog0_.Id        as Id0_0_,
 2         posts1_.Id       as Id1_1_,
 3         blog0_.Name      as Name0_0_,
 4         blog0_.Author    as Author0_0_,
 5         posts1_.Title    as Title1_1_,
 6         posts1_.Blog_id  as Blog3_1_1_,
 7         posts1_.Blog_id  as Blog3_0__,
 8         posts1_.Id       as Id0__
 9  from   [Blog] blog0_
10         left outer join [Post] posts1_
11            on blog0_.Id = posts1_.Blog_id
```

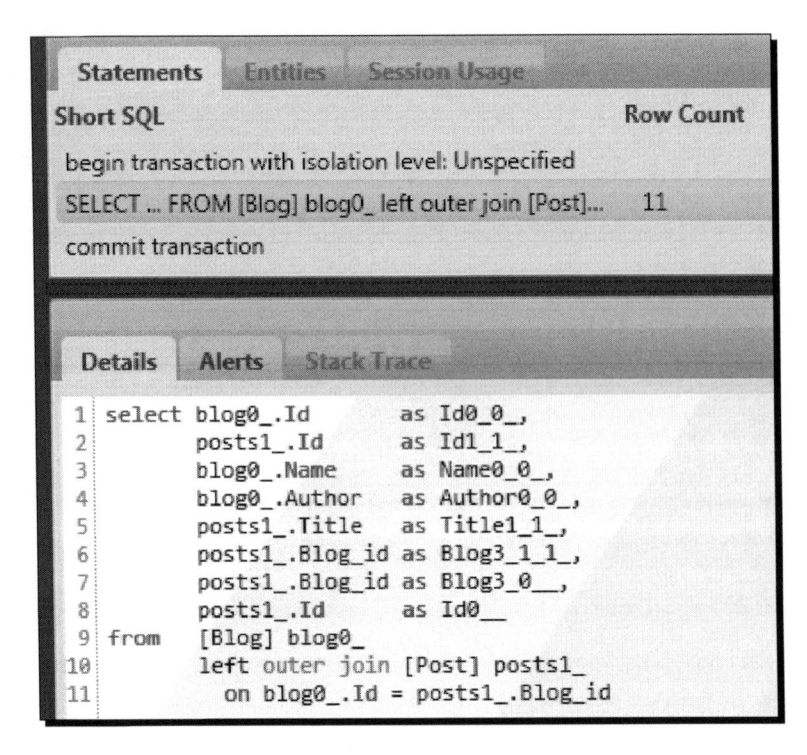

Note that only one single query is generated which retrieves all blogs and all posts in a single go. This is a huge improvement over the first approach when dealing with large lists of entities.

## Accessing lazy loaded parts after the session is closed

One other common trap that developers fall into when using NHibernate is when they try to access properties or collections of an entity that are lazy loaded, and the session that was used to retrieve the entity has already been closed. In this situation, NHibernate throws an exception, as shown in the following screenshot:

```
LazyInitializationException was unhandled
Initializing[LazyLoading.Blog#1001]-failed to lazily initialize a collection of role:
LazyLoading.Blog.Posts, no session or session was closed
Troubleshooting tips:
```

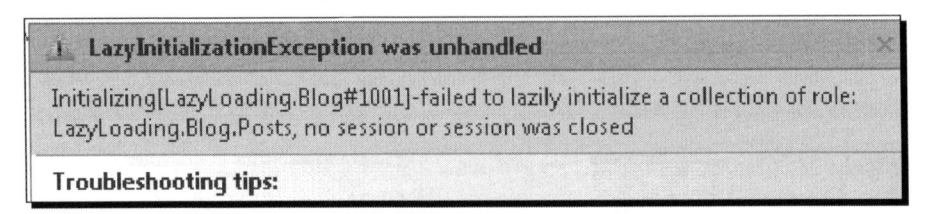

What can we do to avoid such situations? There are a few possible ways to avoid this scenario:

- Close the session at the last possible moment, after all data has been loaded and consumed. In a web application this can be achieved if we use the session per request pattern, open the session when the request starts, and close the session when the request ends.
- Use the hints shown in the preceding section to cause NHibernate to eagerly load data that normally would be lazy loaded.
- Use the `NHibernateUtil` class to force the initialization of a lazy loaded collection or property. Use this code in the case of our blog sample: `NHibernateUtil.Initialize(blog.Posts);`.
- Use database views to load your data as discussed earlier in this chapter and avoid using lazy load at all when mapping those views.

## Did I just load the whole database?

If we have a complex domain and use the domain model to query data, it can easily happen that one single NHibernate request triggers hundreds, if not thousands of queries on the database. All these queries are caused by lazy loading while wandering through the domain.

In a domain model, it is easy to walk from one entity to another via the relations defined in the object model. This following code snippet looks quite harmless but it can cause a lot of trouble in the database:

```
LineItem.Order.Customer.CustomerName
```

It is very important to limit the number of dots in an expression.

## Using one model for read and write operations

In Chapter 3, *Creating a Model* we have introduced the concept of a domain model. In the code samples of all subsequent chapters, we have used this domain to write or update data, as well as to read data from the database. This makes sense as long as the domain is of limited complexity or the solution we build is merely a forms-over-data type application.

If, on the other hand, our domain is very complex then this approach quickly reaches its limits.

## CQRS

The CQRS pattern has been quite successful to address and solve the problem of a single and overly complex domain which is used for read and write operations. When using the CQRS pattern the domain model is exclusively used for write operations. All read operations—here called queries—bypass the domain model and directly hit the database through a thin data layer.

Since the domain model is now freed from the burden of being used to query data it is much simpler. Domain entities are much less coupled by relations. The whole domain can be segregated into mini clusters of related entities, also called aggregates. These aggregates are independent of each other. Each complex problem that can be divided into a set of independent subproblems is much easier to master.

An aggregate is a set of related entities that can be changed in a single business transaction. Let's have a look at a realistic sample. In previous chapters of this book, we have often used an ordering system as our domain. Let's use this example once again to discuss the concept of aggregate and business transactions.

A customer placing an order is a typical business transaction in our selected domain. Which entities are affected by this transaction? We have the order entity containing a list of line item entities. Those two types of entities are created or updated during the process of placing an order. It is clear that these two entities form an aggregate.

Each line item references a product and the order is placed by a customer and handled by an employee of the seller, thus the order references this customer and the employee. Are now the product, the employee, and the customer part of the aggregate we are currently looking at? The answer is a clear no! In a typical ordering system products are maintained by the inventory system. Thus, the product entities are not changed at the same time and in the same transaction as the order is placed. Customer data, on the other hand, is often maintained by a CRM system and not changed when placing an order. Similar things can be said about the employee. That said, we can clearly see that the customer and the product entities lie outside of the aggregate boundaries.

## Diagram

A class diagram shows:
- **Employee** (Class)
- **Order** (Class, Aggregate root) with Properties: OrderDate
- **Customer** (Class) with Properties: CustomerName
- **LineItem** (Class) with Properties: Order, Quantity, UnitPrice
- **Product** (Class) with Properties: Discontinued, Name, ReorderLevel, UnitPrice, UnitsOnStock

Relationships: Order → Employee (Employee), Order → Customer (Customer), Order → LineItem (LineItems), LineItem → Product (Product). An *Aggregate* encircles Order, LineItem, and Product.

---

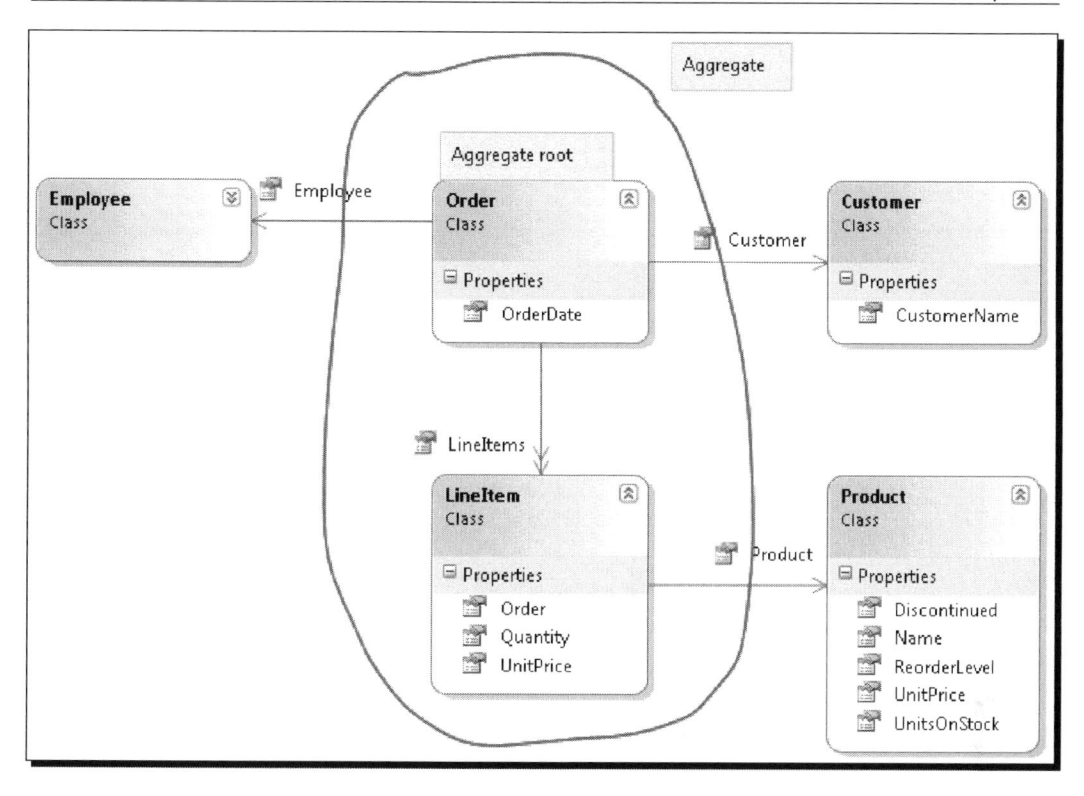

The data we display onscreen and the data that we use to update the system are often very different. When taking an e-commerce site like Amazon as an example, we see that a web page where the user can place an order contains much more data than the system needs to create the shopping cart and from the shopping cart the order when the user checks out. The web page (or to be more general, the view) where the user selects items to place into his shopping cart not only displays a list of available products but also a lot of related information about the products that can be ordered such as reviews, images, or related products.

From our own experience with, for example, e-commerce sites we can deduce that read operations are by far more frequent than write operations. We browse through the product catalogue and request loads of data prior to placing an order. Often, we abandon the web shop without even placing an order.

It is very difficult to tune a system which uses the same domain model for read and write operations. If we optimize the model for read operation, then the write operations become much more complex and also tend to feel unnatural. If, on the other hand, the model is optimized for data manipulation then the queries become slow, or even very slow.

# Phantom updates

Sometimes NHibernate thinks an entity that we loaded from the database and did not explicitly change is dirty. How can this happen? Most of the time it is due to the fact that our mapping between the entities and database tables are wrong or incomplete.

Although we think we did not change the entities, NHibernate will send update statements to the database the moment the session is flushed. This behavior is unnecessary at best, but can lead to false positives if we, for example, monitor each data change to comply with audit requirements.

## Time for action – Causing a phantom update

In this exercise, we want to create a situation where NHibernate creates a phantom update. The cause of the phantom updates will be an inconsistency between the database table column and the respective property of the entity. In the database table, the column is defined as nullable, but the corresponding property of the entity is not nullable. We have to "cheat" and use some SQL bulk operation to prepare our data the way that the scenario is possible. Let's start now.

1. Open Visual Studio and open the `Chapter11` Samples solution.

2. Add a new Console Application type project to the solution. Call the project `PhantomUpdates`.

3. Add references to `NHibernate`, `NHibernate.ByteCode.Castle`, and `FluentNHibernate` to the project. All the references can be found in the `lib` folder.

4. Add a `Product` class to the project, as shown in the following code snippet:

    ```
    public class Product
    {
      public Guid Id { get; set; }
      public string Name { get; set; }
      public int ReorderLevel { get; set; }
      public decimal UnitPrice { get; set; }
    }
    ```

**5.** Add a fluent mapping for the `Product` entity to the project, as shown in the following code snippet:

```
public class ProductMap : ClassMap<Product>
{
  public ProductMap()
  {
    Not.LazyLoad();
    Id(x => x.Id).GeneratedBy.GuidComb();
    Map(x => x.Name).Not.Nullable();
    Map(x => x.ReorderLevel);
    Map(x => x.UnitPrice).Not.Nullable();
  }
}
```

**6.** Please note that the `ReorderLevel` property is defined as `int`, and thus not nullable. On the other hand, the mapping will cause NHibernate to generate a database table creation script where the `ReorderLevel` database table column is nullable.

**7.** Add a static field `factory` to the `Program` class to hold the session factory instance:

```
private static ISessionFactory factory;
```

**8.** Add a string constant `connString` to the `Program` class defining the connection string, as shown in the following code snippet:

```
private const string connString =
    "server=.\\SQLEXPRESS;database=Chapter11Samples;" +
    "integrated security=true;";
```

**9.** Add a static method `CreateSessionFactory` to the `Program` class:

```
private static void CreateSessionFactory()
{ }
```

**10.** Add code to the preceding method to configure NHibernate and use the already existing SQL Server database `Chapter11Samples`, as shown in the following code snippet:

```
factory = Fluently.Configure()
    .Database(MsSqlConfiguration.MsSql2008
      .ConnectionString(connString)
      .ShowSql()
    )
    .Mappings(m => m.FluentMappings.Add<ProductMap>())
    .ExposeConfiguration(c => new SchemaExport(c)
      .Execute(false, true, false))
    .BuildSessionFactory();
```

11. To reduce the amount of code we need to write, create a helper method `WithTx` that accepts an `Action<ISession>` as a parameter, opens a new session object, and starts a new transaction. It then calls the action and passes the session object to it. Finally the transaction is committed, as shown in the following code snippet:

    ```
    private static void WithTx(Action<ISession> action)
    {
      using (var session = factory.OpenSession())
      using (var tx = session.BeginTransaction())
      {
        action(session);
        tx.Commit();
      }
    }
    ```

12. Add a static method `CreateData` to the `Program` class. In the method instantiate a product:

    ```
    private static void CreateData()
    {
      var product = new Product {Name = "Coca Cola",
        UnitPrice = 0.75m, ReorderLevel = 10};
    }
    ```

13. Call the `WithTx` method and pass as a parameter an action to persist the product:

    ```
    WithTx(session => session.Save(product));
    ```

14. The above method will cause NHibernate to create a product record in the `Product` database table. The content of the `ReorderLevel` column will be 10. Now we will use an HQL bulk update query to set the `ReorderLevel` field of all product records to null. Add the following code snippet at the end of the `CreateData` method:

    ```
    WithTx(session =>
             session
                .CreateQuery("update Product p " +
                         "set p.ReorderLevel = null")
                .ExecuteUpdate());
    ```

15. Now we need to add more code at the end of the `CreateData` method to load the product from the database and print some of its properties to the console. The printing shall be a placeholder for any other (complex) operation which only reads the content of the entity but does not change the entity itself, as shown in the following code snippet:

    ```
    WithTx(session =>
      {
        var p = session.Load<Product>(product.Id);
    ```

```
        Console.WriteLine("Loaded product {0} with " +
            "reorder level {1}.",
            p.Name, p.ReorderLevel);
    });
```

**16.** At the end of the `Main` method of the `Program` class, add code to call the `CreateSessionFactory` and `CreateData` methods:

```
CreateSessionFactory();
CreateData();
```

**17.** Finally, add code at the end of the `Main` method to prevent the application from exiting without the user's consent:

```
Console.Write("\r\n\nHit enter to exit:");
Console.ReadLine();
```

**18.** Run the application and review the output in the console window:

**19.** Note the last update statement. This is our phantom update. We didn't change the product and thus would not expect to see this update. The update is caused by our inconsistent mapping of the product entity, specifically the `ReorderLevel` property, as shown in the preceding screenshot.

## What just happened?

We have created a sample application which causes a phantom update. The phantom update is caused due to the inconsistent mapping of a field of the product entity we used in the sample. The unnecessary update of the product record in the database happens even though we did not change the loaded product entity in the code.

## Using NHibernate to persist any type of data

*If the only tool I have is a hammer then everything to me looks like a nail. And if I can't find any nails then I start to invent them.*

The above saying can be easily applied to the usage of relational databases as the one and only way to persist data. We have been told that relational databases are the only type of data stores that makes sense in a business application. Everything else was considered as unreliable.

Lately, more and more alternative ways of storing data have emerged and have been used quite successfully by many well known and respectable companies on the market. A few of them are Google's Big Table or document databases such as Mongo DB, Couch DB, and Raven DB.

Companies that are using these products have requirements that just cannot be fulfilled by the traditional RDBMS. Thus, these companies and other individuals started to look out for some alternative ways to efficiently store and retrieve data. They were willing to trade in some of the features that the traditional databases provide such as, for example, transaction support or they did not need fully normalized data.

In a document database we typically store a whole aggregate. We do not have to convert our object hierarchy into a relational set of data but can just serialize the whole object tree and dump it into the data store in one go. This is a very fast operation and causes one single write operation to happen instead of potentially hundreds when we try to save a complex aggregate to a RDBMS.

If we deal with a lot of hierarchical data, then a document database might be preferable to a relational database.

Also, RDBMS have limited horizontal scalability. Either the desired scalability cannot be achieved at all, or the system becomes overly complex to handle and extremely expensive to buy. Other storage mechanisms such as document databases have proven to provide nearly limitless horizontal scalability.

Nothing is free, we always have to trade in something. If we want unlimited scalability, then we probably have to trade in consistency and accept that our system will only be **eventually consistent**.

The decision of which data store mechanism is best suited for our case, depends on many factors. A careful discussion with the business representatives is necessary to clarify what aspects are most important and where the business is ready to accept some trade-offs.

# Summary

In this last chapter, we have learned a lot about the possible pitfalls when using NHibernate. We have discussed under what circumstances we can fall into traps and how we can avoid this.

Specifically, we covered:

- How to avoid too verbose and inefficient mappings. We learned that lean mappings are easier to understand and maintain.
- Common anti-patterns encountered in the usage of NHibernate. We learned that we should hardly ever use database-generated IDs and always explicitly defined the boundaries of our transactions.
- The correct handling of lazy loading. We learned that under certain circumstances we need to give NHibernate a hint to avoid lazy loading altogether, we were shown how we can achieve that.
- There exist situations where the domain is so complex that it makes sense to separate the concerns for querying data versus updating or writing data. We learned that in such situations we might want to use two models, a read model and a write model, to keep things simple and manageable.

This has been the last chapter of this book. Now you should be ready to go and successfully use NHibernate in your day-to-day job. I wish you all the best and don't forget, there is plenty of information available on the web about the usage of NHibernate.

# Pop Quiz Answers

## Chapter 2

### A First Complete Sample

| 1 | b & c |
|---|-------|

## Chapter 3

### Creating a Model

| 1 | c |
|---|---|

## Chapter 4

### Defining the Database Schema

| 1 | b, e, f & g |
|---|-------------|

# Chapter 5

## Mapping the Model to the Database

| 1 | a & d |

# Chapter 6

## Sessions and Transactions

| 1 | c |
| 2 | b or c |
| 3 | c |

# Chapter 7

## Testing, Profiling, Monitoring, and Logging

| 1 | e |

# Chapter 8

## Configuration

| 1 | b & c |

# Chapter 9

## Writing Queries

| 1 | The data a user collects with the aid of an application only has a business value if it is retrieved from the database and presented in a meaningful way on the screen or on paper. Thereby the raw data is filtered, aggregated, sorted and mapped. All these operations are part of the query process. |
|---|---|
| 2 | Use the ToFuture and the ToFutureValue extension methods to instruct NHibernate to not execute a query individually when we iterate over it but to send all queries that have been defined as futures in one single batch to the server. The server in turn will then return the results also in a batch. |
| 3 | When we have an entity which contains a collection of child entities then when we load a list of those entities and while iterating over this list of entities access not only properties of the respective entity but also of its child entities then NHibernate will trigger the loading of the child collection of the entity we are currently dealing with. In other words, NHibernate will not load all the data in one go but load the list of all entites and then issue a separate query for to retrieve the collection of child entites of each entity. |
| 4 | We can define a batch query in HQL and use the ExecuteUpdate method of the IQuery interface to execute this batch insert, update or delete query. |

# Chapter 10

## Validating the Data to Persist

| 1 | e |
|---|---|

# Index

## Symbols

**1NF** 83
**2NF** 83
**3NF** 83

## A

**ACID property** 147
**ADOConnection** 145
**ADO.NET connection** 155
**anemic domain model** 60
**Apache project** 202
**application**
  logging, adding to 203-206
**AsEnumerable method** 251
**AsEnumerable statement** 321
**attribute-based mapping**
  about 97-99
  advantages 97
  disadvantages 97
**AutoMapper** 124
**auto-mapping**
  about 102
  advantages 102
  disadvantages 102
  Fluent NHibernate 124, 125
  using 125-128

## B

**base entity**
  creating 48-50

**base framework**
  creating, for mapping tests 191-195
**batch**
  multiple queries, executing in 277-279
**BeginRequest handler** 318
**benefits, NHibernate Profiler** 210
**bound context** 147
**BrokenRules method** 302
**BuildSessionFactory() method** 30
**byte code provider** 220

## C

**cache**
  about 152
  clearing 154
  entities, refreshing in 154
**cache regions** 177
**caching mechanisms**
  about 152
  first level cache 152, 153
  second level cache 176, 177
**Castle** 18
**Castle proxy generator** 220
**Categories table**
  creating 68-71
**category**
  about 20
  adding, to database 34, 35
**category list**
  loading, from database 36-38
**CausePhantomUpdate method** 330
**check constraints** 76

CheckProperty method  191
classes, fluent mapping  107
classes, XML-based mapping  134
class tag  134
CLR  42
code
   NHibernate, configuring in  227-233
collections, fluent mapping  111, 112
columns  67, 72
Command object  145
Command Query Responsibility Segregation (CQRS) pattern  326, 327
commercial support, NHibernate  13
Commit method  148
Common Language Runtime. *See* CLR
common mistakes, NHibernate
   database-generated IDs, using  318
   dependent  317
   domain model, using for r/w operations  325
   implicit transaction, using  317, 318
   lazy loaded parts, accessing after closing session  324, 325
   LINQ, using  319, 320
   NHibernate, using for persisting any type of data  332
   phantom update  328
   select (n+1) problem  321- 324
   troubles, with lazy loading  321
   unnecessary attributes  314
   verbose mappings  314
   whole database, loading  325
   wrong mapping  315, 316
complex business rules
   validating  297, 298
   validation classes  299, 300
   valid entities, enforcing  298
configuration elements, NHibernate
   about  218
   byte code provider  220
   database  218, 219
   proxy factory  220
configuration, NHibernate
   need for  217
ConfORM
   about  9, 129
   domain, mapping with  129-131
constraints
   about  76
   adding, to product table  77, 78
   check  76
   data type  76
   foreign key  76
   not null  76
Count() method  279
CreateCriteria method  281
CreateData method  256
CreateQuery method  273
CreateSchema method  27
criteria queries  260
criteria query API  246
Customer entity
   creating  50, 52

# D

data
   about  63, 67
   loading, on demand  103
   locations, for validating  288
   reading, from database  149
   retrieving, with QueryOver API  265-272
   selecting, for validation  287
   updating, in database  151
database
   about  184, 218, 219
   category, adding to  34, 35
   category list, loading from  36-38
   creating  26-30
   data, reading from  149
   data, updating in  151
   including, in tests  184
   new data, adding to  149
   objects, persisting to  33
   reading from  36
   session, opening to  32, 33
database entity  67
database-generated IDs
   avoiding  89
database owner  64
database schema
   about  64, 93
   creating  25-30
   OrderingSystem database, creating  64-66
database schema creation scripts

creating  104, 105
database session
  versus NHibernate session  155
database table
  entity, mapping to  107
database tests
  SQLite, using in  196, 198
database trigger  90
Data Definition Language. *See* DDL
Data Manipulation Language. *See* DML
data type  76
data types, table columns  72, 73
DDL  71
Delete method  152
development environment, NHibernate
  setting up  15-19
Discontinued method  279
DML  71
domain
  mapping, with ConfORM  129-131
domain model
  mapping  114-120
DriverConnectionProvider class  220

# E

eager loading
  versus lazy loading  279-281
embedded resource  95
EndRequest handler  318
entity
  about  43, 152
  applications  43
  base entity, creating  48-50
  creating  47
  customer entity, creating  50-52
  mapping, to database table  107
  refreshing, in cache  154
Entity Framework  8
entity level settings, fluent mapping  107, 108
Entity Relationship Diagram (ERD)  42
environment
  preparing, for testing  186-189
Equals method  46-50
ETL tool  286
exceptions
  handling  175

ExecuteUpdate method  282
existing record
  deleting, from database  152
ExposeConfiguration method  27
Extract, Transform, and Load. *See* ETL tool

# F

features, NHibernate 3.0  8, 9
Fetch method  280
first level cache  152, 153
First Normal Form. *See* 1NF
fluent mapping
  about  99, 100, 105
  advantages  101
  classes  107
  collections  111, 112
  disadvantages  101
  entity level settings  107, 108
  expressions trees  106
  ID columns  108, 109
  many-to-many relations, mapping  113
  properties  109, 110
  references  111
  value objects, mapping  113, 114
Fluent NHibernate
  about  18, 99, 121
  auto mapping, performing with  124, 125
  mapping code, defining  23
  mapping, testing with  191, 192
  NHibernate, configuring with  242
  URL, for downloading  18
FNHConfigurationSample.sln  242
foreach loop  247
foreign key  74
foreign key constraints  76
foreign key conventions  123
full table scan  79

# G

Genome  8
GetHashCode method  46, 49
Get method
  versus Load method  150, 151
Given method  189

given-when-then syntax  187
Global Unique Identifiers (GUIDs)  318
Google Big Table  63
group by keyword  274
GroupBy method  250
GuidComb generator  108, 318
Guid generator  108, 149

## H

hashtable  152
Hibernate Query Language. *See* HQL
High-Low generator  116
HiLo generator  108, 318
HiLo method  108
HQL  246, 272, 274

## I

IBM DB/2  217
ICriteria API  9
ID columns, fluent mapping  108, 109
ID conventions  121, 122
Id method  108
ID property  48
id tag  134
IEnumerable<T> interface  247
impedance mismatch  8, 93
index
  adding, SSMS visual designer used  80-82
  script, adding to  82
indices  79
in-memory mode  197
in-memory objects
  querying  251
InnerException property  175
inner join  281
installing
  NuGet Package Manager Extension  292
Integrate keyword  238
IoC container  167
IPropertyConvention interface  122
IQueryable<T> interface  247
IQuery interface  282
IsComponent method  125
ISession interface  198, 247, 273

## L

Language Integrated Queries. *See* LINQ
lazy attribute  275
lazy evaluation  247
lazy loading technique
  about  18, 103, 220, 321
  properties  275, 276
  proxies  103
  versus eager loading  279-281
left join fetch operation  281
left outer join  281
Length attribute  290
LineItems collection  112
LinFu
  URL  220
LINQ  106, 246
LINQ provider  8
LINQ query
  executing, immediately  250, 251
LINQ to NHibernate
LINQ to NHibernate provider
  about  246, 247
  record set, filtering  248
  record set, mapping  249
  records, grouping  250
  resulting dataset, sorting  249, 250
  used, for creating report  252-260
LLBLGen Pro  8
Load method
  about  149
  versus Get method  150, 151
log
  need for  202, 203
Log4Net
  about  203
  logging, performing with  203-206
log files
  analyzing  209
logging
  about  202, 203
  adding, to application  203-206
  performing, with Log4Net  203-206
  setting up, for NHibernate  206-209
Loquacious
  NHibernate, configuring with  233-242

# M

many-to-many relations
  about 55, 56, 75
  mapping 113
Map function 106
mapping
  about 94, 221
  testing 189, 190
  testing, with Fluent NHibernate 191, 192
  types 94
mapping classes
  creating 23-25
mapping conventions
  foreign key conventions 123
  ID conventions 121, 122
  implementing 123
  property conventions 122
  using 121
mapping information 221
mapping tests
  base framework, creating for 191-195
mapping, types
  attribute-based 97-99
  auto-mapping 102
  fluent 99-105
  XML-based 94-133
materialized view 90
MbUnit
  URL 186
MemCache 178
Message parameter 290
Microsoft SQL Server 63
Microsoft SQL Server 2008 R2 Express
  installing 16
mock 198
model
  about 42, 93
  defining 20
  elements 43
  mapping 22-25
  order entity model 56
  order entity model, implementing 56-61
  product inventory model, creating 20-22
model, elements
  entity 43, 44
  value objects 44

Model-View-Presenter (MVP) pattern 174
MonoDevelop 16
MS SQL Server 89, 217
multiple queries
  executing, in batch 277, 279
MySQL 217

# N

name attribute 134
Name value object
  about 52
  creating 45-47
natural keys 43
new data
  adding, to database 149
NHibernate
  about 7, 8
  benefits 9, 10
  caching mechanisms 152, 153, 176, 177
  category list, loading from database 36-38
  commercial support 13
  configuring, in code 227-233
  configuring, with Fluent NHibernate 242
  configuring, with Loquacious 233-242
  configuring, XML used 222-227
  convention, over configuration 243
  criteria queries 260
  database, including in tests 184
  database schema, creating 25-30
  database schema creation scripts, creating 104, 105
  data, modifying in bulk 282
  development environment, setting up 15-19
  documentation 11, 12
  environment, preparing for testing 186-189
  exceptions, handling 175
  Fluent configuration 233-242
  help 12, 13
  HQL 272, 274
  lazy loading technique 18, 103, 275, 276
  lazy loading, versus eager loading 279-281
  log files, analyzing 209
  logging 202
  logging, setting up for 206-209
  log, need for 202, 203
  mailing list 12, 13

mappings 94
model 42
model, defining 20
model, mapping 22-25
multiple queries, executing, in batch 277-279
objects, persisting to database 33
queries, testing 198-202
relational databse support 16
second level cache, implementing 177
second level cache, using 178-182
session, creating 148
session factory 147
session factory, creating 30-32
session, opening to database 32, 33
sessions 145, 146
SQL Server Profiler 210
strongly-typed criteria queries 260-265
transactions 145-147
untyped criteria queries 260-263
URL, for FAQ 11
URL, for meta blog 11
users 13
XML configuration 221-227
**NHibernate**
  pitfalls 313
  verbose mappings, avoiding 314, 315
**NHibernate 3.0**
  features 8, 9
**NHibernate 3.1.0**
  URL, for downloading 17
**NHibernate configuration**
  elements 218
  need for 217
**NHibernate contribution project**
  resources 10
**NHibernate Contributions 288**
**NHibernate logo 8**
**nhibernate-mapping.xsd file 94**
**NHibernate Profiler**
  about 237
  benefits 210
  monitoring with 211-214
  profiling with 211-214
  URL, for downloading 210
**NHibernate Profiler support**
  adding 212-214

**NHibernate project**
  resources 10
**NHibernate session**
  about 145
  versus database session 155
**NHibernate session management 166**
**NHibernate Users Mailing List group 12**
**NHibernate.Validator 289**
**normal form**
  1NF 83
  2NF 83
  3NF 83
  about 83
**normalization 83**
**not null constraints 76**
**NuGet logo 11**
**NuGet Package Manager Extension**
  installing 292
**NuGet project 11**
**null 72**
**NUnit**
  URL 186

# O

**Object Relational Mapper.** *See* **ORM framework**
**objects**
  about 7, 8
  persisting, to database 33
**one-to-many relations 53, 74**
**one-to-many restriction criteria 261**
**one-to-one relations 54, 75**
**OpenSession method 148**
**open source project (OSS) 10**
**Oracle 89, 217**
**OrderApprovalValidator class 299**
**OrderByDescending method 250**
**order by keyword 274**
**OrderBy method 250**
**order entry model**
  about 56
  implementing 56-61
**order entry system**
  schema, creating for 83- 89
**OrderingSystem database**
  Categories table, creating in 68-71

creating  64-66
ORM framework  8
OSS options  16

## P

PersistenceSpecification class  191
persistent entities  49
Persistent Object ID. *See* POID generator
persistent object identifier. *See* POI
Persist method  149
phantom update
  about  328
  causing  328-331
Plain Old CLR Objects. *See* POCO
POCO  42
POI  43
POID generator  89, 219
post mortem analysis  203
predicate  248
presentation layer  288
Prevalence  178
primary key  74
product inventory model
  creating  20-22
product table
  constraints, adding to  77, 78
property conventions  122
property tag  134
property validation
  using  292-297
proxy  103
proxy factory  220

## Q

QL Server Management Studio (SSMS)  64
quality assurance (QA)  202
query
  root, defining for  247
  testing  198-202
QueryOver API  9
  about  246
  data, retrieving with  265-272

## R

RDBMS  63
ReadOnly() method  316
record
  deleting, from database  152
  grouping  250
record set
  filtering  248
  mapping  249
reduce function  248
references, fluent mapping  111
relational database  8
relational database management systems. *See* RDBMS
relational table  75
relations
  about  74
  types  53-56, 74
relations, types
  many-to-many  55, 56, 75
  one-to-many  53, 74
  one-to-one  54, 75
ReorderLevel property  329
report
  creating, LINQ to NHibernate used  252-260
ReSharper  105
resulting dataset
  sorting  249, 250
root
  defining, for query  247
rows  67

## S

SaveCategoryValidator class  302
Save method  149
schema
  creating, for order entry system  83-89
SchemaAction.None() statement  316
SchemaExport class  159, 290, 316
scope  42
script
  adding, to index  82
  creating, for check constraint addition  78, 79
  defining, for product table creation  71, 72

**second level cache**
  about  176
  cache regions  177
  enabling  176
  implementing  177
  using  178-182
**second level caching  221**
**Second Normal Form.** *See*  **2NF**
**SelectedCategory property  307**
**Select function  249**
**select (n+1) problem  321-323**
**SELECT statement  241**
**session**
  about  145, 146
  creating  30, 148, 156-165
  Commit method  148
  CRUD operations, performing  156-165
  entity, removing from first level cache  154
  opening, to database  32, 33
**session factory**
  about  147
  creating  30-32
**session management**
  about  166
  implementing, for web application  166-174
  Windows services  174
  WinForm  174
  WPF applications  174
**session object**
  about  146
  data, reading from database  149
  new data, adding to database  149
**SetDecimal method  273**
**SetMaxResults function  260, 273**
**SetMinResult method  273**
**SetProjection method  262**
**SetString method  273**
**SetUp attribute  187**
**SharpDevelop  16**
**simple domain**
  mapping, XML used  139-143
**single properties**
  validating  288
**single responsibility principle (SRP)  299**
**singleton pattern  167**

**Spring.Net**
  URL  220
**SQL  246**
**SQLite**
  about  185
  downloading  185
  URL, for downloading  185
  using, in database tests  196, 198
**SQL Server driver  16**
**SQL Server Management Studio Express.** *See*
    **SSMS**
**SQL Server Profiler**
  using  210
**SSMS**
  URL, for downloading  17
**SSMS visual designer**
  index, adding with  80-82
**stored procedure  91**
**strongly-typed criteria queries  260-265**
**stub  198**
**Subsonic 8**
**surrogate keys  43**
**sut  201**
**SysCache  177**
**SysCache2  177**
**system under test.** *See*  **sut**

# T

**table**
  about  67
  layouts  68
**table attribute  134**
**table columns**
  about  72
  data types  72, 73
**table layouts  67, 68**
**Take function  248**
**TearDown attribute  187**
**test driven development (TDD)  183**
**TestFixtureTearDown attribute  187**
**testing**
  environment, preparing for  186-189
**tests**
  database, including in  184
  need for  183

ThenByDescending method  250
ThenBy method  250
Third Normal Form. *See* 3NF
ToDictionary function  251
ToList() method  150
transaction.Commit() statement  148
transaction object  145
transactions
  about  145, 146
  ACID property  147
  characteristics  147
  example  146
transient entities  49

# U

UI validation logic  288
undefined value  72
Unit of Work  149, 175
unit test
  about  186
  parts  186
unit test, parts
  act  186
  arrange  186
  assert  186
UnsavedValue function  109
untyped criteria queries  260-263
user input
  validating  300-310
using statement  148

# V

validation
  about  285
  data, selecting for  287
  enforcing  291, 292
  need for  287
validation classes
  user input, validating  300-310
  using  299, 300

validation messages
  localizing  297
validation rules
  configuring, fluently  291
  defining  290
validator
  configuring  289, 290
value objects
  about  44
  mapping  113-143
  Name value object, creating  45-47
  samples  44
value type  235
Velocity  177
VerifyTheMappings method  191
views  90
Visual Studio  105

# W

web application
  session management, implementing for  166-174
Web.config file  221
When method  189
Where keyword  248

# X

XML
  simple domain, mapping with  139-143
  used, for configuring NHibernate  222-227
XML-based mapping
  about  94-96, 132, 133
  classes  134
  ID columns  135
  many-to-many relations  138, 139
  one-to-many relations  136
  properties  134
  value objects, mapping  139-143
XUnit
  URL  186

# [PACKT] open source*
### PUBLISHING
### community experience distilled

# Thank you for buying
# NHibernate 3 Beginner's Guide

## About Packt Publishing

Packt, pronounced 'packed', published its first book "*Mastering phpMyAdmin for Effective MySQL Management*" in April 2004 and subsequently continued to specialize in publishing highly focused books on specific technologies and solutions.

Our books and publications share the experiences of your fellow IT professionals in adapting and customizing today's systems, applications, and frameworks. Our solution based books give you the knowledge and power to customize the software and technologies you're using to get the job done. Packt books are more specific and less general than the IT books you have seen in the past. Our unique business model allows us to bring you more focused information, giving you more of what you need to know, and less of what you don't.

Packt is a modern, yet unique publishing company, which focuses on producing quality, cutting-edge books for communities of developers, administrators, and newbies alike. For more information, please visit our website: www.packtpub.com.

## About Packt Open Source

In 2010, Packt launched two new brands, Packt Open Source and Packt Enterprise, in order to continue its focus on specialization. This book is part of the Packt Open Source brand, home to books published on software built around Open Source licences, and offering information to anybody from advanced developers to budding web designers. The Open Source brand also runs Packt's Open Source Royalty Scheme, by which Packt gives a royalty to each Open Source project about whose software a book is sold.

## Writing for Packt

We welcome all inquiries from people who are interested in authoring. Book proposals should be sent to author@packtpub.com. If your book idea is still at an early stage and you would like to discuss it first before writing a formal book proposal, contact us; one of our commissioning editors will get in touch with you.

We're not just looking for published authors; if you have strong technical skills but no writing experience, our experienced editors can help you develop a writing career, or simply get some additional reward for your expertise.

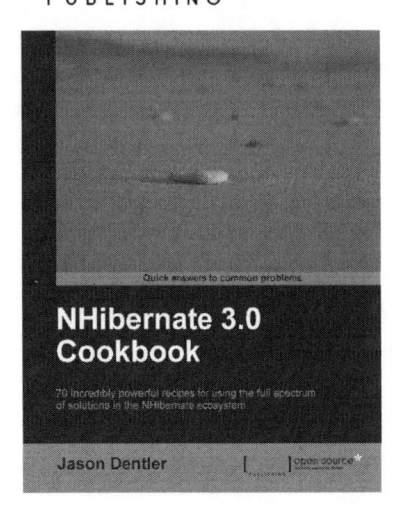

# [PACKT] open source
community experience distilled
PUBLISHING

## NHibernate 3.0 Cookbook

ISBN: 978-1-849513-04-3  Paperback: 328 pages

70 incredibly powerful recipes for using the full spectrum of solutions in the NHibernate ecosystem

1. Master the full range of NHibernate features
2. Reduce hours of application development time and get better application architecture and performance
3. Create, maintain, and update your database structure automatically with the help of NHibernate
4. Written and tested for NHibernate 3.0 with input from the development team distilled in to easily accessible concepts and examples

## Scribus 1.3.5: Beginner's Guide

ISBN: 978-1-849513-00-5  Paperback: 348 pages

Create optimum page layouts for your documents using productive tools of Scribus

1. Master desktop publishing with Scribus
2. Create professional-looking documents with ease
3. Enhance the readability of your documents using powerful layout tools of Scribus
4. Packed with interesting examples and screenshots that show you the most important Scribus tools to create and publish your documents

Please check www.PacktPub.com for information on our titles

# [PACKT] open source
## community experience distilled

## ChronoForms 3.1 for Joomla! site Cookbook

ISBN: 978-1-849510-62-2       Paperback: 376 pages

80 recipes for building attractive and interactive Joomla! forms

1. Develop feature-rich Joomla forms with the help of easy-to-follow steps and ample screenshots
2. Publish forms, that let you interact with your users, to a website using ChronoForms in minutes, not in hours
3. Explore the versatility of ChronoForms and use them to make your web site an interactive one
4. Part of Packt's Cookbook series: Each recipe is a carefully organized sequence of instructions to complete the task as efficiently as possible

## PostgreSQL 9.0 High Performance

ISBN: 978-1-849510-30-1       Paperback: 468 pages

Accelerate your PostgreSQL system and avoid the common pitfalls that can slow it down

1. Learn the right techniques to obtain optimal PostgreSQL database performance, from initial design to routine maintenance
2. Discover the techniques used to scale successful database installations
3. Avoid the common pitfalls that can slow your system down
4. Filled with advice about what you should be doing; how to build experimental databases to explore performance topics, and then move what you've learned into a production database environment

Please check **www.PacktPub.com** for information on our titles